The Left Behind

T0287883

'A well written and engaging account that tackles the stereotyping of so-called "left behind" communities by journalistic and political opinion-formers. James Morrison questions how the most disadvantaged sections of society have been framed (or blamed) for delivering Brexit and in doing so he demonstrates why this kind of media representation is both over simplistic as well as problematic. *The Left Behind* identifies and explores the inadequacies of this account and in doing so examines the motives of those largely responsible for it. As Morrison observes, it was ironic that "such stout defences of the disenfranchised masses should be mounted by elite commentators in papers which had long been passionate cheerleaders of the very neoliberal free-market policies that had so immiserated the erstwhile industrial towns they now championed".'

—Dominic Wring, Professor of Political Communication,
Loughborough University

The Left Behind

Reimagining Britain's Socially Excluded

James Morrison

PLUTO PRESS

First published 2022 by Pluto Press
New Wing, Somerset House, Strand, London WC2R 1LA

www.plutobooks.com

Copyright © James Morrison 2022

The right of James Morrison to be identified as the author of this work has been asserted in accordance with the Copyright, Designs and Patents Act 1988.

British Library Cataloguing in Publication Data
A catalogue record for this book is available from the British Library

ISBN 978 0 7453 4463 8 Hardback
ISBN 978 0 7453 4462 1 Paperback
ISBN 978 0 7453 4466 9 PDF
ISBN 978 0 7453 4464 5 EPUB

This book is printed on paper suitable for recycling and made from fully managed and sustained forest sources. Logging, pulping and manufacturing processes are expected to conform to the environmental standards of the country of origin.

Typeset by Stanford DTP Services, Northampton, England

Simultaneously printed in the United Kingdom and United States of America

Contents

List of tables

About the author

James Morrison is a Reader in Journalism at Robert Gordon University, Aberdeen. His research focuses on media-political discourses around stigmatized groups – primarily people experiencing poverty and other forms of inequality – and their intersection with public deliberation, social attitudes and government policy. Before becoming an academic, he was a full-time journalist, working for a succession of newspapers, including *The Independent on Sunday*, before going freelance. He has since written for numerous publications, including the *Guardian*, *The Times* and *Telegraph Magazine*. He is a senior examiner and member of the National Council for the Training of Journalists' Public Affairs Board and author of *Essential Public Affairs for Journalists* (Oxford University Press). His other published research includes the monographs *Familiar Strangers, Juvenile Panic and the British Press: The Decline of Social Trust* (Palgrave Macmillan) and *Scroungers* (Bloomsbury), as well as articles in *Digital Journalism*, the *British Journal of Politics and International Relations* and *Social Semiotics*.

Acknowledgements

In embarking on this book, I have been indebted to the many eminent academics (and more enlightened journalists) who have attempted to wrestle before me with the complexity of what one might call the 'left behind question'. I am particularly grateful for the inspiration gained by reading the thoughtful contributions of Professors Danny Dorling, Peter Golding, Gurminda Bhambra and Imogen Tyler, and Drs Lisa McKenzie and Tracey Jensen, as well as the seminal earlier writings of McKenzie and Silver, Coates and Silburn, and Goldthorpe and colleagues. Thanks also to John Harris and John Domokos, whose insightful 'Anywhere but Westminster' podcasts for the *Guardian* have always treated their subjects with a level of empathy and respect missing from many other 'mainstream' media narratives – refusing to stereotype or patronize the residents of towns and communities battered by austerity, COVID-19 and years of wrangling and division over Brexit. Thanks are also due for the insightful advice, feedback and (above all) patience of other academics who heard me out as I harped on about 'the left behind' through the various conference papers, articles and proposal drafts that led to this book. Chief among these have been my editor at Pluto Press, Ken Barlow; Dr Kayleigh Garthwaite at the University of Birmingham, Dr Kostas Maronitis at Leeds Trinity, Dr Jay Wiggan at Edinburgh, and Dr Ceri Davies at the National Centre for Social Research; Professor Darren Lilleker and Dr Antje Gluck at Bournemouth; and (again) Professor Golding (who must have read more of my book proposals and grant applications than any other single academic!) I would also like to thank the Political Studies Association for the Research and Innovation Fund grant which provided the resources to enable me to carry out the Scottish interviews which contributed to the testimony explored in Chapter 5, and charities and user-led groups that helped me recruit interviewees, including the Poverty Alliance, Inclusion Scotland, the Black Triangle Campaign, and Mo Stewart of the Centre for Welfare Reform.

More importantly, this book would have been much less substantial (let alone 'useful') had it not been for the honest and incisive contributions made to it by the various people who found time to speak to me, often while juggling extraordinary personal challenges in the midst of a global pandemic. Of the many interviewees whose testimony contributed, directly or indirectly, to the findings presented in Chapter 5, I am particularly indebted to Janet Mason from Bentilee, Stephen Ruffley from Leigh and Keri Anderson from Edlington – all of whom went above and beyond granting me a single interview to offer additional pointers and insights that helped enrich the final result, by providing additional background and context.

Beyond this, I want to thank the family, friends and colleagues who have bolstered and encouraged me as I've ploughed on with this project – despite all the difficulties presented by the COVID-19 backdrop against which it was researched. As ever, I owe everything to my wife, Annalise – a frontline social worker who helps people affected by poverty and inequality every day of the year – and our three children, Scarlet, Rosella and Ivor Munro, who have been through so much themselves during the period in which this book was written, from prolonged periods of home schooling to (in Scarlet's case) final National 5 assessments. Of friends and colleagues, my thanks go out especially to Dr Fiona McKay, my partner in crime at RGU, and Kenny Lindsay – for keeping me sane during lockdown(s) with our weekly tennis matches.

Above all, though, I would like to close with a call-out to the various distinct and/or overlapping groups (and millions upon millions of *individuals*) whose lives are needlessly and unjustly affected, day to day, by economic and other disadvantages it is well within our power to end. If we want to heal the political and cultural divisions that have so toxified latter-day social relations and public debate, we need to get serious about redressing the long-term industrial decline; precarious, low-waged, unsatisfying work; digital, health and educational disparities; and racial, gender and disability-related injustices that (for want of more precise or elegant epithets) have led so many people, for so long, to feel left behind.

Introduction
Inventing and appropriating 'the left behind'

Residuum, underclass, forgotten people, precariat: journalists and politicians have a compulsive predilection for inventing labels to classify (and disparage) people experiencing poverty, insecurity and alienation. But of all the popular imaginaries constructed to describe the nature and condition of latter-day social exclusion, few have risen to prominence so swiftly, or come to dominate public debate so comprehensively, as 'the left behind'.

While use of the term 'left behind' only became common currency during the weeks and months succeeding the 2016 European Union referendum – primarily as a go-to shorthand for neglected and/or economically ravaged post-industrial communities that had overwhelmingly voted for Brexit – its most recent origin in a UK context can be dated to several years earlier. In their 2014 book *Revolt on the Right*, political scientists Robert Ford and Matthew Goodwin argued for the growing significance of an 'ageing, shrinking and left behind white, working class': a social group sharing 'a distinct set of social attitudes' and viewing 'a cosmopolitan, multicultural and globalised Britain as an alien and threatening place' (Ford & Goodwin, 2014: 132). This they contrasted with the 'younger, university educated and more secure middle-class professionals' who had hitherto set 'the political and social agenda' (ibid.: 126). In a near-contemporaneous report, the Institute for Public Policy Research (IPPR) identified a similar pattern of social and political disengagement among two-thirds of the 'white working class' who, they contended, felt '"left behind" by politics' and no longer believed 'democracy works for them' (Griffith & Glennie, 2014). Significantly, around half of this sizeable population segment had become resigned to 'success' being 'mostly reserved' for 'people from privileged backgrounds who know the right people', rather than 'talented people from poorer backgrounds' (ibid.) – a finding that reflected the stubborn persistence of barriers to the acquisition of social capital by those encumbered with 'the symbolic baggage' of their 'past' that has led more and more sociologists to dismiss the contemporary discourse of 'social mobility' and 'meritocracy' as an illusory myth (Friedman, 2014: 363). Three years earlier, a similar conceptualization of 'the left behind' had surfaced in a report by researchers at Sheffield Hallam University. A scarcity of secure, well-paid jobs outside South-East England's 'economic powerhouse', combined with workforce immobility caused by personal circumstances (and exacerbated by ongoing benefit changes), had, it argued, left 'many people and places' at risk of being 'left behind' (Beatty et al., 2011: 7).

A crucial dimension of the 'left-behind condition' such studies spotlighted was that people were in this position not just because their *economic* circumstances were precarious (though they certainly were), but due to being left out of *cultural* and *political* discourses – or what contemporary commentators like to call the 'national conversation'. According to this argument, the 'left behind' had been taken for granted by the mainstream political establishment and, in many instances, wilfully ignored, as party leaders and candidates relentlessly pursued the fabled middle-class 'floating voter' throughout the 1990s and 2000s (barring occasional flirtations with elusive working-class imaginaries, such as 'Essex man' – Biressi & Nunn, 2013), in the blinkered belief that it was they who would decide all future elections. 'In fifty years', wrote Ford and Goodwin, Britain had been 'transformed from a society where poorly skilled and blue-collar voters decided elections' to one in which they had 'become spectators in electoral battles for the educated middle-class vote' (2014: 117).

Significantly, this hybrid economistic-culturalist analysis has since been acknowledged by some of those culpable for sidelining these working-class groups. In *Beyond the Red Wall*, her book exploring the concerns and values of disaffected 'left-behind' voters following Labour's loss of dozens of core constituencies in the 2019 general election, Deborah Mattinson, a onetime adviser to Prime Minister Gordon Brown (later rehired by Sir Keir Starmer), confessed that 'other than the occasional by-election, at no point in the decades that I spent advising Labour did we ever consider running focus groups or polling in any of the Red Wall seats' (2020: 9). As a result, she confessed, 'red-wall' voters had been 'neglected by the entire political class': while Labour 'felt that they didn't need to worry about their "heartland constituencies"', Conservatives 'ignored them' because they deemed them 'totally unwinnable' (ibid.). In a subsequent book touching on the 'red wall' collapse, but adopting a wider purview to consider forms of economic precarity experienced by 'workers' *everywhere* (not just in Labour's former electoral strongholds), Jon Cruddas, Labour MP for Dagenham and Rainham, conceptualized his party's 1990s shift in political priorities as one that sought to target the beneficiaries of the then emerging 'knowledge economy' (today reincarnated as the 'Fourth Industrial Revolution'). In so doing, Labour had both exploited and contributed to entrenching an 'hourglass' labour market that had worsened in later years, with serious long-term consequences for its rapidly depleting working-class base (Cruddas, 2021: 74–5). Arguing that 'the political strategy of New Labour' had been 'focused on the top end of this hourglass' – the 21 per cent of 'knowledge workers' with 'significant discretion over their hours and work patterns' – Cruddas accused the party of having short-changed those lodged in the 'secondary labour market' of 'service-related elementary occupations, administrative and clerical occupations, sales occupations, caring personal service occupations and the like'. By ignoring this 'growing trend' towards 'low-paid, routine and much unskilled work' in once 'pre-eminent' occupations – and failing to engage with those it affected – the Left had assured itself of 'disastrous' long-term 'political consequences', as a working class disempowered and sidelined by the new post-industrial economic settlement slowly 'deserted the party' (ibid.).

At the point Ford, Goodwin and others were first conceptualizing 'the left behind', a key concern was that this grouping might offer an incipient recruiting ground for radical right-wing political forces – primarily the then ascendant United Kingdom Independence Party (UKIP) – and that the slow-burn, decades-long marginalization of working-class voters, their values and concerns by an out-of-touch London-centric political elite could provide a recipe for populist uprisings. This was an all-too-familiar thesis, most recently floated following the British National Party's (ultimately short-lived) breakthrough in the 2006 Barking Borough Council elections, in which it had won 12 seats and set itself up as (semi) official opposition to the ruling Labour group, and the similarly ephemeral rise to infamy of Tommy Robinson (aka Stephen Yaxley-Lennon) and the English Defence League. During the feverish public debates surrounding these developments, the 'liberal' media-political establishment fell over itself to navigate a tortuous discursive path that (belatedly) 'recognized' the condition of white working-class alienation, while trying not to pander to the bigotry and racism it potentially fostered. Of the more questionable editorial contortions by the BBC alone, two stood out: the decision to offer then BNP leader Nick Griffin his most public platform to date, on BBC1's *Question Time*, and, a year earlier, the devotion of a whole season of BBC2 documentaries, under the collective banner *White*, to the provocative question, 'Is the white working class in Britain becoming invisible?' (quoted in Lawler, 2012). Indeed, the latter films achieved the near-impossible feat of attracting criticisms accusing them of racism towards *both* ethnic minorities and white people themselves (ibid.; socialistworker.co.uk, 2008).

If *Revolt on the Right* was responsible for reviving the 'invisible whites' debate, within two short years it had been thoroughly reheated, as pundits raced to apply similar diagnoses to the outcome of the Brexit referendum, through the proliferation of a discourse of post hoc rationalization attributing the result (over-simplistically) to a backlash by 'left-behind' working-class voters against a take-your-pick medley of factors. These ranged from the long-term impact of de-unionization and globalized labour markets on post-industrial communities to pressures on public services and rapid cultural change in areas disproportionately affected by immigration.

Whatever the truth of the matter, today 'the left behind' (if such a crudely homogenizing imaginary can be considered valid) is less a marginal or peripheral phenomenon – the clichéd angry older white man hollering at the ministerial motorcade from beneath a 'We Voted Leave!' placard – than the foremost protagonist in the battle for the UK's future political direction. By the time of the 2019 election, all major parties were belatedly battling for the 'left-behind' vote, with Boris Johnson's Conservatives audaciously pitching for former Labour heartlands in northern England and elsewhere with pledges to both deliver Brexit and pursue a 'Levelling Up' agenda – explicitly framed, in his subsequent Queen's Speech, as a way of spreading 'opportunities and investment' more equitably across 'the regions of England' beyond the prosperous South East (gov.uk, 2019: 12). Indeed, there were two abiding narratives to emerge from that election, which delivered the biggest Conservative majority since 1987. One was the borderline absurd idea – road-tested three years earlier by the Brexit battle-bus but mobilized even more effectively in the dreary door-stepping rituals of the wintry 2019 campaign – that a Cabinet of millionaires, led by an old Etonian ex-Oxford Union president, could plausibly frame themselves as champions of an 'anti-elite' working-class backlash. The other was the collapse of the 'red wall': a never-before-used but now ubiquitous term, coined earlier that year on Twitter by ex-Tory pollster James Kanagasooriam to reframe a disparate swathe of northern English, Welsh and Midlands constituencies that had once formed a supposedly unbreachable bulwark against Tory encroachment into Labour territory as newly ripe for annexation following the tectonic political upheavals of preceding years.

The sub-Disraelian discourse of 'Levelling Up' would grow ever more audible during the ensuing Parliament – alternately pilloried and parroted by a Labour Party racing to keep up (rhetorically and politically) with the Conservatives' newly (re)discovered devotion to the concerns of 'left-behind' areas. Even in the thick of the COVID-19 pandemic and its attendant economic shocks, Ministers continued to invoke this egalitarian mantra – miraculously stumbling on the 'magic money tree' so oft-derided by their frugal predecessors (May, quoted in Dearden, 2017) to promise generous helpings of taxpayer-funded largesse aimed squarely at investing (and solidifying their support) in their newly assembled 'blue wall'. First there were pledges (subsequently downsized) to spend £500 million reversing regional railway closures dating back to the 1960s Beeching cuts, including the Ashington, Blyth and Tyne line running through the Blyth Valley in Northumberland: a one-time coal-mining, shipbuilding and fishing hub, and perhaps the most surprising defector among all erstwhile red-wall strongholds to crumble in the face of Johnson's assault. Then, in the early days of COVID, came the 'One Nation' rhetorical flourishes accompanying Chancellor Rishi Sunak's announcement of emergency support for households plunged into economic insecurity by the ensuing UK-wide lockdowns. Unveiling an initial £1,000 one-year boost to Universal Credit, the main working-age social security benefit, and a £35 billion Job Retention Scheme paying up to 80 per cent of the wages of workers temporarily 'furloughed' due to the enforced closure of 'non-essential' businesses, he reflected that the government would be 'judged by' its 'capacity for compassion' (quoted in Partington, 2020). Eight months later, Sunak would train his sights more narrowly on 'left-behind' areas, by using an otherwise downbeat inaugural Spending Review to launch a £4.8bn 'Levelling Up Fund' to boost regeneration projects in deprived areas – even as many of those same places continued to weather harsh COVID restrictions and the government's own Office for Budget Responsibility (OBR) issued baleful warnings of impending economic doom.

Yet, while an affinity with working-class 'angels in marble' (McKenzie & Silver, 1968) might reasonably have been claimed by Benjamin Disraeli, Harold Macmillan and other Conservatives of a more charitable (if condescending) disposition, sceptical observers were quick to emphasize the irony that many of Johnson's self-styled 'champions of the people' had been enthusiastic cheerleaders, or in some cases architects, of a long period of neoliberal governance which had entrenched the very inequalities they now pledged to address – not least during the decade of Tory-led austerity immediately preceding their 2019 electoral triumph. Indeed, even as Ministers continued to insist they were putting their 'arms around the people of this country' through a pre-vaccine COVID winter (Johnson, quoted in Roach, 2020), the mask of compassion began to slip, as 'left-behind' areas of England that had scarcely been out of lockdown since the previous March were plunged into a bleak December of 'tier-3' restrictions (the toughest in the land) and the small-print of policies introduced to help struggling, newly unemployed workers began to reek of familiar punitive, behaviouralist approaches to welfare. As 50 Tory MPs from the so-called 'Northern Research Group' stressed in a letter to Johnson, by November 2020 – shortly before a second England-wide lockdown – all areas under the strictest measures were in the North and Midlands, including numerous newly 'blue-walled' towns widely recognized as among the most 'left behind' in the land (localtrust.org.uk, 2019). These included Blyth itself, Leigh in Greater Manchester and Doncaster, South Yorkshire. The letter stressed how COVID had exposed 'the deep structural and systemic disadvantage faced by our communities' and threatened to 'continue to increase the disparity between the North and South still further' (cited in Pidd, 2020).

Such concerns appeared to fall on deaf ears: when conditions surrounding England's three-tier system were toughened still further in December 2020, numerous other local authority areas encompassing 'left-behind' wards, from Newcastle-upon-Tyne to Stoke-on-Trent, were shunted into the highest tier, defying figures suggesting that many of them had lower infection rates than parts of the (less restricted) South-East and London. As the revised tier system sparked a fresh revolt among Tory backbenchers, the reaction from Johnson's political opponents was blunt. 'They used the same scare tactics against Greater Manchester when they tried to browbeat us into accepting their original flawed tier-3 proposals', declared the city's metropolitan mayor, Andy Burnham, adding that continued relegation to the highest tier of so many already struggling areas would 'decimate' them, in 'a deliberate act of levelling down' (Kirby, 2020). Some academic commentators were similarly indignant. 'Why does the late November map of the three-tier system in England look so much like a depiction of the north-south divide?' asked social geographer Danny Dorling in the *Observer*. The answer, he concluded, could be found in the multiple, intersecting inequalities disproportionately affecting communities in the North, the Midlands and a handful of post-industrial areas in southern England, including much of Kent, south Gloucestershire and northern Somerset. In 'poorer, more often northern, parts people have jobs that cannot be done from home and more use public transport', he pointed out, while fewer could afford to retire early and childcare was 'provided by the extended family' (including vulnerable older relatives), as wages and benefits were too low to fund paid-for cover (Dorling, 2020). Dorling added that 'overcrowding in homes' was more common in high-density urban areas – an echo of concerns about 'multigenerational' and 'multi-family' households previously highlighted by others as partial explanation for COVID's disproportionate impact on Black and South Asian groups that had hitherto baffled pundits and politicians (e.g., Razaq et al., 2020).

Reflecting on these interconnected dimensions of 'the left-behind condition', columnist Andrew Rawnsley drew attention to Johnson's vow that 'no one will be left behind' and 'what happened in 2008' would not be repeated – that is, the sweeping austerity, wage freezes and benefit cuts that had become the default neoliberal response to the global financial crash. A 'further sharpening' of inequalities, 'accompanied by even deeper feelings of unfairness', was, he warned, 'a formula for more of the corrosive bitterness that was already disfiguring society before the epidemic began' (Rawnsley, 2020).

Indeed, the persistent positioning of the North and Midlands as somehow aberrant and deviant in the context of COVID – as hotspots of infection letting down the national side in its fight against the virus – would translate into an increasingly overt discourse of othering as the pandemic approached its second wave. In an interview on BBC Radio 4's *Today* programme on 27 November (the day after the revised tiers were confirmed), then Communities and Local Government Secretary Robert Jenrick repeatedly advised residents in tier-3 areas to 'work hard' to cut infection rates so they might earn the greater freedoms that came with lower-tier status – including a then proposed five-day Christmas respite from lockdown. This effective designation of deviant areas, through the prism of the tier system, followed a familiar Conservative script of both *individualizing* responsibility for complex *society-wide* issues and spatially othering named communities, through a discursive practice sociologist Loïc Wacquant describes as 'territorial stigmatization': the construction of 'isolated and bounded territories', including 'social purgatories' and 'leprous badlands', at the heart of the 'post-industrial metropolis' (2008: 43). Moreover, as ministers busied themselves on the breakfast media rounds justifying their 'exclusion' of the geographically marked 'imperfect people' from basic societal freedoms (Sibley, 1995: 69), critical commentators began scrutinizing the conditions and caveats in the latest package of labour-market and welfare interventions aimed at furloughed workers and the unemployed. The devils in the detail of a blizzard of snappily titled initiatives – from a KickStart programme for young 'job-seekers' to a Job Entry Targeted Support scheme for people facing longer-term unemployment – included a melange of re-sharpened sticks wielded during the heyday of Coalition Work and Pensions Secretary Iain Duncan Smith's coercive Work Programme. Instead of a Keynesian programme of public investment-led job *creation*, there were job 'coaches' for those recently made redundant – again individualizing responsibility onto unemployed people to 'search' for work, as if it might magically (re)appear against a backdrop of pre-COVID zero-hours precarity, during COVID economic contraction and slow-burn post-COVID recovery.

Meanwhile, younger people were offered 'placements', rather than apprenticeships, under a scheme promising them the minimum wage for internships of up to six months but otherwise eerily redolent of Coalition-era 'mandatory' work activity. While Opposition MPs fixated on Universal Credit's impending slump back to pre-COVID levels, there was also the end of a nine-month moratorium on the household benefit cap and the headline 'cut' in Sunak's economically hawkish spending review: the reintroduction of a disproportionately red-wall/blue-wall-pummelling public-sector pay freeze, legitimized (in terms reminiscent of Coalition Chancellor George Osborne's divide-and-rule rhetoric) by a race-to-the-bottom assertion that, as COVID had 'deepened the disparity between public and private sector wages', he could not 'justify a significant across-the-board pay increase for all public sector workers' (fenews.co.uk, 2020). Indeed, the entire basis of Sunak's comparison was spurious: the supposed relative generosity of public-sector wages was based on notional private-sector comparators including the most precarious, poorly paid 'employees' in Britain, from care-workers and security guards to drivers of Deliveroo mopeds and Uber taxis in the gig economy. Yet, amid all the understandable criticism of such measures, and their likely impact on 'left-behind' groups, one of the earliest manifestations of the imagined post-pandemic 'new normal' was scarcely noticed: the return of punitive benefit sanctions for unemployed and disabled people, sneaked out by the Department of Work and Pensions (DWP) the moment the first lockdown ended.

How long, then, before sympathy for 'left-behind' areas at the macro level of towns and regions is undermined by a renewed emphasis on conditionality and coercion – regardless of the background reality of a structurally damaged labour market – and the revival of 'scrounger discourse' (Morrison, 2019a) at the micro-level of the individual households and neighbourhoods making up these semi-mythologized domains? Is the electorally expedient imaginary of 'the left behind' ultimately doomed to be recast (once its usefulness expires) as the latest incarnation of a long-running continuum of stigmatized social groupings, from the nineteenth-century 'residuum' through the 'underclass' to the 'socially excluded' communities Tony Blair problematized as 'forgotten people' (quoted on bbc.co.uk, 1997)? This is to say nothing of the yawning national-to-local democratic deficit magnified by COVID – devolution of *responsibility*, not *power*, to metropolitan authorities – as lockdown restrictions, and the terms and conditions of state support, were imposed on territorially stigmatized regions by a centralized Whitehall-based government machine: one helmed (lest we forget) by a premier who won his mandate by championing 'the will of the people' against the condescending, we-know-best diktats of a 'metropolitan elite' (Grieve, 2019).

These incipient mobilizations of 'left-behind' discourse for more divisive political purposes are merely one reason why the concept is problematic. Even when applied in a well-intentioned (if patronizing) way, dominant media and political narratives about 'the left behind' fail to adequately acknowledge the full range and diversity of groups that might be described in such terms – or, in the perhaps more suitable phraseology of Nottingham housing estate residents interviewed by ethnographer Lisa McKenzie, 'left out', 'invisible', or 'not existing' (McKenzie, 2017: 199). As several recent interventions by race-equality charity the Runnymede Trust rightly query, where in the prevailing left-behind narrative framed around a 'somewhat mythical "white working class"' is there mention of the similarly economically marginalized and politically disenfranchised ethnic minority groups with whom they increasingly coexist – including in once more mono-ethnic industrial areas that today exhibit 'significant racial and ethnic diversity' (Barbulescu et al., 2019; Snoussi & Mompelat, 2019)? And what of the much wider spectrum of groups that have, for some years, weathered insecure, low-paid work and periodic bouts of unemployment? Where is the space in this narrative for the zero-hours, payday loan-dependent gig-economy workers of Guy Standing's universal 'precariat' (2011); the similarly precarious 'emerging service workers' seen as slowly supplanting the 'traditional working class' by Britain's leading class analyst, Mike Savage (2015: 169); and the multi-ethnic, multifaceted 'new working-class' conceived of as a catch-all umbrella for all these subgroups by Claire Ainsley (2018), Labour adviser and ex-director of the Joseph Rowntree Foundation? In the words of a former coalminer interviewed for this book, any worthwhile definition of 'the left behind' must move beyond stigmatizing 'a supposed underclass', framed as having 'fallen out of the "working class"' – by recognizing that this term increasingly describes the position of a '*majority* of employees in the UK'.

UNDERSTANDING 'THE LEFT BEHIND'

What, then, is the purpose of this book? As ever, it is simplest to set out what it is *not*. It does not aim to prove or disprove the empirical existence of a normatively quantifiable 'left-behind' group, or even a kaleidoscope of related groupings. For detailed explorations of the multidimensional characteristics of today's complex, rapidly evolving British class system, cast a critical eye over the aforementioned works by Savage, Ainsley and Standing. Neither is this a book about Brexit, who voted for it and why, the collapse of Labour's 'red wall', the supposed 'culture war' between social conservatives and social liberals, or how the 'workers' party' (and the Left generally) might reconnect with their one-time working-class base. Again, authoritative and nuanced accounts of these seismic democratic events – and the contribution (decisive or overstated) of 'left-behind' voters – can be found in the work of Danny Dorling, economist Sascha O. Becker, social policy scholar Lorenza

Antonucci and a slew of reports by the Resolution Foundation and other think-tanks (e.g., McCurdy et al., 2020). For diagnoses of the growing disconnect between big-L and small-l Labour (especially the 'traditional' working class), and how this might be repaired, look no further than Mattinson's *Beyond the Red Wall* (2020), trade unionist Paul Embery's polemical *Despised* (2020), Sebastian Payne's *Broken Heartlands* (2021), or the extensive work of Maurice Glasman's Blue Labour 'advocacy group' (www.bluelabour.org, 2020). You might also consult Ainsley's manifesto for winning over 'the new working-class' (2018), Jon Cruddas's prospectus for the future of meaningful work, *The Dignity of Labour* (2021), and David Goodhart's provocative dissection of the 'tribes' defining modern Britain: *The Road to Somewhere* (2017).

What this book *does* offer is an attempt to unpack the symbolism and substance of a contentious archetype that rose to prominence in the 'shadow' of the referendum – and the deep social divisions that vote exposed and exacerbated. In doing so, it examines how 'the left behind' have repeatedly been (re)constructed as a problem in media coverage and political rhetoric – by both detractors and defenders – and analyses the key traits that have come to be associated with them in the discourse(s) of the press, Parliament and social media. Perhaps most significantly, it explores how 'the left behind' have been appropriated and mobilized for multiple, often conflicting, ideological purposes – by different actors, at different times. The book's central proposition is that the term 'left behind' – like 'Levelling Up', the equally nebulous imaginary that Ministers repeatedly invoke as a 'solution' to the problems 'left-behind' communities face – is no more than an 'empty signifier' (Dabirimehr & Fatmi, 2014). It is a malleable, at times meaningless, discursive construct that insults the real-world individuals, families and communities afflicted by economic disadvantage by weaponizing them as rhetorical pawns in a relentless game of political chess.

The remaining sections of this introduction set out the core themes and debates that guide us on this journey. Before turning to them, though, a quick word about terminology: from now on, the book drops the use of inverted commas whenever it uses the term 'left behind'. Henceforth, please assume that this label is used critically, rather than normatively: in other words, its relevance, precision and suitability are implicitly questioned, even when reference is made (as it frequently is) to its matter-of-fact usage by others.

Chapter 1 begins by exploring the roots of left-behind discourse. It does so by locating this, in part, in the evolution of historical conceptualizations of lower-income social groups, communities and/or geographical areas – including those framing them as successive iterations of the 'undeserving poor' and, latterly, 'underclass' (Welshman, 2013) – while relating it to the seismic socioeconomic and cultural upheavals of recent decades that have contributed to genuine transformations in the nature of what it means to *be* working class.

In Chapters 2 to 5, the book switches focus to the recent past, to examine how the concept of the left behind rose to prominence in the context of the 2016 Brexit referendum and commensurate political upheavals in the United States, mainland Europe and elsewhere – including the election of US President Donald Trump. To achieve this, the book interrogates popular conceptions of the left behind through a framing and critical discourse analysis of local and national newspaper coverage and parliamentary discussions of this concept clustered around key political events during the three-and-a-half-year period between the referendum and the 2019 'Brexit election'. This is followed by a sentiment analysis of the ways in which the public both responded and *contributed* to these moments in the evolution of the left-behind debate, via newspaper comment threads and Twitter.

Finally, the book goes 'in search of' the left behind, by drawing on individual interviews with people who can make stronger claims than most to speak on behalf of economically disadvantaged groups – from representatives of foodbanks, residents' associations and local businesses to councillors, MPs and other community actors based in areas of England, Wales and Scotland identified in recent independent audits of the indices and dimensions of what it means to be left behind. But it also goes beyond this, to speak to out-of-work former Staffordshire potters, retired miners from Wigan and Doncaster, disabled people, struggling single parents and other hard-pressed, hard-working individuals – employed and unemployed alike – from towns and hinterlands as geographically widespread as Leigh in Greater Manchester, the east coast resort of Great Yarmouth, Torridge in North Devon and the Rhondda valley in South Wales. In so doing, it purposely adopts as inclusive an approach as possible to addressing what it means to be (or feel) left behind in today's Britain: one which takes account of legitimate recent criticisms of the disproportionate (at times, exclusive) emphasis in popular discourse on the white, post-industrial working-class(es) to embrace groups and communities of a more multicultural and multidimensional character.

The book concludes by making a case for a more socially and culturally inclusive narrative around the position of areas, communities and groups affected by inequalities of opportunity, education, health, income and status: one which moves beyond one-size-fits-all labels like 'left behind' or 'red wall' to meaningfully speak *up for* the widest possible range of people affected by economic and other inequalities, but without speaking *for* them (let alone simply *about* them). In doing so, it advocates a more 'public-led' approach to reframing the dominant discourse(s) and refocusing the substance of media and political debates: one that both recognizes and responds to the full diversity and complexity of the needs, challenges and – yes – opportunities facing the multifarious groups currently locked out of the good life, to improve the lives of the people (formerly) known as the left behind.

FRAMING THE BLAME FOR BREXIT: REVOLT OF THE WORKING CLASS OR RISE OF A NEW 'UNDERCLASS'?

While the term 'left behind' may have been circulating before the referendum in the rarefied realms of policy think-tanks and academia, it was only widely popularized in the context of Brexit. As those on both sides of the Leave–Remain divide struggled to digest the enormity of the referendum result, the belated recognition that many areas of the UK had suffered decades of economic neglect suddenly seemed to become common currency – albeit less as a wake-up call demanding policy action to redress resulting social injustices than a convenient explanatory framework for the high concentrations of Brexit support in post-industrial towns, defunct ports and faded coastal resorts. 'A howl of rage and frustration by one half of the country' against a 'system of power, wealth and privilege perceived to be controlled by an elite residing, well, elsewhere' was *Guardian* columnist Raphael Behr's apocalyptic reading of the slender Leave majority on the morning after the 23 June vote (Behr, 2016). But it took his colleague (and fellow arch-Remainer) Polly Toynbee to crystallize what soon became the dominant *economistic* diagnosis of the outcome, characterizing it as 'an uprising of resentment by the left-behind' that had 'torn us in two' – exposing 'a country wrecked by a yawning class divide stretched wider by recession and austerity' (Toynbee, 2016).

One of the earliest commentaries leaning towards a more *culturalist* interpretation of events came from another liberal broadsheet, the *Independent*. In an explainer article headlined 'Brexit: 5 things we learned from a night that shook Europe', policy correspondent Jon Stone introduced into the mainstream public sphere an argument that would soon be the most widely debated alternative narrative about the nature of left-behind disenchantment – but had, up to this point, largely only been voiced by a handful of academics. This was the suggestion that the Leave–Remain split 'cleaves to a wider emerging divide', between politically 'forward-looking cosmopolitans and those left behind by globalisation, terrified of immigration and seeing their communities change' (Stone, 2016a).

Within hours, a 'left-behind thesis' of one shade or other had become so widely accepted by pundits, politicians and public that it was being reduced to a common-sense, taken-for-granted truth requiring little elaboration. In quotes reproduced across several national and regional newspapers, from the *Daily Mirror* to the *Newcastle Chronicle*, Bridget Philipson, Labour MP for Leave-voting Houghton and Sunderland South, responded to the result with an economistic reading strongly reminiscent of Toynbee's: rationalizing it as reflecting the fact 'people in the North East feel that time and time again we're left behind', with years of austerity having further drained 'jobs and investment' from the region (Kelly, 2016a). Quoted in the *Northern Echo*, shellshocked fellow North-East Labour MP Alex Cunningham spoke of his constituents as people 'not sharing in the wealth of this country' – while hinting at other, by turns subtler and broader, aspects of their disconnect from the London-based political class, by arguing that they felt 'left behind and cut off' by 'the political establishment in Brussels and Westminster' (Blackburn, 2016).

There was also no shortage of voices ventriloquizing normative definitions of the left behind on Twitter. 'It's no surprise that Sunderland has voted for Brexit', tweeted one *Guardian* reader as results flooded in shortly after midnight on Friday, 24 June, 'it's an old shipbuilding and coalmining city full of the "left behind"'. More sobering was this hard-truths assessment from another tweeter, as the sun rose on Brexit Britain at 6.20 a.m.: 'Globalization has been so elitist that the working class left behind just stabbed everyone from behind.' Among the more authoritative voices monitoring the live results was political scientist Matthew Goodwin, who noted at 2.05 a.m. that a 'big story tonight is Wales', where 'lots of left behind, blue collar & anxious voters' seemed to have 'moved to Brexit in [a] big way'. Even then-Democratic Party US presidential hopeful Bernie Sanders contributed to the debate. In tweeted interview excerpts from *CBS News*, he qualified his 'concerns' about the result with the observation that 'a lot of people are being left behind in this global economy.'

For others (notably those manoeuvring themselves for party leadership contests ahead), the righteous anger of the left behind presented useful discursive tools for furthering their own political ends. Within days, Brexiteer ministers Michael Gove and Andrea Leadsom – both veterans of a government that arguably had done more than most to stoke the grievances of economically marginalized communities by presiding over ten years of austerity – were hastily restyling themselves as champions of the left behind, while launching rival bids to succeed outgoing Prime Minister David Cameron. Leadsom rebooted the 'Northern Powerhouse' rhetoric she had helped co-author as Economic Secretary in Osborne's Treasury with an over-the-rainbow promise that, on her watch, 'parts of the country which felt left behind' would all receive 'shares in our economic prosperity' (quoted in Kelly, 2016b). Gove, a key architect of the official Vote Leave campaign, revived the 'Take back control' slogan so instrumental in its success to align himself with the same hitherto disenfranchised groups in a divisive, rhetorically charged battle between 'two Britains': those who 'reap the benefits of globalisation' versus 'those who are flotsam and jetsam in its powerful flows of global capital and free labour' (quoted on conservativehome.com, 2016). The eventual victor, Theresa May, drew on her own backstory of upward social mobility (grammar school to Oxford University) to emphasize how the lives of working-class households were 'much harder than people realise', before itemizing a list of 'burning injustices' – ranging from variations in educational attainment to life expectancy (Butler, 2016). These would ultimately form the basis of a mission to transform the lives of struggling groups that were 'just about managing', crystallized in her maiden address as prime minister (quoted in Ferrari, 2019).

Meanwhile, the left behind provided a useful trope for candidates on the other side of the political divide, as the initial rush to succeed Cameron as premier was drowned out by the opening salvoes in a drawn-out battle for the leadership of the Labour Party – whose incumbent, Jeremy Corbyn, had been widely criticized for his lacklustre contribution to the Remain campaign. For Jon Trickett, Corbyn loyalist and Labour's election coordinator, the prospect of an un-elected Tory prime minister being crowned amid post-referendum chaos underlined the urgency of uniting to ensure the millions 'left behind by the Tories' failed economic policies' had the chance 'to elect a Labour government' (Pope, 2016). This amplified Corbyn's own message, in fending off his challengers: the promise of a Utopian 'economic revolution' to ensure that 'no one and nowhere' was 'left behind' (Cecil, 2016).

Suddenly, everyone had something to say about the left behind. Beyond the Westminster village, Ruth Davidson, leader of a Scottish Conservative Party newly emboldened after leapfrogging Scottish Labour to become the official Opposition in the Holyrood parliament, contrasted the obscene wealth of 'dotcom millionaires' and 'the Middle Eastern super-rich' with the plight of an 'awful lot of people' who felt they had been 'left behind' and saw no 'means or opportunity or anybody helping them to catch up'. Interviewed in *The Times*, Davidson patented her own variation of the 'howl of rage' Brexit thesis to describe the collective 'yelp of pain' against injustice she also attributed to disparate groups ranging from Trump supporters to devotees of Spanish Left-populist party Podemos (Thomson & Sylvester, 2016). And it was not just politicians claiming to speak up for left-behind groups. For priest and social commentator Giles Fraser (who, five years earlier, had resigned his post at St Paul's Cathedral in solidarity with Occupy protesters encamped on its doorstep), this was an 'angry roar for attention' from people who had been 'left profoundly unattended by the political process' and 'taken for granted, patted on the head – by the Labour party as much as the Conservatives' (Fraser, 2016a). Continuing his commentary on Twitter, Fraser provoked a lively debate by arguing that, while UKIP had 'shamelessly exploited' such resentments, they were 'not about immigration' but 'about people being left out by globalisation' – to which Philip Pullman, award-winning author of the *His Dark Materials* trilogy grumpily retorted, 'of course they were about immigration.' Even Sir Simon Stevens – the sober mandarin helming England's National Health Service – seemed to normatively buy into the new national obsession, by announcing plans for NHS apprenticeships to help '"left-behind" communities alienated from modern Britain' (quoted on itv.com, 2016).

But while these early reactions strained to display empathy – a recognition of the *existence* of left-behind communities paired with attempts to divine the *causes* of their frustrations – it took little time for initial waves of self-recrimination in Remainer circles to yield to a more natural state of disbelief. 'The day after the EU referendum I was sitting in ... shocked company with colleagues at the Joseph Rowntree Foundation headquarters in York', recalled Claire Ainsley in *The New Working Class*, describing how 'no one could quite believe' the city had turned out to be one of 'only two places in the whole of North Yorkshire that did not vote to leave' (2018: 1). In going on to quote journalist and writer Caitlin Moran's concept of the '"Attenboroughisation' of places outside the immediate purview of the London-based media' (ibid.), Ainsley crystallized the state of wide-eyed, Orientalizing bewilderment increasingly worn by the liberal intelligentsia and commentariat as they began their long, obsessive post-referendum inquest. Over ensuing weeks, the mystique attached to the supposed authors of Britain's misfortune – the newly discovered left behind – came to mesmerize the media. Suddenly London-based newsrooms were dispatching reporters well beyond the M25, venturing into forgotten fringes, post-industrial ghost towns and low-rent suburbs: their mission to seek out the lost tribes intent on dragging Britain back to the Dark Ages. It was soon impossible to open a newspaper or switch on the television without stumbling on mention of the left behind, as camera crews ambushed as many people fitting the white working-class stereotype as possible – like boom mike-wielding Victorian social explorers. 'As a result of the referendum the media suddenly became interested in people on lower incomes and those living in parts of the country less well known to them', observed Ainsley, all 'because they had chosen to vote against the "established" view' (2018: 2).

Predictably, these early (performative) displays of concern and understanding for the plight of disadvantaged communities thrust into the spotlight by Brexit did not last. The mix of soul-searching and studied concern that had characterized the earliest stage of the Remainer hangover soon gave way to simpler, less conflicted, emotions of condescension, resentment and blame. There was, after all, only so much empathy even those genuinely disturbed by the economic and political inequalities that seemed to have fuelled the Leave vote could muster for people determined to vote against their own interests. Perhaps unsurprisingly, the bitterest recriminations were to be found on social media: 'ah the poor misunderstood persecuted English working class tories ... you have [to] feel sory for them [*sic*]', read one sarcastic tweet just hours after the referendum polls closed – heralding a simmering strain of resentment in the Twittersphere that would continue to fester for years to come. By the time of the fabled 'red-wall' collapse in the December 2019 election, any pretence of empathy for left-behind voters determined to pursue the Brexit folly seemed to have vanished in uber-Remainer circles, to be replaced by bitter and vengeful expressions of disdain. 'The gobshites up in working class areas like Grimsby who today have voted tory so you can "get Brexit done" will be the first left behind by the tory party if brexit [*sic*] causes a recession and you lose your jobs', wrote one angry poster shortly after the YouGov exit poll forecast an 86-seat Conservative majority. Such voters would, they predicted, 'look back on this moment' when they found themselves 'in a que [*sic*] for a food bank'.

All the while, a subtler vein of criticism was running through the op-ed pages of the *Guardian*, where on 25 June – two days after the referendum – lead opinion writer Jonathan Freedland had already portrayed many Leave voters as regretful handmaidens of the Brexit mayhem ahead: a supposed phenomenon of mass contrition one tweeter had waggishly termed 'Regrexit'. 'There are leave voters who confessed to reporters that they never thought their side would actually win, that their vote had only ever been intended as a protest, presumed to be safe because surely everyone else would vote the other way', he asserted, citing BBC interviews with 'leavers in Manchester who admitted that they woke up thinking, "What have I done?"' The questions exercising many denizens of 'rundown English towns that were left behind decades ago' were, he said (speaking for them), 'are you content with the status quo? Are you comfortable with immigration? Do you feel you have anything to lose?' And yet, he warned, 'already it's become clear that the verdict they delivered will not answer the questions they want answered' (Freedland, 2016b). In a similar but more succinct assessment a few hours earlier, one tweeter had distilled the same argument thus: 'Brexit is a disaster that will impact all of us, but especially the "left behind" who voted for it.'

Some Remain-supporting commentators continued to speak up for Leave-voting working-class communities – among them *Guardian* columnist Owen Jones and his colleagues, John Harris and John Domokos, whose long-running 'Anywhere but Westminster' films managed to capture more nuanced drivers of Brexit support in left-behind places. Their most vocal defenders by this stage, however, were an alliance of disputably Left- and Right-leaning libertarians. Among their number were the contrarian columnists of *Spiked Online*, notably its then editor, Brendan O'Neill, self-proclaimed 'left-leaning' Brexiteer Ella Whelan and soon-to-be Brexit Party MEP Claire Fox, director of the Academy of Ideas think-tank. In a throwback to their years defending the masses as members of the Revolutionary Communist Party, Fox and O'Neill leapt to the defence of working-class voters during the earliest stages of the post-Brexit Remainer backlash – the latter with a defiant November 2016 blog-post on his website, entitled 'In defence of the crowd'. In it, O'Neill likened condemnation of

Leave voters by 'the new elites' to a process of othering: 'hand-wringing over the rage of Them', of the 'swarm of folk brutishly disturbing politics and business as usual' (O'Neill, 2016). Brexit and Trump's ascendancy had left everyone 'freaking out about the howling little people and their ripping-up of the political script', he fumed. Three years on, these words found striking echoes in comments by Trump's hawkish national security adviser, John Bolton. Asked about the prospect of a 'no-deal' Brexit, he observed that the 'fashion' in the EU, whenever 'people vote the wrong way from the way' the 'elites want to go', was to 'make the peasants vote again and again until they get it right' (quoted in Rahim, 2019). In these early exchanges of fire between the likes of Freedland and O'Neill could be glimpsed the opening salvoes of a protracted battle over British values later crystallized as the new 'culture war' (Sobolewska & Ford, 2020) or (by some on the Right) as 'the war on woke' (Payne & Wright, 2020).

Amid all the initial post-referendum hubbub about 'working-class' or 'blue-collar' revolts, however, one inconvenient truth was in danger of being lost: the fact that, while many disadvantaged towns and areas had indeed backed Brexit, the majority of Leave votes were *not* cast by the (real or imagined) left behind. As Professor Dorling noted in an early academic article crunching the granular demographic data underpinning the vote, 'the outcome of the EU referendum has been unfairly blamed on the working class in the north of England', when 'most people who voted Leave lived in the south' (Dorling, 2016). Not only this: some 59 per cent of Leave voters had come from what latter-day socioeconomic indicators would define as 'the middle classes' (those in A, B and C1 occupations), while less than a quarter derived from 'the lowest two social classes (D and E)' (ibid.). Others were soon noting similar patterns – even while maintaining that 'key drivers of the Vote Leave share' were voters' 'education profiles' and 'historical dependence on manufacturing employment as well as low income and high unemployment' (variables normatively associated with left-behind groups) (Becker et al., 2017: 601). In a ground-breaking 'comprehensive district-level analysis' of the referendum vote, Sascha O. Becker and colleagues drew on both Dorling's argument and extensive data from Conservative pollster Lord Ashcroft to repeat the finding that 'the typical Leave voter' was 'white, middle class and lives in the South of England' (ibid.: 606).

Two years later, a journal article on spatial planning drew on hyper-local analysis of contiguous electoral wards with similar levels of economic deprivation in the Liverpool city region to challenge deterministic notions that disadvantaged areas were necessarily more likely than affluent ones to have backed Brexit, while also showing how 'some areas and populations voted to leave the EU' just as 'others with comparable profiles voted to remain' (Nurse & Sykes, 2019: 589). Earlier that year, in a trenchant letter to the Darlington-based *Northern Echo* newspaper (cited in ibid.), four northern Labour MPs had derided the blanket 'stereotyping and caricaturing' of areas later dubbed the 'red wall' – condemning 'journalist after journalist' and 'broadcaster after broadcaster' in the 'London-based metropolitan media' for having 'declared' the North to be 'Brexitland' (thenorthernecho.co.uk, 2019).

Moreover, while a growing academic consensus was emerging that Brexit voters represented a 'cross-class coalition of middle-aged and older men and women' (Virdee & McGeever, 2018: 1803), not a homogenous left behind, a more segmented analysis soon identified the contribution of another latter-day political imaginary: 'the squeezed middle'. Locating their re-reading of the data in the context of ongoing debates about non-class-specific precarity, social policy researcher Lorenza Antonucci and colleagues concluded that, contrary to dominant readings of Brexit as the will of the 'left behind', 'outsiders', or 'globalization losers', it was actually *declining* economic position – not *static* measures of disadvantage – that typified Leave voters. 'Brexiters' were, they concluded, primarily 'voters in intermediate positions' who had 'declined in economic terms and experience a general feeling of social malaise' (Antonucci et al., 2017: 212–13).

VOTING AGAINST ONE'S OWN INTERESTS? THE ROOTS OF 'WORKING-CLASS CONSERVATISM'

While the extent to which Brexit can be *attributed* to low-income groups is open to debate, of one fact there can be little doubt: some of the highest concentrations of Leave voters were to be found in areas of England and Wales widely considered left behind. These included swathes of Britain which, despite having undoubtedly experienced some negative outcomes from globalizing processes promoted by the European Union, had also disproportionately benefited from EU initiatives *addressing* economic inequalities. Among them were regular recipients of generous European Regional Development Fund grants, such as the North East, South West and Wales, and, in Greater Manchester, a metropolitan region selected as one of twelve pilot areas for a new programme entitled 'Regions in Industrial Transition' in the months following the Brexit vote. Why, then, would communities that had been some of the UK's largest net beneficiaries of EU regional investment – not to mention employment rights safeguarding annual leave and sick pay for their many precarious, low-waged workers – so overwhelmingly choose to vote Leave? However illogical such behaviour might appear, at least two long-standing currents of historical thinking might help explain the sentiments fuelling these left-behind Leave-backing majorities.

Firstly, there is the protectionist, so-called 'Lexiter' strand of Left economic thinking favoured by politicians such as the late Tony Benn, his protégé Jeremy Corbyn, and trade unionists ranging from Len McCluskey, former general secretary of Britain's biggest trade union, Unite, to Arthur Scargill, who led a year-long miners' strike opposed to the rapid globalization of energy markets in the 1980s. But of perhaps greater relevance to a consideration of the motivations of many Brexit-backing left-behind households, Britain boasts a curious tradition of 'small-c' (and, in some cases, 'big-C') working-class conservatism. As we shall see in the next chapter, political campaigners and social scientists alike have long puzzled over the fact that, throughout the life of the Labour Party, the Conservatives have continued to attract consistently high numbers of working-class votes – while dissuading many 'working people' from supporting a movement formed with the explicit aim of representing them. In their classic study into the typologies and motivations of 'working class Conservatives in urban England', *Angels in Marble*, psephologist Robert McKenzie and sociologist Allan Silver observed how the Tories had consistently succeeded in presenting 'an image of themselves' and 'the society they believe in' that was 'more consistently attractive to the electorate – and to working class voters in particular – than their opponents have ever seemed able to realize' (1968: 15). Defying warnings that, by extending the working-class franchise, they were committing a 'great betrayal' – by allowing 'the working man' to 'outvote all other classes put together' (ibid.: 8–9) – Tory sponsors of the Second Reform Bill 1867 actually ushered in a system that, within a year, was being decried by class warrior Friedrich Engels for having *improved* their electoral fortunes, following an 1868 election at which 'the proletariat' had 'discredited itself terribly' (cited in ibid.: 14).

Over the next century-and-a-half, this pattern of general disinterest towards labourist politics – punctuated by occasional lukewarm swings in its favour and more frequent (occasionally dramatic) ones towards the Conservatives – would continue to characterize the ambivalence of many working-class voters towards a 'people's party' forged in their name. By the time Margaret Thatcher's Tories won their third successive landslide in 1987, she could count on the support of 42 per cent of working-class voters – leading to what social anthropologist Gillian Evans describes as a sense of 'double betrayal' among (then still class-conscious) voters in northern and Midlands Labour heartlands, who found themselves 'abandoned by the ruling government' and 'facing a loss of solidarity' with other working-class voters edging 'toward the new consensus of self-determination through personal gain' (2017: 216). But while Thatcher's appeal to material aspiration would form the bedrock of a new, very particular, strand of working-class Conservative support rooted in the democratization of property ownership and individualistic forms of social mobility, it can have had little to do with the fact that, by 2019, C2DE voters accounted for just 33 per cent of the Labour vote, compared to 48 per cent of that for the Tories – as numerous people who had never voted for anyone but the Red team (whatever baubles were dangled before them) finally defected to the Blues (McDonnell & Curtis, 2019). Neither can the peculiar attractions of neoliberal self-advancement explain more *ingrained* strands of working-class conservatism that long pre-dated the advent of the 'New Right' and 1980s mass consumerism – surviving the gestation and expansion of the Labour movement, thirty years of post-war social-democratic consensus, and Blair's attempt to pick it off with 'New' Labour's more centre-right economic agenda.

Partial answers to the question of what 'makes' or 'characterizes' a working-class Conservative – or how the rationales underpinning their politics might be better understood – lie in nuanced typologies successive social scientists developed in the late 1960s, at a time when the phenomenon of 'blue-collar' conservatism was first attracting meaningful attention. The crucial distinction drawn by many academics was between traditional or instinctive Tory voters on the one hand, and clubbable social climbers on the other: think car-driving, TV-owning 1950s consumers, or 1980s council tenants offered the chance to purchase council homes through the 'Right to Buy' scheme. For McKenzie and Silver, emerging from reams of in-depth interview transcripts in the late 1960s, the key distinction was between habitual, cloth cap-doffing Tories they dubbed 'deferentials' – people who appeared to view the Conservatives as somehow 'born to rule' – and a more intriguing type they dubbed 'seculars'. The latter were voters who based their Tory leanings, conditionally, on 'a pragmatic assessment of their performance in office' (1968: 164). By definition, the nature and depth of seculars' allegiance to the party was therefore judged to be qualitatively different to that of 'deferentials': an instrumentalist antecedent, perhaps, of the aspirational working-class and lower-middle-class floating voters who would come to hold sway from the 1980s.

In analysing working-class voting patterns in then recent elections, however, McKenzie and Silver identified two further voter categories common to both major parties: 'changers' and 'constants'. But, while the term 'changer' denoted those who had historically voted for more than one party and were therefore less constrained by loyalty (or habit) to backing the Conservatives, perhaps surprisingly they did not necessarily correspond with 'seculars'. As the authors explained in a nuanced analysis detailed in Chapter 1, while almost all 'deferentials' were 'constants' – people committed to voting Tory based on the party's 'traditional status and intrinsic qualities' – only around one-half of 'seculars' were 'changers' (ibid.: 228–9).

The 'deferentials' and 'seculars' of *Angels in Marble* overlapped with categories identified in a contemporaneous study with a subtly different focus. This was a series of interlinked monographs exploring the self-described class and political leanings of upwardly mobile Luton-based factory employees by sociologists John Goldthorpe, David Lockwood, Frank Bechhofer and Jennifer Platt, entitled *The Affluent Worker*. Goldthorpe and colleagues devised a typology distinguishing between two broad categories of 'traditional worker' – dubbed 'proletarian' and 'deferential traditionalists' (1968: 74). While the former were those who retained a strong sense of solidaristic working-class consciousness, and (more or less solid) loyalty to the Labour Party, the latter were (like McKenzie and Silver's 'deferentials') more 'socially conservative' in their values and worldviews – and, by extension, more likely to be swayed towards (big-C) Conservatism. One of this study's key findings was that most skilled and semi-skilled 'affluent' factory workers showed little or no evidence of 'embourgeoisement' in their voting behaviour (contrary to expectations based on Marxist theory): despite earning higher wages, often being house-owners and having 'more durable consumer goods than the majority of manual workers', they still registered 'a notably high and solid Labour vote' (ibid.: 38). Significantly, it was another type of worker entirely – those based in 'small-scale enterprises', often 'in a relatively close personal relationship' with their employers 'and less subject to trade union influences' – that the authors found leaning towards conservatism. It was these they labelled 'deferential' – albeit as a typological category of 'traditional worker' rather than (as in McKenzie and Silver's case) Tory voter (ibid.: 51). However, as 'deferential' workers were more likely to vote Conservative than class-conscious 'proletarians' – and *both* forms of 'deferential' were portrayed as content with the prevailing order – there was substantial overlap between this aspect of both books' theses, and many of those to whom they applied their distinct definitions of 'deferential'.

On the face of it, Goldthorpe and colleagues' Tory-inclined 'deferential' workers seem to share little in common with working-class people who backed Brexit – and (in some cases) have since switched allegiance from Labour to Conservatives. If widely accepted accounts of these disruptive democratic events are believed, they were (at least partly) rebellious spasms from angry discontents lashing out at elites and establishments – and hardly the acts of timid 'deferentials' who knew their place and had minimal day-to-day interest in politics. Of course, as recent polling evidence emphasizes, the *specific* 'elites' against which they were railing were much less likely to be Queen and country, or even UK governments, than the hegemonic 'metropolitan elites' and 'Brussels bureaucrats' of tabloid legend (see, for example, Mattinson, 2020). Indeed, much of the same polling emphasizes the *patriotism* of these groups: both that of a *hyper-local* kind, rooted in a sense of place, and networks and traditions based in their communities, and the more flag-waving *national* variety, that takes pride in security, defence and the Royal Family. Moreover, the image of habitual (if not especially engaged) Tory-voting 'deferentials' bears little resemblance to that of latter-day lifelong Labour voters who (we are endlessly reminded) would never have deviated from the cause until the point that they finally 'fell out of love' with the party, as it left them behind to court city-based graduates and prioritize 'identity politics' over their more socially (if not economically) conservative values (Glasman, 2016). Nonetheless, where Goldthorpe and colleagues' 'deferential worker' model may have something useful to tell us about both the *general* drivers of working-class conservatism and *particular* trends that have contributed to its recent resurgence is in its focus on the kinds of working cultures in which such individuals were typically found. The authors' characterization of the 'deferential worker' as an employee in a small-scale enterprise, with a 'relatively close personal relationship with his employer' and lack of union engagement, could easily be describing the circumstances of many people in today's increasingly de-unionized labour market (Goldthorpe et al., 1968: 51).

One of the biggest stories about the transformation of working life since the 1980s has been the decline of large-scale manufacturing-based employment, and with it 'the one-industry town' which, even when Goldthorpe and colleagues were writing in the 1960s, had 'become less and less a familiar aspect of British industrial society' (ibid.: 76). In its place is a mix of (often involuntary) self-employment in small-scale trades (frequently sub-contracted by bigger companies) and insecure zero-hours work in retail, hospitality, deliveries and small-scale service industries. As a result, many workers are now *their own* employers, have direct stakes in small businesses employing them, or work in sectors considered incompatible with – or actively opposed to – trade unionism. Where big employers *do* still exist, they tend to be out-of-town call-centres, distribution depots and retail parks owned by multinational companies that often pointedly refuse to recognize or negotiate with unions. According to a November 2020 labour force breakdown by the Office for National Statistics (ONS), more than 83 per cent of all workers in North-East England – a region consistently labelled left behind, based on measures of economic disadvantage – were employed in the service sector, compared to fewer than 10.5 per cent in 'production' (ONS, 2020). Similar splits were recorded in all other regions that were once the heartlands of Britain's manufacturing and energy sectors – Scotland, the North West, Yorkshire and the Humber, the East Midlands and Wales – with production shrinking to 8.3 per cent in (left-behind) eastern England. There have, then, been many recent workplace shifts that have contributed to transforming – and *complicating* – typologies of working-class conservatism. Mostly, these relate to familiar stories rehearsed above: the dismantling and disintegration of heavy industries, the failure to replace these with high-quality alternative forms of mass employment, and the progressive decline of union membership that has both accompanied and enabled these developments. But there have also been other, insidious, forces conspiring to undermine the cohesion of 'traditional' working-class communities, fragmenting their identities and political affiliations – ones we explore in Chapter 1.

WHO *ARE* THE LEFT BEHIND? THE DECLINE AND FALL OF THE 'TRADITIONAL' WORKING CLASS

In interrogating the phenomenon of the left behind, its emergence as a real or imagined consequence of de-industrializing, precarity-fuelling neoliberal economics, and the extent and limits of its relationship to twenty-first-century blue-collar conservatism, it is impossible to sidestep the biggest question of all: in what respects does this concept describe, or otherwise relate to, the contemporary *condition* of the 'traditional' industrial working class?

Much has been written elsewhere about the decline or shrinkage of the post-war working class following the free-market industrial reforms, mass privatizations and globalization of the 1980s, and the emergence of various other, fragmented working-class formations since – from Standing's 'precariat' (2011) to Savage's 'emerging service workers' (2015) and Ainsley's intersectional, more all-encompassing 'new working class' (2018). However, interwoven with this has been the, at times conflicting, story of how the traditional working class (though it may indeed have shrunk) has not so much vanished as become progressively ignored, marginalized and, at times, stigmatized – by politicians of both Left and Right. Adherents of the latter 'schools' see in recent expressions of popular discontent, from Brexit to the 2019 election (and, elsewhere, the election of Trump and other populist insurgents), a spectrum of more or less justifiable backlashes. These range from those fuelled by nativist (at times, racist) sentiments directed against foreigners who have supposedly stolen jobs, destabilized communities and (through the EU) dictated the terms of their economic and political identities, to more rational expressions of concern about the impact on households and businesses in post-industrial areas of rights guaranteeing the free movement of goods, services and labour, and the rapid pace of cultural and/or ethnic change. According to many commentators and activists, not only does the traditional, one-time industrial working class still *exist*: so too do its oft-discussed 'class consciousness' and many (if not all) aspects of its sense of locally rooted, collective solidarity. While recent elections may have tested the limits of its continued loyalty to the Labour movement – and, if some are believed, the 2019 poll has endangered this for good – such popular eruptions may also be viewed as signifying many communities' determination to reassert 'values' that, as *Guardian* associate editor Julian Coman puts it, have 'an honourable history on the British left', including 'stability, locality, honour, loyalty and patriotism' (Coman, 2020). In both the referendum and the 2019 election, Coman has argued, 'it was something neglected during the past three decades' that 'angrily resurfaced, demanding attention'. This was a 'sense of communal identity and associated values' that 'characterised' working-class communities during the post-war period: ones that 'social democratic parties' were once 'seen to represent'.

Such arguments cut to the heart of two key debates running through the rest of this book. The first of these is the question of where we should *place* the concept of the left behind, in relation to past discourses about economically disadvantaged groupings – including those, like the long-running narrative of 'underclass', that have othered, stigmatized and, in many cases, blamed 'the poor' for their own poverty. The second is the distinct, but related, question of how we can best understand – and, where necessary, address – the *phenomenon* of left-behind areas and communities, in terms of the facets that characterize them and the factors causing them to be left behind in the first place. In essence, which features are most dominant: the economic or the cultural? Is 'being' or 'feeling' left behind mainly a *material* condition – the nuts-and-bolts experience of finding life a perpetual struggle to retain secure work, make ends meet, pay the bills and have some sense of being valued? Or does it denote a deeper, profounder state of mind: a psychological malaise caused by the cumulative impact of decades of economic and political neglect, disrespect and/or attrition of cherished norms and traditions by forces beyond one's control? Moreover, even if the *manifestations* of left-behind or red-wall disenchantment seem to be cultural – expressed in terms of 'values' and 'identities' – to what extent are its *drivers* nonetheless down to neoliberal economics?

To the extent that there is any 'official' literature on what the term 'left behind' actually *means* – and how we might measure or visualize it as a condition – perhaps the most detailed definition was given in a 2019 report by the Local Trust, the charitable body established in 2012 (under then Prime Minister Cameron's 'Big Society' agenda) to deliver Big Local: a National Lottery-funded programme initially designed to allocate 150 renewal grants worth £1 million each to 'communities without significant existing civil society activity' (Local Trust, 2019: 2). Entitled *Left Behind? Communities on the Edge*, this identified a range of specific measures beyond annually published government indices of deprivation or unemployment claimant counts that, occurring in combination, were judged to characterize left-behind areas – including poor connectivity and a lack of basic community infrastructure (ibid.: 4–5). Echoing a refrain familiar from media and political narratives, the trust emphasized the 'concentration of such left-behind areas' in 'post-industrial districts in northern England' and 'coastal areas in southern England', while emphasizing how it was specifically 'a phenomenon of post-war social housing estates on the peripheries of cities and towns' and 'predominantly white populations'. These were communities that had not (it argued) 'traditionally been the focus of debate about deprivation', which 'tended to be multicultural and based in city centres' (ibid.: 5). The report's most refreshing contribution was its self-conscious acknowledgement of the *limitations* of the term 'left behind' – which it described as 'controversial and contentious' and open to accusations that it could be seen as 'patronising' for suggesting that 'residents of left-behind areas' were 'trapped in rosy nostalgia for past glories'. Nonetheless, it mounted a stout defence of its decision to use the label itself, in place of potential alternatives such as 'held back' – based (questionably) on previous research showing it to be a term that people 'instinctively understand', as well as one recognized by 'at least some' of those living in 'the areas commonly described as such' (ibid.: 7).

While the trust's definition identified *aspects* of the left-behind condition that might broadly be termed 'cultural' or identity-based, its overall diagnosis was arguably *economistic* in nature – a reading echoed in several subsequent reports by government agencies, non-government organizations (NGOs) and think-tanks. In the Resolution Foundation report *Painting the Town Blue*, which presented 'an audit of the demography, economy and living standards' of the 'Blue Wall' of former Labour seats annexed by the Tories in 2019, the term 'left behind' was repeatedly used as a normative corollary for *economic* decline and disadvantage (McCurdy et al., 2020). And in a broadly contemporaneous chapter of its 2020 'Green Budget' document focusing on the Johnson government's 'Levelling Up' agenda and the economic impacts of COVID-19, the Institute for Fiscal Studies (IFS) explicitly elided the left-behind concept with 'regional inequalities' – describing 'left-behind places' as 'particularly concentrated in large towns and cities' in 'former industrial regions' and 'coastal and isolated rural areas' outside London and the South East (Davenport & Zaranko, 2020: 315–16). Meanwhile, the inaugural report of the All-Party Parliamentary Group for 'Left Behind' Neighbourhoods proclaimed itself 'the voice at Westminster' for 'those deprived communities' that 'for far too long' had lacked 'the things that most of us take for granted' – before reeling out a lengthy shopping-list mirroring the community infrastructure-focused, hybrid economistic-cultural typological variant conceptualized by the trust. Its definition of what left-behind places *lacked* embraced 'accessible places and spaces' for 'people to meet and interact'; shops and amenities serving 'the needs of local residents'; 'active and vibrant community groups, organisations and institutions that strengthen local civic, social and cultural life', and 'good connectivity, both digital and physical' (Howell & Johnson, 2020).

There is, then, substantial agreement about many *economic* dimensions of what defines a left-behind place or community, but considerable dispute over the extent to which their condition is also *cultural*. While this book cannot 'answer' any of these questions, what it does offer is a consideration of the origins and antecedents of left-behind discourse; an analysis of the ways the left behind have been discursively constructed in the present, by politicians, press and public, and an exploration of the lived experiences and perceptions of the people who matter most in this debate: residents, businesses and other representatives of communities commonly framed in these terms, as well as some of those currently excluded from the narrative but to whom it should arguably be extended, including people battling disadvantages who do not neatly conform to the white working-class left-behind archetype.

In problematizing the left-behind imaginary in this way, the book deliberately raises additional questions – not least that of whether we should seek to decouple the term 'left behind' from its current associations with the post-industrial working class, to acknowledge the extent to which this one-dimensional, exclusivist definition embeds racialized narratives that privilege 'white workers', while denying the experiences of exploitation, abandonment and economic disadvantage they share with '*all* workers' (original emphasis), including minority-ethnic working-class people, migrants and immigrants (Bhambra, 2017: 227). Relatedly, it aims to consider the extent to which the term 'left behind' (used as verb or noun) might now be applied not just to *communities* but to myriad economically precarious, politically and/or culturally marginalized people who can be found right *across* society – in 'metropolitan' cities as often as former pit towns, fishing ports and faded coastal resorts.

In examining these interlocking considerations, the book adopts the widely accepted definition of 'marginalization' used by the United Nations Development Programme, which characterizes this condition as 'the state of being considered unimportant, undesirable, unworthy, insignificant and different', resulting in 'inequity, unfairness, deprivation and enforced lack of access to mainstream power' (as cited in Messiou, 2012). Underlying these issues is a deeper question: in the lingering shadow of COVID-19, as Britain finally leaves the EU to embrace a new world of bilateral trade deals against the backdrop of renewed calls for Scottish independence and growing demands for more English regional autonomy, what kind of country does it want to be – and for how much longer will it tolerate the obscene inequalities that lead us to expend so much energy debating the left behind?

1

Working-class, 'underclass' and collapsing-class identity: The roots of the left behind

In excavating the roots of contemporary debates about left-behind places, communities and groups, a good place to start is by examining two evolutionary trails. One is a recent history documenting the shrinkage and fracturing of the traditional working class in the post-war era, particularly since the period of deindustrialization and market liberalization that commenced in the late 1960s. Intertwined with this is the widely discussed topic of how this (post-) industrial working class slowly fell out of love with the political movement formed to represent it, the Labour Party – and how this complex story, in turn, relates to a long tradition of 'small-C' (and, in some cases, 'big-C') working-class conservatism. The second is a deeper-rooted history charting the reproduction of an unfolding continuum of narratives dating back beyond the Victorian age that have stigmatized economically disadvantaged households, neighbourhoods and, at times, entire areas – by framing them as culturally backward, pathologically poor and undeserving.

While this chapter's principal focus is the interplay between these two fundamental debates around class, in considering the complexities of disadvantage in the late-capitalist era it also touches on two other important dimensions beyond the purely socioeconomic: geography and race. Just as no account of the evolution, or dissolution, of conventional class categories would be complete without considering the increasingly spatial and/or regional manifestations of economic inequality, it is equally crucial to recognize that poverty, lack of opportunity, underinvestment and working-classness itself are far from the exclusive preserve of white people – and, if anything, affect certain Black, Asian and minority ethnic (BAME) groups *disproportionately*. To illustrate, a 2022 report commissioned by the Labour Party, based on granular analysis of official data, revealed that more than half of British Black children were growing up in poverty, compared to just over a quarter of young whites (Sparrow, 2022).

To return to our overarching histories of class, though, how exactly have these played out – especially during the sustained socioeconomic turbulence of the past fifty years? In addressing this question, we must recognize the wider social, economic, cultural and political backdrops against which these histories have unfolded, and the extent to which trends in class reconfiguration witnessed in Britain reflect analogous experiences in other (post-) industrial states. One of the most widely discussed socio-political phenomena of recent years has been the resurgence of authoritarian populism and the mobilization of politically and economically marginalized 'traditional' working-class groups through various forms of (more or less organized) backlash. In his recent book *Post-democracy After the Crises*, sociologist Colin Crouch conceptualized forms of marginalization that contribute to such backlashes as outcomes of 'post-democracy': the process by which democratic processes are 'hollowed out' in western societies, as institutions are co-opted by closed political and economic elites (Crouch, 2020). Elsewhere, the factors motivating such backlashes have been conceived (and evidenced) as everything from disenfranchisement arising from the highhanded actions of said distant, unrepresentative elites (D. Kellner, 2017) to economic neglect and/ or insecurity (Halikiopoulou & Vlandas, 2017); the pace of social and cultural change (Inglehart & Norris, 2016); or any combination of these and other, contextually specific, triggers (Goodwin & Heath, 2016). The similarly myriad actors held *responsible* for these concerns have included everyone from political and economic elites themselves – national governments, state bureaucracies, 'Eurocrats', casino bankers and traders, big businesses and a 'woke' intelligentsia – to social groupings recognizable to the public from their own direct or vicarious experiences. In a UK context, *Guardian* columnist John Harris has helpfully characterized these as a 'grimly familiar' rogues' gallery of folk devils ranging from 'naïve and idealistic middle-class students' to immigrants and 'scroungers' (Harris, 2020).

While there has been a distinctly British *version* of this 'backlash politics' – and it is this that forms part of our focus here – the processes of globalization, industrial decline, class fragmentation and economic and cultural disruption that have contributed to the emergence (and recognition) of Britain's left behind has occurred, to varying degrees, across the 'developed' world. Nativist and/or nationalism-tinged populist backlashes against the regressive effects of globalization on jobs and wages, and the supposed threat posed by mass migration to indigenous identities and values, have been stirring across mainland Europe since at least the 1990s – finding latter-day expression through the strong electoral showings of (among others) Geert Wilders's Party for Freedom in the Netherlands, various parties of government in Poland, Austria and Hungary, the breakthrough for the far-right Alternative fur Deutschland (AfD) in Germany's 2017 federal elections and the prolonged waves of protests by '*gilets jaunes*' ('yellow-vest') protesters in France, where Marine Le Pen's Front National has long held a popular appeal. Most notorious was billionaire businessman Donald Trump's triumph in the 2016 United States presidential election – trumpeting a heady mix of 'America first' messages cynically designed to exploit the insecurities of precarious workers in economically ravaged 'rust-belt' states, such as Michigan and Pennsylvania. His smorgasbord of policy pledges ranged from promises to introduce protectionist tariffs to safeguard jobs in the steel, aluminium and automotive sectors, and other industries struggling to compete with cheap Asian imports, while erecting a physical wall along the country's porous Mexican border and issuing a near-abstract vow to 'make America great again' (quoted in Restad, 2016).

In his 2020 book *The New Class War*, political scientist Michael Lind confronts these populist insurgencies through a post-Marxian lens, insightfully arguing that, while 'the immediate issues that animate mostly native working-class populism in particular countries' might appear to be immigration, post-Brexit sovereignty, French fuel prices, or 'other domestic policies' that chiefly penalize 'the peripheral working class', the underlying *driver* of resentment is a latter-day iteration of 'class conflict', focusing on 'social power' – as exercised through 'three realms', of 'government, the economy, and the culture' (Lind, 2020: xi). This diagnosis – and the helpful distinction between what *fuels* support for Brexit, Trump, Le Pen et al. and its public *expressions* – is worth keeping in mind in coming chapters.

Deliberating the causes of populism's geographical advance in the West is only part of the story. As political scientists Roger Eatwell and Matthew Goodwin argued in their 2018 book *National Populism*, not only did this problem start to emerge 'long before' the financial crisis and ensuing 'Great Recession', but its 'supporters' are 'more diverse than the stereotypical "angry old white men" who, we are frequently told, will soon be replaced by a new generation of tolerant Millennials' (Eatwell & Goodwin, 2018). While continuing to argue (as Goodwin had previously) that 'white workers' lie at the core of electoral coalitions that have delivered recent national populist triumphs, they drew on rich psephological data to propose a five-fold typology of Trump supporters and a three-fold one of Brexit voters. These emphasized both the wide variations in wealth and income across these groups (from 'affluent Eurosceptics' to the 'older working-class' and 'economically declined' in Brexit's case) and, crucially, the *multigenerational* makeup of each coalition: the fact that, contrary to popular stereotypes, a strong current of national populism prevails among some *younger* segments of the population, not just the old and middle-aged. Although much of the wider data strongly supports the argument that it was primarily older voters – from *various* socioeconomic segments – who backed Brexit (and the Conservatives in 2019), Eatwell and Goodwin's point about the appeal of backlash politics to some younger people is worth remembering as we move on to consider the more homogeneous conceptualizations of the working-class left behind that typify how this nebulous grouping is framed in public debate.

In addition, if we consider the concept of left-behind communities more broadly, the phenomenon of unequally dispersed, often severe pockets of economic disadvantage is now much more *globally* widespread than mainstream media and political narratives typically recognize. As economic geographer Andres Rodriguez-Pose has observed, the world of the twenty-first century – a globalized marketplace evangelists once predicted would offer undreamt-of opportunities for universal material and social advancement – has become pockmarked with numerous 'places that don't matter' (2018: 192). As national and global elites become increasingly preoccupied with the revival and expansion of cities, often to the detriment of peripheral smaller towns and post-industrial regions, he argues they implicitly mark out '"lagging-behind" areas the world over' as having 'no future'. In so doing, they further embed 'persistent poverty, economic decay and lack of opportunities', fuelling the 'considerable discontent' that has increasingly led to the 'revolt against the status quo' (ibid.: 189). There is much in this 'places that don't matter' thesis – which we might usefully broaden to embrace 'groups' or 'people who don't matter', *wherever* they happen to reside – that recalls the now-notorious policy (and accompanying discourse) of 'managed decline' strategically pursued by Margaret Thatcher's UK government in the 1980s across northern regions it subjected to a process of accelerated de-industrialization (Howe, quoted in bbc.co.uk, 2011).

In a global context, Rodriguez-Pose emphasized the differences between 'generally better-off and emerging countries' that had 'shown some concern for territorial inequality' – and 'acted on it' – and countries that had neither 'means' nor 'will' to intervene 'to promote economic development in their less developed regions' (2018: 193). Within the European Union alone, he argued, numerous regions had suffered disproportionately negative impacts from the unequally distributed dividends of globalized trade and investment – from low growth that had become 'the norm' in Bulgaria, east Germany, eastern and southern Hungary, central Greece and southern Italy (all left-behind regions in which populist movements had gained traction) to the plummeting employment rates attending industrial decline across large tracts of otherwise wealthy countries, including France and Germany. Citing evidence from a then recent study 'covering virtually all countries in the world' (Lessmann & Seidel, 2017), he argued that, while 'many less-developed regions' had 'caught up with richer regions in their respective countries', a 'greater polarisation' of 'within-country' disparities persisted in Africa, much of South Asia and eastern Europe (Rodriguez-Pose, 2018: 193). In other words, the condition of being left behind is no longer confined to 'developing' nations and regions in the 'Global South' on the one hand and *relatively* impoverished regions of 'developed' countries on the other. Instead, across 'Bihar in India, the central lowlands of Thailand, parts of East Germany, Champagne-Ardenne or Lorraine in France or Michigan and Ohio in the US', a globe-spanning '"geography of discontent"' is emerging – linked to 'crises' in agricultural and/or industrial sectors, 'significant outward migration and brain drain' and feelings of 'no future and no hope' (ibid.: 196, citing Essletzbichler, 2018; Los et al., 2017).

Britain's ongoing debate about its own 'geography of discontent' – its left-behind areas and communities – is, then, intermeshed with an increasingly *multinational* one about lagging-behind, neglected places (and groups) 'that don't matter'. So, too, is its wider preoccupation with the decline of its traditional industrial working class and the growth of more atomized, precarious work and class formations. It has long been commonly observed that there is something uniquely tenacious about Britain's class system, that its historically ingrained 'upper/middle/lower-class' distinctions, derived from a combination of inherited titles and property rights and near-abstract ideas like 'breeding', have shown a peculiar capacity to survive the repeated reconfigurations of other measures of social privilege and stratification that have occurred since the Middle Ages. Such transformations have included everything from the insurgence of new forms of wealth derived from the acquisition, ownership and exploitation of capital in the Industrial Revolution to the emergence of levels of (qualified) social mobility, based on widening educational and employment opportunities in post-war Britain, to the slow-burn democratization of political representation, participation and, latterly, decision making. For all their disruptive force, such developments failed to overturn the more stubborn class-based certainties ancestrally inscribed by accidents of birth. And yet, as resilient as these class identities undoubtedly are, they clearly *have* been challenged more than ever before in recent decades – by the disruptive forces of neoliberalism, globalization and de-industrialization. In the hyper-capitalist 'Wild West', people from humble backgrounds set up successful global businesses, and fortunate families from modest historical roots break into the ranks of the global 'super-rich'; yet, at the same time, work for the many becomes ever less secure and worse paid, while the traditional trappings and shared associations of working-class life, from trades unions to worker education programmes, are effaced. How, then, have working-class people *themselves* been affected by these developments – and what has happened to their 'culture' along the way?

FROM SOLIDARITY TO FRAGMENTATION: WHATEVER HAPPENED TO THE TRADITIONAL WORKING CLASS?

It is a truth universally acknowledged – to paraphrase English literature's most celebrated chronicler of class, Jane Austen – that Britain's social structure is no longer as rigid and immutable as it once was (or was once *imagined*). In the words of psephologist Robert McKenzie and sociologist Allan Silver, writing more than six decades ago, 'the problem of understanding the post-war working class stems not from its poverty but its "affluence"': specifically, 'the contrast between its customary status' and its (by then) 'unprecedented prosperity', which carried with it 'the possibility of new working-class values, goals, and demands' (1968: 77). For social scientists working during this period of rising incomes, emerging consumerism, technological change and (for a time) narrowing economic inequality, a key preoccupation in the study of class was a Marxian concept dating back to the 1930s: *embourgeoisement*. Put simply, this is the process by which middle-class aspirations, and 'a bourgeois standard and style of life', become 'institutionalized' among segments of 'the working class' (encyclopaedia.com, 2020). Viewed through McKenzie and Silver's political lens, embourgeoisement was a potential corollary for the medium- to long-term defection of people from once hardwired Labour-loyalist backgrounds to the established ranks of intergenerational/lifelong working-class Conservatives (a subject to which we turn shortly).

In normative terms, the 'embourgeoised worker' was most clearly defined by psephologists David Butler and Richard Rose as 'working class in terms of occupation, education, speech and cultural norms' but 'middle class in terms of income and material comforts' (1959: 15–16). For the post-war baby-boomer generation, this manifested itself in what sociologists John Goldthorpe and colleagues characterized as 'the familiar history' of a 'relatively rapid rise in living standards' and the 'marked increase in the number of families achieving "middle range" incomes' – leading to 'considerable overlap, in terms of income, between those in manual and nonmanual occupations' and a growing 'pattern of working-class consumption' (1968: 33). Materially, this led to many more households being able to afford their own homes, motor vehicles and 'durable consumer goods' – from washing machines to record players and television sets. More significantly, it saw the steady erosion of 'wide differences in the spread of ownership' between 'more prosperous manual' and 'lower white-collar strata' (ibid.). By the 1980s, material embourgeoisement would, of course, reach a new level entirely, through the rocket-boosted aspirationalism of the 'Right-to-Buy' generation – as upwardly mobile blue-collar workers and self-employed tradesmen (the 'Mondeo men' of popular folklore) raced to buy video recorders, foreign package holidays, British Gas shares and the previously rented council homes many had lived in since childhood.

The differences between the pre-war and post-war working-classes – and the process of embourgeoisement itself – turned out to be markedly more nuanced than predicted by McKenzie and Silver's emphasis on the pre-eminent factor of rising 'affluence'. In their near-contemporaneous multi-volume account of the lives and values of (newly) 'affluent workers', Goldthorpe and colleagues observed that there had long been more heterogeneity *within* the working class than was widely acknowledged, adding that their focal grouping – 'traditional' workers – should be viewed as both a 'sociological rather than a historical concept' and one of *several* working-class categories (1968: 74). Noting that 'by no means all of the pre-war working class were traditional in our sense', they argued that 'distinctive elements of working-class traditionalism' still persisted in various parts of post-war Britain, while the concept of traditional workers encompassed not just 'the most class-conscious' and 'radical sections of the working class' (a sub-category they designated 'proletarian traditionalists'), but also its 'socially more conservative elements', which they termed 'deferential traditionalists' (ibid.).

The concept of social conservatism among the working class(es) is one to which we return in the next section – and not simply in the sense applied by Goldthorpe and colleagues, in whose study it was also synonymous with a greater long-term inclination towards *voting* Conservative. For now, there are two key points worth unpacking in this important qualification of 'traditional worker' status. Firstly, even *before* the transformative changes that followed the Second World War – from the birth of the Welfare State and comprehensive education to the rise of early forms of mass consumerism – Britain's working class was by no means homogenous in character or outlook. Secondly, for all the incipient social mobility and materialism that contributed to rising embourgeoisement among *segments* of the 'traditional' working class, 'proletarian traditionalism' had turned out to be remarkably persistent.

Qualifications aside, there is no doubt that recent decades have subjected the working class(es) to a near-continual bombardment of disruptive external forces – and that these have contributed to substantial and often surprising *internal* realignments, including in relation to collective identities and value systems. One significant development, closely linked to the (limited) patterns of embourgeoisement Goldthorpe and colleagues noted more than half a century ago, has been the increasing importance attached not just to financial and physical badges of middle classness – the accumulation of *economic* capital, such as the 'savings devices' and 'homeownership' McKenzie and Silver (1968: 95) emphasized as indicators of potential Conservative voting – but less tangible, more symbolic, measures of advancement that often carry greater long-term material value. For Goldthorpe and colleagues' affluent workers, such forms of *social* and/or *cultural* capital were advantages acquired primarily through 'white-collar affiliations' – whether these took the form of 'close contact with middle-class persons', being 'brought up in' or marrying into 'a white-collar family', or by 'having worked in' (or had a wife in) 'a white-collar job' (1968: 56–7). While conceding that only 'a minority of manual workers' had 'extensive ties with the middle class' in the late 1960s, the authors thought it 'highly probable' that this represented 'a growing minority in the country' – concluding that it was 'precisely such changes in the occupational structure, rather than affluence itself' that should be regarded as 'the most influential factor in encouraging the spread of middle-class values and life-styles among the working class' (ibid.: 81). Equally important (especially in light of more recent developments), they argued that the still solid levels of Labour support among affluent workers was 'of a less "solidaristic" nature' than among 'the traditional working class' – and more based on 'instrumental attitudes' relating to 'the "pay-off" to be expected from a Labour Government' in better living standards and services (ibid.: 80).

What Goldthorpe and colleagues described in the context of a late 1960s period of rising prosperity and rapid social change was, then, a foretaste of socio-political trends that would be *accelerated*, rather than spawned, by the disruptive neoliberal gear-shifts of ensuing eras. As they wisely concluded, it was (and arguably *is*) 'the extent of workers' family or occupational "bridges" with the middle class', not just their 'level of earnings or standards of consumption', that appear to hold 'the key' to potential changes 'within the working class in the direction of embourgeoisement' – and, with it, the growing disconnect with conventional working-class political alignments reflected in their finding that men with 'particularly extensive white-collar affiliations' were 'markedly less likely to vote for the Labour Party' than those with 'entirely blue collar' backgrounds (ibid.: 81). Touring former Labour heartlands more than half a century later for her 2020 book *Beyond the Red Wall*, pollster Deborah Mattinson met several newly converted Conservative voters who admitted their shifting loyalties reflected the fact that they (and others like them) 'had changed'. These included one ex-miner and a middle-aged electrician who told her, 'we've all moved on', because 'we're better off than our parents could ever have dreamt of being' (2020: 132).

Yet the 'affluent worker' thesis (however enduringly valid) only addresses one aspect of what has happened to traditional working-class identities during the ever-escalating tug-of-war over their values and loyalties. Embourgeoisement certainly helps illuminate the *pull*-factors that have disrupted the industrial working class as a cohesive political entity: specifically, the incentives and mechanisms encouraging people to migrate willingly from an intergenerational, solidaristic loyalty to labourism, cemented by routinized trade unionism, towards more instrumentalist, individualistic lifestyles and attitudes. But the peeling away of ingrained labourist allegiances is only part of the story. What of the *push*-factors that have more recently assailed the traditional working class – conspiring in a pincer-movement with embourgeoisement to undermine its solidarity and fragment it into multiple disparate components? What of the disempowering forces – worlds away from liberating ones like upward mobility, home ownership, consumption and accumulation – that have conspired to *reduce* incomes, security and opportunities for working-class people, by removing stable jobs, eroding the social security safety-net and dissolving long-standing workplace and community-based networks? What, too, of the *wider* aspects of working-class culture that such processes have eroded and lost – notably the steady disappearance of the educational, artistic and social opportunities promoted by trades unions and workers' educational associations, and the deeper forms of 'self-improvement', beyond the purely material and aspirational, to which these sometimes led? To put it another way, while social mobility (real and imagined) helps explain how some people *proactively* leave behind their working-class roots to pursue more middle-class careers and lifestyles, what of the many others who are *being* left behind – both by erstwhile neighbours/colleagues and the process of neoliberalization itself?

To begin with the point about wider working-class culture, there was much more to the industrial-age British working-class tradition than mere hard graft and workplace solidarity – let alone the valorized 'patriotism' and 'social conservatism' retrospectively ascribed to it by the likes of Mattinson and Blue Labour theorist Maurice Glasman. The shared sense of class consciousness that once informed the mindsets of many (if not most) working-class people also had *intellectual*, even scholarly, origins and expressions. Moreover, the solidarity it espoused focused on promoting and preserving a culture of dignified, rewarding, secure, fairly paid labour and was often as outward-looking and internationalist in its worldview as it was rooted in a 'sense of place' – at least, in the rather insular and parochial vein that this tends to be characterized by revisionist academics and pollsters today.

Though often normatively defined in relation to their economic status and mode(s) of employment, the working class – like the trade unions and, later, Labour movements with which they were long associated – have a proud history of autodidacticism, intellectual curiosity and recreational artistic and cultural self-expression. During the heyday of the industrial era, this was fostered through (among other things) voluntarist libraries, reading societies, writing workshops and art classes run by unions themselves and worker coops. Its staggered apotheosis came with, first, the 1899 founding of a working-class university – Ruskin Hall (now Ruskin College), Oxford – and the 1903 formation of the Workers' Educational Association. As literary historian Jonathan Rose argued in his book *The Intellectual Life of the British Working Classes*, by 1822 some 51 working-class libraries had been founded in Scotland alone (where literacy rates had reached the heights of 74 per cent for weavers and 94 per cent for wrights during the eighteenth century), while cities like Sheffield had a 'long tradition of independent working-class education' prior to the introduction of any form of nationwide formal state schooling, thanks to the Sheffield People's College, founded in 1842, which was 'governed democratically by its students' and whose president was a shoemaker (Rose, 2001: 59, 190). In Chapter 5 of this book, several interviewees vividly recall the worker-centred cultural (as well as industrial) infrastructure that once infused the fabric of their towns, before factories and mills – and union libraries, art galleries and social clubs alongside them – were demolished or converted into luxury apartments, business parks and Amazon warehouses.

The triumphs of working-class autodidacticism have latterly inspired several award-winning dramatizations for stage and screen, notably the works of playwright Lee Hall. In the film (now musical) *Billy Elliot*, Hall told the fictional story of the son of an 1980s miner from County Durham who follows his dream to become a ballet dancer, while his 2007 National Theatre play *The Pitmen Painters* focused on the true-life story of the Ashington Group of artists from Newcastle-upon-Tyne. The spirit of intellectual and cultural inquiry that propelled such (real or imagined) achievers did more than anything else, over time, to foster a sense of international connectedness among the working class. Fuelled by the 1848 Europe-wide 'revolutions' (whose British expression was the Chartist uprising), the rise and fall of the Paris Commune and the emergence of the incipient Labour and union movements, the go-to reading lists of book groups in the Welsh collieries alone steadily absorbed Marx and Engels, 'Victorian best-sellers' like Dickens, Hardy and Eliot, and Fabian playwright George Bernard Shaw – before undergoing a 'more striking shift' in the 1930s, when ledgers showed them turning to authors preoccupied with 'a world in crisis' (Rose, 2001: 152). During this period, they took in everyone from Emile Zola to Upton Sinclair and Mulk-Raj Anand, author of *The Coolie*, a celebrated novel about life at the bottom of the Indian caste system.

For all these admirable traditions, though, it would be naïvely over-romantic to characterize working-class culture as having been relentlessly progressive throughout the industrial era. Indeed, the zealous, but often futile, efforts of working-class autodidacts *deprived* of collectivist institutional avenues were frequently immortalized in the literature of their day, whether as stonemason Jude Fawley's earnest (and ultimately fatal) pursuit of a liberating academic Utopia symbolized by the fictitious Oxbridge amalgam, Christminster, in Thomas Hardy's 1894 novel *Jude the Obscure*, or the futile efforts of house-painter Frank Owen to educate other exploited workers in the similarly fictional backwater town of Mugsborough in Robert Tressell's *The Ragged-Trousered Philanthropists* (1914). As Rose acknowledged, while there had been a widespread and relatively enduring 'Victorian ethos of mutual improvement', the 'intellectuals and Marxists among the Welsh colliers' who had been 'prime movers behind the miners' libraries' were 'minorities concentrated in certain places and certain intervals in time'. Similarly, 'the proletarian internationalism of the Welsh coalfields' may well have been 'exaggerated' by some histories – though 'it certainly existed' in the case of the Markham Miners' Lodge, which bore a banner proclaiming 'The World is Our Country: Mankind are Our Brethren' (Rose, 2001: 253).

Six decades on from *The Affluent Worker*, then, much of its prognosis for the slow-burn dissolution of traditional class bonds and loyalties has turned out to be prescient. If anything, though, it underestimated the scale and rapidity of these transformations – particularly those caused by later disruptions it could not have foretold. Although Goldthorpe and colleagues found limited evidence for widescale embourgeoisement among 1960s affluent workers – especially in terms of altered *voting* behaviour – they were writing at a time when the nature of *work* (for all its faults and inequities) was generally more stable and secure; income inequality was narrowing; trade union membership was standard in most workplaces; and incipient post-war consumerism was still some way short, in scale and pervasiveness, of the mass consumer era which eventually followed. Wind forward to the third decade of the twenty-first century and the world of employment is fundamentally different. In place of the highly unionized, more collegiate, workplaces of old, many people work for public, private and third-sector organizations with work cultures that are more marketized, managerialist and hierarchical. At the same time, entire modes of employment, and whole industries that once employed hundreds of thousands, have drastically shrunk or vanished, to be replaced by 'flexible' (or casualized), often short-term forms of work – primarily in an amorphous, ever-expanding service sector embracing everything from telesales and taxi-driving to retail and hospitality. Over the twentieth century as a whole, the proportion of manual workers in Britain's working population halved – from 75 to 38 per cent – while the number of professionals and managers quadrupled, from 8 to 34 per cent (Sveinsson, 2009: 8). De-industrialization began earnestly more than half a century ago, leading to the loss of 6 million manufacturing and coal-mining jobs between 1966 and 2016 (Beatty & Fothergill, 2016). More than 2 million more went in coal during the Thatcher-dominated 1980s, and another 2.5 million followed in the 1990s and ensuing 13-year 'New Labour' interregnum (Froud et al., 2011: 18). As sociologist Kjartan Sveinsson argued in a 2009 pamphlet for the Runnymede Trust, 'to be a "manual worker" at the beginning of the 20th century was to hold a position shared by three-quarters of the working population', but by its end most people held 'more privileged jobs' (2009: 8).

The ensuing (and ongoing) 'labour-market restructuring' has latterly led to 'a shift in the composition of the working classes' and, with it, a cumulative and profound status loss for many working-class people – with traditional male roles particularly, both within families and wider communities, undergoing dramatic transformations alongside the contraction of Britain's industrial base (Sveinsson, 2009: 9). These changes have deepened class disadvantages, notably among younger men, who have increasingly become concentrated in low-level manual work, where their relative pay has fallen behind that of older colleagues. Equally significantly, shifts in the 'culture' of manual labour have undermined some of the historic claims for working-class status, including one-time attractions of heavy industries, which – though 'dirty, dangerous and tough' – had 'nourished "heroic" images of men's manual labour' (ibid.). Such nostalgia for masculine work was echoed more recently in the words of many of those interviewed by Mattinson, with one ex-industrial worker telling her that, in the 'tough' world of 'long hours, hard work, dangerous work' he once inhabited, he felt he was 'doing something important' that was 'valued – and well paid' (2020: 86).

An intersecting development, traceable to much earlier than the rise of the twenty-first-century gig economy, was the onset of mass automation that commenced in many industries during the 1960s and '70s, as well as the philosophies underpinning them – notably 'Taylorism', developed in the early twentieth century by North American mechanical engineer Frederick 'speedy' Taylor, which sought 'to organize production into the most routine tasks', depriving the worker of 'any human discretion or creativity' (Cruddas, 2021: 101). In his 2021 book *The Dignity of Labour*, Labour MP Jon Cruddas traces the resultant transformation of one-time manpower-heavy industries through the prism of his Barking and Dagenham constituency. Drawing on lessons from the 1973 book *Working for Ford*, which chronicled the post-war mechanization of the Dagenham and Halewood car plants through the process of 'Fordism', he chronicles unionized workers' 'political struggle to retain human dignity' (not to mention basic health and safety standards) by mounting an 'organized resistance to the degradation intrinsic to Ford's production technologies' using their local shop stewards to maintain 'greater discretion and autonomy' from their supervisors and managers (ibid.: 100).

Reflecting on the more *de*-unionized workplace of the present day, writer and journalist David Goodhart's *The Road to Somewhere* made the more prosaic observation that, 'as we have evolved from an industrial to a post-industrial society', most British people have become 'much richer', with 'more comfortable, healthier and freer lives' – leading to 'less drudgery and physical strain and much greater probability of a career rather than just a job' (2017: 149). At the same time, he argued, the 'more fluid and competitive' working world promoted by de-industrialization privileges a less rooted, more mobile, university-educated middle class – an amorphous grouping he dubbed 'Anywheres' – while eating away at the old securities (including fabled 'jobs for life') once enjoyed by the traditional working-class component of their similarly nebulous equal and opposite: 'Somewheres'. The new 'knowledge economy', Goodhart argued, is 'increasingly organised around Anywhere assumptions about cognitive ability, creativity and work' as expressions of 'individual fulfilment' – depriving 'more basic jobs' of their 'meaning and status' (ibid.: 150).

The sheer scale of the transformations these accounts describe can be illustrated by data compiled for the most comprehensive review of the composition of Britain's latter-day class system to date: the Great British Class Survey (GBCS), an Internet-based public census co-run by the BBC and academics at the London School of Economics and Political Science. Based on an initially contentious, but now widely accepted, 'seven-class model', this identified not one but three distinct sub-classes *within* the contemporary working class: the precariat, emerging service workers and the 'traditional' working class (Savage, 2015). Between them, this trio of sub-categories accounted for nearly half the working population (48 per cent) – though, tellingly, the traditional working class (those still employed in older industries and manufacturing) comprised a mere 14 per cent of all adults, compared to 15 per cent categorized by Mike Savage and colleagues (after Goldthorpe) as 'new affluent workers' (ibid.). Accompanying and enabling the seismic shifts that had shaped this new, more complex, class structure was the previously described pincer-movement of workplace-based trends that might almost have been deliberately engineered to dilute working-class consciousness and solidarity. The introduction of market-based metrics and target cultures, combined with creeping de-unionization, has fostered *advancement* for the few – picking off able, ambitious individuals who play by the rules, through performance-related pay rises, expansion of middle management and other forms of superficial workplace-based social mobility. Concurrently, the ability of the many to organize for their *collective* benefit has been eroded by mass privatization, deregulation and dismantling of one-time state-owned industries; the fragmentation of collective bargaining units through subcontracting and outsourcing of key functions to third-party providers; the refusal of employers to formally recognize and consult with unions, and, above all, the proliferation of insecure, precarious and/or part-time positions in place of the stable, unionized, industrial jobs of old.

Though this widespread precarity is one of many long-term consequences of neoliberal reforms introduced by the Thatcher governments, these changes remained largely unchallenged by successive subsequent administrations. As political scientists Ford and Goodwin have argued, later governments remain culpable for the fact that, even during periods when 'unemployment fell steadily and incomes rose', the 'yawning inequalities between classes and regions' which emerged during the Thatcher-Major years 'did not narrow' – and many working-class families 'remained in poverty', untouched by the recovery that was 'benefiting the middle classes' (2014: 130). Moreover, not only was 'no large-scale policy effort' made to ameliorate the impact on 'millions of former manufacturing workers living in economically depressed northern towns and cities', guaranteeing that they 'never recovered from deindustrialisation' and were left lacking 'the skills and experience necessary to prosper in the new services economy', but social security changes introduced in the 1980s (in part, to disguise the true scale of structural unemployment) shifted many ex-industrial workers onto a new disability payment, Invalidity Benefit. Over time, 'claimant numbers rose remorselessly even as unemployment fell' – creating 'a displaced army of unwanted workers' who had (in their words) 'withdrawn altogether from the labour market' (ibid.).

The 'reinvention' of class in the later decades of the twentieth century, and with it the re-imagining of old definitions of what it means to *be* working or middle class (or to work in working/middle-class occupations) has, then, been a tale of two parallel realities. While many people have experienced *improved* living standards and opportunities for advancement – including large numbers of the 'embourgeoised', who would once have been expected to settle for life as members of a largely immobile 'industrial' working class – others have grown accustomed to *diminished* opportunities, security and incomes, often exacerbated by periodic or prolonged unemployment. Interwoven with these trends is the equally unhappy story of ever-widening economic inequalities – again, disproportionately affecting the various segments of this multifaceted 'new working class' (Ainsley, 2018). While traditional workers like those Goldthorpe and colleagues interviewed in the 1960s still make up part of this demographic, today the lowest-placed class (or sub-class) is the bottom 15 per cent: the grouping economist Guy Standing terms 'the precariat' (2014). This new category – itself an umbrella, encompassing everyone from low-waged cleaners and care-workers to intermittently paid zero-hours contractors in the gig economy – has been neatly summed up by Savage as having little if any savings, the lowest household incomes, the least social ties to people in higher-status jobs (social capital) and less cultural capital 'than any of the other classes' (2015: 171).

While the exact nuances of class composition have blurred with the decades, stubborn forms of economic inequality still demonstrably persist – and what remains of the traditional working class are among those most adversely affected. As Sveinsson put it, 'the marked rise in affluence and increasing social opportunities' since the post-war period sit alongside 'class inequalities' that continue to 'sharply affect people's chances in life', with unequal 'distribution of income and property opportunities' harming everything from 'life expectancy' to 'chances of educational success' and 'risk of falling victim to crime' (2009: 9).

DE-RACIALIZING THE LEFT-BEHIND WORKING CLASS: CHALLENGING 'METHODOLOGICAL WHITENESS'

The complication of old-style class formations through the addition and interweaving of post-industrial sub-categories, such as the precariat and new service workers, is still only part of the story. As Savage and others rightly note, one 'unintended consequence' of the schema developed by Goldthorpe, both through *The Affluent Worker* and his later efforts to devise the occupational class scheme that today forms the basis of the officially sanctioned National Statistics Socio-Economic Classification (NS-SEC), was 'to weaken analyses of the relationship between the study of class, and the study of gender, race and ethnicity' (Savage, 2015: 40). In reality, it is unwise and misleading to divorce class-based inequalities from these various other forms of inequality, as doing so denies the complex identities and multiple, intersecting disadvantages experienced by many of the tens of millions of people who (in broad terms) constitute today's working class. By failing to recognize these multidimensional experiences of inequality, researchers, campaigners and politicians effectively privilege some groups over others – introducing false divides between closely related and/or coexisting segments.

A specific critique is that mounted by critical race theorists who question the disproportionate emphasis in recent media and political narratives about the left behind on the plight of white working-class communities. 'One hundred and fifty years since the creation of the term "working class", we are confronted with a new class reality', argued economist, activist and ex-Labour parliamentary candidate Faiza Shaheen in her introduction to a 2019 Runnymede Trust report entitled *'We are Ghosts': Race, Class and Institutional Prejudice* (Shaheen in Snoussi & Mompelat, 2019: 3). 'Rather than "working class" being redundant, as Margaret Thatcher suggested 40 years ago', it had 'mutated' from being a term 'used to foster solidarity' and denote 'those working in industrial jobs' into 'a divisive concept' – pitting the 'white working class' against immigrants and 'the minority ethnic population'. In reality, she added, 'the "white working class" and "ethnic or migrant working class"' no longer live 'different or separate lives'; instead, their 'everyday lived experiences' have 'significant overlap' (ibid.: 4). Moreover, this overlap extended beyond the common difficulties they face to the fact that, in many areas, white and minority-ethnic households (UK-born, immigrant and/or migrant) live – and often work – not in segregated silos or on neighbouring streets, but side by side. As sociologist Lisa McKenzie argued in a paper *critiquing* the trust's work – specifically, what she saw as its continuation of narratives of '"lack", "decline" and "division"' familiar from 'policy and political language' about the white working class – Black, Asian, and white working-class people are more likely to live in 'connected communities' than separate ones, with the archetypal 'Pakistani taxi driver' living next door to the white 'ex-miner' and 'their children likely school friends' (McKenzie, 2019).

The argument that preoccupations with the plight of the white working class risk appearing intrinsically racist was forcefully made in a 2017 critique by Gurminder Bhambra, Professor of Postcolonial and Decolonial Studies at the University of Sussex. In a much-cited paper, she challenged the 'pervasive "methodological whiteness"' present in 'social scientific accounts of both Brexit and Trump's election victory' – arguing that, by implicitly accepting as 'legitimate' the 'claims of the [white working-class] "left behind" or those who had come to see themselves as "strangers in their own land"', academics (often unwittingly) bought into the underlying assertions of the 'rhetoric of both the Brexit and Trump campaigns' (Bhambra, 2017: 214). As both these populist causes had reinvented the past as constructed of 'white' nations 'into which racialized others had insinuated themselves and gained disproportionate advantage', social scientists risked legitimizing 'analyses that might otherwise be regarded as racist' – by 'skewing' these examples of 'white majority political action' as those of 'a more narrowly defined white working class' (ibid.).

Bhambra's argument was important not just because it rightly drew attention to the disproportionate white *privilege* afforded to Britain's oft-described traditional working class, through the singular media, political and academic focus on the economic plight of post-industrial and (now) 'red-wall' areas. More significantly, she argued that any degree of acceptance of the ahistorical claims on which Trump, Nigel Farage and Boris Johnson built their cases for 'taking back control' of their countries did a disservice to *both* minority-ethnic communities and the very (white) working-class voters they claimed to represent. Reflecting the findings of Dorling, Becker and others, she underlined the false premise underpinning many taken-for-granted assumptions about the profile of Leave voters: essentially, the suggestion that white working-class groups could be *blamed* for Brexit, even if they should also be understood. Instead, she pointed to detailed analyses demonstrating a much more varied pro-Leave coalition, summed up by Swales as 'affluent Eurosceptics, the older working class, and a smaller group of economically disadvantaged, anti-immigration voters' (2017: 2). Similarly, she drew attention to Gusterson's analysis of data from the US-based Pew Research Center showing that, while the mainstream media 'put disproportionate weight on a single narrative thread' – the 'role of free trade and factory closings in alienating a post-industrial white working class' – it was actually 'middle-class communities' that 'overwhelmingly shifted to Trump' and were 'largely responsible for his victory' (Igielnik & Kochhar, 2016, cited in Bhambra, 2017: 216). Taken together, these realities showed that 'claims about a (white) working-class backlash' were 'not supported by a thorough analysis of the available empirical evidence either in the UK or the US' (ibid.: 215). Bhambra's overriding argument was that 'the empirical category of the "left behind"' – understood in socioeconomic terms – contained 'significant proportions of the Black and minority ethnic population', with the latter 'more likely to suffer the effects of austerity' and to have worse health, education and employment outcomes than 'white populations' (ibid.: 216). Further consideration is given in coming chapters to the dubious assessments of relative 'deservingness' that continue to be applied to white and minority-ethnic groupings through homogenous portrayals of the left behind.

THE CURIOUS CASE OF THE 'WORKING-CLASS C/CONSERVATIVE'

The story of working-class conservatism is a tangled tale of two distinct, if often overlapping, sets of values. On one hand, there is the intriguing persistence of a long-standing strand of big-C working-class Conservatism: support for Britain's Conservative and Unionist Party. On the other is the tradition of 'social' conservatism: a well-documented, if somewhat elusive, concept which has been associated with everything from a generalized sense of patriotism (towards family, community and/or country) to a pick-and-mix set of small-c conservative instincts, embracing everything from authoritarian attitudes towards punishing crime and disorder to concerns about immigration and welfare dependency. Such instincts are arguably 'political' only insofar as they relate to issues that are easily politicized – and, significantly, they are as often associated with Labour voters as supporters of the Tories or other parties.

To commence with the former, the most authoritative attempt to anatomize and explain the phenomenon of working-class Conservatism to date remains McKenzie and Silver's ambitious 1968 study *Angels in Marble*. This proposed a typology of more or less ideological forms of Conservative support among what were then commonly termed 'blue-collar' voters, based on a sweeping multi-phase longitudinal survey and interview-based analysis of shifting patterns of Tory support throughout much of the 1960s. The authors' first order of classification distinguished between two broad types of blue-collar Conservative: 'the secular' and 'the deferential' (McKenzie & Silver, 1968: 164). The latter, defined by a term derived from nineteenth-century constitutional historian Walter Bagehot's concept of 'social deference' (ibid.: 16), tended to be those most likely to have habitually supported the Tories over long periods, perhaps even throughout their adult lives. This perhaps puzzling loyalty was based on 'certain *a priori* assumptions' – including a curiously subservient tendency to credit Tory leaders with 'an innate and transcendent superiority over all possible political rivals which borders on the magical' (ibid.). As such, deferentials often abdicated 'any right to pragmatic evaluation and criticism' of the Tories – in marked contrast to 'seculars', who based their support for the Tories 'not upon *a priori* assumptions about their innate superiority' but 'a pragmatic assessment of their performance in office' (ibid.: 164).

When assigning their survey respondents and interviewees to categories, McKenzie and Silver applied six criteria to distinguish between responses indicative of secular or deferential voters. These ranged from the primacy some individuals placed on the 'socially superior' class 'origins' of their political leaders and their attitudes towards 'traditional symbols of authority', such as the monarchy and House of Lords, to whether they attributed the success of policies benefiting 'ordinary people' to sound administration and 'successful management of the economy', or 'the generosity and benevolence' (even 'personal wealth') of 'politicians of elite origins' (ibid.). While deferentials adopted presumptions of upper-class altruism and intrinsic fitness to govern, seculars based their Tory leanings on evidence of their *competence*, rather than any deference to class determinism or breeding. Moreover, far from viewing the Conservative Party as a 'unique custodian of the national interest and traditions' (as deferentials generally did), they considered it 'one of several legitimate contenders for office' (ibid.: 165). Indeed, a primary factor motivating secular voters explored in the book was a concern about 'mobility frustration': the obstacles and opportunities impeding or enabling their own children's future social advancement, through education and employment (ibid.: 202). As several interviews demonstrated, this 'secular concern with achievement' and 'mobility frustration' defined itself not just against submissive assumptions that Tories had a divine right to rule, but 'both kinds of traditionalism' – that is, 'pre-industrial deference' and 'the view of some Labour voters' that class was 'immutably determined by birth' (ibid.).

It is perhaps worth pausing briefly here to note that McKenzie and Silver were not alone in noting the coexistence of 'seculars' and 'traditionalists'. In a near-contemporaneous book *The Working Class Tories* (1967), political scientist Eric Nordlinger identified the same distinction, while important work carried out by psephologist Mark Abrams from the mid-1950s onwards had exposed how, despite being 'overwhelmingly a working-class party' at that time, Labour's 'support from this group' between the elections of 1945 and 1955 was, in fact, 'far from solid' – with one-third of manual workers backing the Conservatives (1961: 343).

But where McKenzie and Silver's thesis became more revealing than those of their contemporaries – offering clues about more complex and *fluctuating* aspects of working-class Conservatism –

was in its investigation of a related, more nuanced, dimension of Tory support: the question of longevity and loyalty. Interlaced with their analysis of the broad distinction between seculars and deferentials was their exploration of two other forms of working-class voter, both Labour and Conservative: 'constants' and 'changers'. While they defined constants as those who had both voted for a particular party at the previous general election and 'expressed a clear intention to do so again at the next', changers were generally those who '"did not know" which party they would support' next time (ibid.: 105–6). What made the ensuing analysis so rich and surprising, though, was that it often confounded correlations one might expect to find between more pragmatic, evidence-oriented Tory 'seculars' and instrumentalist 'changers' willing to switch voting allegiances away from the party whenever more tempting retail offers lured them away. Conservative changers were 'almost twice as likely' as constants to 'prefer a prime minister of working-class background', but also 'more critical of obstacles to social mobility' and less likely to see *themselves* as working class – in keeping with a belief in the virtues of talent, ability and effort, rather than birthright, that one might also expect to find among seculars (McKenzie & Silver, 1968: 160). Yet, while the authors did indeed find that 'almost all' changers were seculars, around *one-half* of seculars, paradoxically, were 'constants' (ibid.: 228–9). This latter finding pointed to the existence of a substantial, highly intriguing subset of working-class Tories that confounded easy pigeonholing – and was arguably under-explored in McKenzie and Silver's otherwise forensic study. This was the segment that, despite claiming to base its Conservative allegiance purely on merit (that is, the party's performance in office – not its natural right to govern), nonetheless *constantly* supported it. Indeed, the existence of this curious hybrid – the 'secular constant' – perhaps offers a partial explanation for some of the authors' other, messier findings. While changers tended to regard themselves as upwardly mobile – as closer, in that respect, to the middle class than their actual class of origin – the secular *constant* sub-category appeared to at least partly correspond with that of 'lower-income seculars' who were 'more likely than any other group to see themselves as "working class"' (ibid.: 196).

For McKenzie and Silver, the significance of secular constants lay in the contrast it struck with the counterintuitive self-image of lower-income *deferentials*, who they found to be 'much more likely than seculars to claim middle class status', in apparent denial of their modest social and material circumstances. This curious correlation was summed up in the authors' ironic observation that 'deference serves to enhance, in their own eyes, the social prestige of those Conservatives who are in fact among the *least* prosperous of the working class' (ibid.; emphasis added). But the existence of secular constants – strongly aware of their intractable proletarian status, but nonetheless fiercely loyal to a party with a questionable record for representing their class interests – perhaps has more to offer us interpretively (including today) than simply a contrast to more bourgeois-identifying deferentials. What it potentially points to is the long-standing existence of a group of working-class voters who, though nominally basing their political support, conditionally, on their perception of the Conservatives' competence and ability to deliver the goods, remain impervious to the appeal of rivals promising to improve their lot: in essence, to a strain of secular (rather than deferential) Tories who appear to 'know their place'. Is this a form of wilful blindness – or even what Friedrich Engels referred to when, in an 1893 letter to communist historian Franz Mehring, he lamented the 'false consciousness' of subjugated peoples who internalized and accepted as given the grossly unequal social order imposed by their oppressors (Marx & Engels, 1977)? At the very least, it seems to find clear echoes in the findings of frustrated miner-turned-sociologist Ken Coates who, following his and colleague Richard Silburn's in-depth research on Nottingham's deprived St Ann's estate for their classic 1970s ethnography *Poverty: The Forgotten Englishmen*, despaired at the fact that a belief in 'our received institutions' as '"natural" even when they affront nature', as '"normal" even when they parody insanity', was 'all too widely prevalent among the poor' (1981: 168).

So what (if anything) might such acceptant, apathetic and borderline apolitical 'secular constancy' have to tell us about the attributes of latter-day working-class voters willing to switch their electoral support towards the Conservatives, and away from the movement that – within *their own* class and/or communities –

would historically have been the 'natural' party of government? To what extent might the position of recently converted 'red-wall' Tories be interpreted as a new variant of secular conservatism? And at what point might their much-discussed falling out of love with Labour be viewed as so complete that they can be considered closer to McKenzie and Silver's Tory 'constants' than 'changers'?

In addition to puzzling over such apparently inscrutable forms of *loyalist* working-class Conservatism, considerable attention has been paid to the question of what factors might persuade blue-collar floating voters, or those with other historical allegiances, to *switch* to supporting the party – including the forms of Labour 'changer' also interviewed by McKenzie and Silver. One obvious explanatory framework relates to the previously discussed concept of embourgeoisement: in essence, the suggestion that the more upwardly mobile and aspirational someone becomes (both socially and materially) the more likely they are to become gameable by the Tories. The evidence for this simple trade-off, however, is far from conclusive – both in 'classic' literature and more recent electoral studies that have charted the ever-rising average incomes of Labour voters and the commensurate increase in Tory support, over many years, among the lower-income working-classes.

In an early finding that now seems somewhat at variance with trends since the 1980s, Goldthorpe and colleagues' *The Affluent Worker* found little evidence of what might be termed *electoral* embourgeoisement among increasingly well-heeled, but still heavily unionized, Luton-based car-workers – even as they rose up the skills and income scale over a period of years. Instead, they observed that 'the average 80% Labour vote of our sample in 1955, 1959, and 1963' was 'still remarkably high in comparison with the level of Labour voting in the working class as a whole' (1968: 14), while (unsurprisingly) their white-collar interviewees were 'predominantly committed' to the Conservatives and Liberals (ibid.: 13). This broadly accorded with McKenzie and Silver's contemporaneous observation that 'subjective' social class was 'strongly related to working-class voting', with 'those *considering* themselves [emphasis added] to be middle class' much 'more likely to vote Conservative' than people self-identifying as working class – and embourgeoisement 'most strongly linked to Conservative voting' among those who, while earning below-average incomes, had experienced levels of 'intergenerational mobility' enabling them to become 'savers and homeowners' (1968: 95–6). The corollary here with Goldthorpe and colleagues' factory workers was, then, that – despite being relatively 'affluent' – Labour loyalists still strongly *self-identified* as working class.

Even more significant than this foretaste of 1980s aspirationalism, though, was *The Affluent Worker*'s emphasis on the findings of an earlier study by Alford (1963): one which now appears hugely prophetic following recent swings towards the Tories within the (increasingly fragmented) 'new working class' (Ainsley, 2018). In it, Alford noted that, while working-class support for Labour had never historically been lower than 57 per cent, it was also 'never higher than 67%' (cited in Goldthorpe et al, 1968: 14). Wind forward forty years and, according to longitudinal polling analysis by YouGov, the proportion of C2DE voters backing Labour fell from 56 per cent in 1970 (already below the party's minimum historical level of support recorded by Alford) to just 34 per cent in 2015. This downward trend was only briefly interrupted by the party's historic landslides in 1997 and 2001, when it again breached the 50 per cent mark (P. Kellner, 2017). Following the 2017 and 2019 elections, moreover, there was a 'further realignment of voters by class', with the Conservatives managing to draw more support from those in the C2DE category than ABC1s (48 compared to 43 per cent), and Labour by then attracting as many voters from each (33 per cent) – pointing to its rising support, over time, among middle-class voters (McDonnell & Curtis, 2019). As YouGov pollster Peter Kellner noted in a 2017 journal article 'Public opinion and the depth of Labour's crisis', the implications of the party's plummeting support among working-class voters presented it with a singular conundrum, given that it had simultaneously maintained a modest but steady middle-class following. While Labour's 'instinct' was 'to revive support among "our people"', this aim implicitly assumed that 'old class divisions still persist, albeit in slightly different forms.' In truth, he concluded, 'the roots and forms of social solidarity' that 'dominated' the 'first fifty years' of Labour's life – lingering 'in progressively weakened forms for the next thirty' – had 'gone' (Kellner, 2017).

Elsewhere, diagnoses of the causes of Labour's growing electoral vulnerability have been attributed as much to the diminishing size of the working class itself as to a growing disconnect with the party and readiness to vote for its rivals – or abstain altogether. In a lively academic debate kicked off by Labour's then historic defeat at the 1983 election, sociologist Anthony Heath and colleagues argued that the primary cause of its woes was the ongoing 'contraction of the working class' (Heath et al., 1986: 162). Indeed, numerous subsequent surveys have shown class to be an increasingly mutable phenomenon, while also demonstrating how (even based on conventional definitions) the working class has drastically declined in size over time. Of these, a recent Ipsos-MORI survey showed how the C2 (skilled manual workers) grade had plummeted from 30.4 per cent of the population in 1968 to just 20.2 per cent by 2015, while Ds had dropped to 15.5 per cent from 23 in 1972 (the first year they were recorded) (Ipsos-MORI, 2016). Conversely, in a robust retort to Heath's original thesis, political scientist Ivor Crewe reinterpreted the same electoral data to dismiss his argument that Labour's path to future electoral success necessitated further *deepening* its support among its traditional working-class base – arguing that 'the implications for Labour's electoral strategy' were actually 'the opposite of those suggested', because 'class dealignment' between the party and working-class voters instead meant it needed to build a wider coalition by courting the middle class (Crewe, 1986: 620). Indeed, Heath himself would later recognize working-class disillusionment with Labour as an important factor, by demonstrating how, even at the party's record-breaking landslide victory in 1997, it failed to persuade many voters in its 'core groups' to back it, with the result that they simply abstained (Heath, 2000: 37).

Some clues as to the reasons for the growing disconnect between the self-styled party of the labouring classes and its erstwhile core constituency might be sought from a brief examination of the other (*small*-C) variety of working-class conservatism: the collective set of values and attitudes commonly characterized today as *socially* conservative. One of the most notable trends visible in the YouGov table is the fact that, barring its brief recovery in the late 1990s and early 2000s (ironically enough, under that most metropolitan and bourgeois of prime ministers, Tony Blair), Labour's fortunes among the class for whose benefit it was originally founded have steadily declined for decades. The most obvious and dramatic drop (from 45 to 36 per cent) occurred between 1979 and 1983, when a combination of accelerating de-industrialization, victory in the Falklands War and the growing popularity of Margaret Thatcher's 'Right-to-Buy' council house policy contributed to a 'khaki election' victory, partly powered by a mass defection from Labour among blue-collar Tory converts. However, the real story of the past fifty-plus years is of a longer-term, creeping erosion in Labour's working-class support – even before the slow picking off of upwardly mobile voters at the top of the pile under Thatcherism, and more recent developments that have left those at the bottom feeling left behind (not least by that party). Indeed, far from having been confined to periods when its policies swung to the Left – as in the early 1980s and under Jeremy Corbyn – the speed and scale of Labour's decline accelerated markedly during the mid to late 'New Labour' period. Between 2001 and 2010, the party's share of the C1DE vote plummeting by 18 percentage points – from 51 to 33 per cent. It is to the task of explaining this trend that understanding the schism between the more liberal and socially conservative values held by newer and older members of the party's increasingly vulnerable electoral coalition is so integral.

The literature on the subject of working-class social conservatism – and its relationship to (and tension with) Labour's own evolving values – is now so extensive that it is impossible to give more than a broad overview here. However, certain features of this debate are widely accepted, so it is with these that we primarily concern ourselves. Two of the clearest definitions of the kinds of attitude commonly ascribed to this social conservatism are the elegant (if simplistic) summaries of traits attributed to the class-straddling communitarian patriots Goodhart categorizes as 'Somewheres' in *The Road to Somewhere* and Mattinson distils as the essence of working-class ex-Labour voters in *Beyond the Red Wall* (2020). Goodhart describes the worldviews of people of *all* classes who value rootedness and sense of place over the increasingly mobile, autonomous and globally facing values of younger, degree-educated 'Anywheres' as those of 'group identity, tradition and national social contracts' – or 'faith, flag and family' (2017: 5). Mattinson crystallizes the core values of working-class social conservatism (a term she avoids using directly) as the similarly alliterative trio of 'pride, place and patriotism' (2020: 71).

Where Goodhart's and Mattinson's values most closely align is their emphasis on 'flag' and 'patriotism': both the former's 'Somewheres' and the latter's 'red-wallers' are patriotic to *hyper-local* degrees, seeing their own identities as intrinsically bound up with the histories, triumphs and tragedies of the places where they were born and raised. For Mattinson's working-class subjects, these local identities tended to relate to the glories of their industrial heritage: she recalls, for instance, how 'everyone' she met in Stoke-on-Trent 'had a parent or grandparent who had worked in a pot bank, the local name for a pottery factory' (2020: 61). More intriguingly, though, this 'small-p' patriotism of locality and place seemed indivisible from the 'big-P' variety: one rooted in the nation as a whole, and both its industrial and imperial legacies. 'Community matters to people around here, but when they're thinking about community they're thinking about the whole country', remarked Graham Jones, ex-Labour MP for Hyndburn, in an interview with Mattinson, adding that locals' ideas about 'patriotism' meant that both 'the country is what happens on their own doorstep and what happens on their own doorstep is the country' (ibid.: 80). Little wonder, perhaps, that a 2018 survey commissioned by Mattinson's polling company, BritainThinks, found that people living in north-east England, Yorkshire and the Midlands were 10 per cent more likely than Londoners to describe themselves as 'proud to be British', while, when asked to write an election strapline listing their priorities, 'red-wallers' on a citizen's jury she convened for Labour came up with this hauntingly Trumpian slogan: 'Make Britain Great Again' (ibid.: 80).

An extension of the 'local-*is*-national' perspective underpinning the patriotism of Mattinson's interviewees – and one which perhaps helps explain their recent anti-Labour backlash – was her finding that such voters' perceptions of the 'establishment' tended to centre more on their *local* politicians (councillors and MPs), rather than *Westminster* governments. This sentiment was neatly encapsulated in the views of Yvonne, a woman who had spent several years campaigning to save Darlington Library with what she saw as little support from the then Labour council and sitting MP, before an ambitious Conservative parliamentary candidate and incoming Tory council leader effectively reversed the earlier decision to close it. To Yvonne (and others like her), Labour had adopted the 'paternalistic', metropolitan-elitist, attitude of 'we know best, we know what's good for you better than you do' – and, crucially, this paternalism had extended to its (national) approach to Brexit, which left 'the little people' feeling 'fed up with not being listened to' (2020: 48).

In a lengthy passage focusing on the importance attached to local-level representation by her 'red-wall' interviewees, Mattinson reflected how, for those who had 'long felt neglected and ignored by national government', what 'happens locally' was of 'greater importance' – because 'place' means more 'when people's lives are contained within the area they come from' and this is where they 'live, work and socialise' (ibid.: 100). In such contexts, she argued, people's judgement of political parties' performance is primarily viewed 'through the lens of local government' (which extends to perceptions of the effectiveness of their local MPs) – with voters assessing their representatives by such prosaic, but important, measures as whether they feel they are on their 'side', share the same 'priorities' and spend their money 'wisely' (ibid.). In essence, then, the 2019 election saw many long-time working-class Labour voters rebelling against a status quo they conceptualized, at least partly, through the prism of *the local* – and their condescending treatment by a *provincial* establishment that, in turn, symbolized wider problems with 'we-know-best' (Labour) politicians *nationally*. They therefore used the election as much as a protest vote against their *local* establishments as a verdict on the *national* one (incumbent and/or insurgent) – an intriguing inversion of long-standing voting patterns familiar from local elections, at which voters often give national leaders a 'bloody nose' before swinging back behind them at general elections.

This conflation of 'the local' and 'the national', and its intersection with ideas about patriotism, elites and (lack of) accountability, is Mattinson's most important finding, as it helps explain an enduring conundrum of the 2019 general election result. This is the question of why people in disadvantaged areas with deep historical ties to Labour abandoned it in such numbers to instead consolidate the hold on power, at UK-wide level, of an 'establishment' party that had already been in government for a decade – during which it had presided over sweeping cuts to public services and the benefits system that had deeply affected them.

A more brutal – not to say specific – illustration of socially conservative attitudes than Goodhart's or Mattinson's had been exposed forty years earlier by McKenzie and Silver, in describing the 'high degree of consensus among working-class voters' around certain issues, notably 'three controversial areas of social policy': 'coloured immigration; flogging as a form of judicial punishment, and the granting of independence to colonial territories' (1968: 152–3). While Labour voters surveyed saw no contradiction in supporting socially progressive policies around the welfare state, intervention in the economy and income redistribution via the tax system, when it came to questions around the extent and limits of British citizenship, 83 per cent of them favoured 'government action to restrict coloured immigration'. Tellingly, 'Labour and Conservative voters supported this view with almost exactly the same frequency' and 'almost half of Labour voters' agreed with the imperialistic, racially problematic statement that Britain had been 'too hasty in granting independence to colonies' (ibid.).

That such manifestly conservative sentiments prevailed among voters across the political spectrum may go some way to explaining other attitudes McKenzie and Silver noted among Labour interviewees – in particular, their overwhelmingly instrumentalist motives for supporting that party. When asked why they voted Labour, many respondents fell back on normative, taken-for-granted assertions such as that it 'stands for the working man', was 'the working man's party' or simply 'runs in the family' (1968: 112). In such testimony, they noted 'an almost complete absence of any reference to "socialism" or a "new social order"' – suggesting that the 'section of the working class which supports Labour' did so 'almost entirely through class loyalty' and 'the expectation of greater social benefits from a Labour government' (ibid.). More curiously, given the heavily unionized 1960s context in which their research was conducted, four out of ten of their most 'hard-core' Labour-supporting interviewees said they disapproved of the 'extent' of 'union power' (ibid.: 126), while people advocating 'class conflict' were almost universally seen (in terms eerily redolent of the language of moral panics) as 'socially deviant' (ibid.: 136). Of particular significance here was the fact that, even during a period of normalized union membership and ingrained support for Labour among the industrial working class, there were already signs of emerging proletarian-bourgeois (in today's terms, provincial-metropolitan) *cultural* fault-lines, as well as wider concerns about groups considered to be a preoccupation of Labour's latter-day 'woke' elites. 'It is the intellectual, so-called educated type of man who stirs it up', remarked one man, when asked who he blamed for promoting class-war rhetoric, while others identified a familiar rogues' gallery embracing everyone from 'younger people' (specifically teenaged boys) to 'the Irish', 'coloured people' and 'agitators' who 'come into the country' (ibid.).

In these small-c, decidedly illiberal, comments from Labour voters, one detects clear echoes of the apolitical working-class tradesmen scabrously satirized in *The Ragged Trousered Philanthropists*: men 'averse from arguing or disputing about politics', who knew 'as much about the public affairs of their own country' as 'the condition of affairs in the planet of Jupiter' and sneered at the polemical outpourings of their socialist co-worker, Frank Owen (Tressell, 2004: 11). There was a foretaste, too, of tensions portrayed in Alan Bleasdale's BAFTA-winning 1982 BBC2 state-of-the-nation drama *The Boys from the Blackstuff*, in which ill-fated Workers Revolutionary Party supporter Snowy Malone was ridiculed by his workmates for ranting about the Toxteth riots, socialism's demise and the prospect of mass unemployment and poverty under a then early-stage Thatcher government.

This mix of parochialism, reciprocal charitability and instrumentalist political allegiances, combined with a neo-colonialist nostalgia for nation and empire, seems eerily redolent of views ascribed (sometimes dubiously) to Britain's latter-day left behind – as exemplified by 'red-wall' Tory converts who told Mattinson of their pride that 'Britain used to own the world' and be 'a force to be reckoned with' and how they saw 'the north' as 'uniquely British' (2020: 80). Yet four decades on – and notwithstanding the echoes of imperialist rhetoric in campaign messages *targeted* at socially conservative voters by actors on the latter-day populist Right – just how insular and nativist *are* these groups?

An increasingly dominant reading of the value-systems of such voters, particularly following the much-debated 'red-wall' backlash, is that the condition of being (or feeling) left behind is not so much *economic* as *cultural*: that it has just as much to do with feelings of disconnection from the dominant worldview in society at large as a sense of being economically disadvantaged or neglected. Indeed, there are glimpses of such feelings of cultural disconnect in many interviews quoted in Mattinson's research – particularly those in which respondents reflect on their one-time support for Labour. 'Politically correct, morally superior and fixated on the wrong priorities' is how she summed up their attitudes towards the party's perceived latter-day dominance by a middle-class metropolitan liberal elite, while time and again she was told that 'Labour no longer really represents its traditional voters' (2020: 130–31). One example given was of a group of men from Accrington, Lancashire, who were 'baffled' about Labour's focus on issues such as trans rights under Corbyn's leadership – with one complaining that its priorities were wrong, when there were 'thousands of kids here with no work and no hope' (ibid.: 130). So far, so much in keeping with the 'culture-war' thesis that has become common currency today, including among those with clear agendas for stoking it (Sobolewska & Ford, 2019). Yet, an equally important finding was that these overwhelmingly pro-Brexit, often self-describing left-behind voters – however aggrieved and angry they might have felt towards Labour and its progressive preoccupations – saw no meeting of minds with Donald Trump. Asked how they viewed Britain's future relationship with America, the opinions they aired were 'almost entirely … negative' towards him (ibid.: 118) – giving the lie to lazy assumptions of a simple *equivalence* to, let alone read-across from, Britain's 'red-wall' voters to blue-collar Trump supporters of the US 'rust belt'.

Indeed, there is much in the (now widely accepted) red-wall thesis – and approaches Mattinson and others have applied in exploring it – that is deeply flawed. Though she acknowledges the origins of the term 'red wall' as the construction of another pollster, the entire premise of Mattinson's 'deep-dive' focus groups was the implicit assumption that, in one way or another, it objectively exists. By contrast, as fellow psephologist Lewis Baston argued in a compelling article for *The Critic* magazine days after the 2019 election, the notion that 'the red wall' corresponds to any kind of cohesive real-world phenomenon is a 'myth' (Baston, 2019). The 'mythical wall', he argued, might be discursively convenient, but is also 'a patronising generalisation about a huge swathe of England (and a corner of Wales)'.

In reality, the wall was (and is) a construct cobbled together to fit a predetermined narrative about renewed Tory electoral ascendancy – based on the party's triumph in a wildly disparate range of seats it managed to win from Labour. Included among these were a handful in which Labour had clawed surprising wins in 2017, when it confounded predictions by coming within 2.5 percentage points of the Tories in national vote-share, and a 'large proportion' of 'traditional marginal seats' that had somehow 'resisted the tide to the Conservatives in the last few elections' – though, historically, they were normally captured by whichever party secured a majority. Indeed, early analyses of the specific demographic characteristics of red-wall seats offer some support for the view that many of them are (or were) far from *typical* of those historically held by Labour across the North and Midlands. In a post-election report entitled *Painting the Towns Blue*, the Resolution Foundation found that, while working-age employment rates and household incomes in 'red-wall' seats that switched to the Conservatives were lower than the national averages, they were slightly higher than in northern seats *retained* by Labour (McCurdy et al., 2020: 27, 58–9). Home ownership rates were significantly above those of other Labour-retained seats, at 54 compared to 43 per cent – suggesting that (as in the 1980s) many red-wall defectors were relatively embourgeoised and/or aspirational people (ibid.: 8). This reading was later consolidated when the ongoing longitudinal British Election Study found that, 'contrary to numerous post-election narratives', most *working-age* low-income adults voted Labour, not Conservative, in 2019 – and only when *retired* people were factored in (a bigger proportion of whom were assumed to be homeowners) did the overall preference of 'poorer' voters switch from Labour to Tories (Fieldhouse et al., 2021). In other words, whatever the dominant left-behind discourse tells us, it was actually *older* voters, *across* the age-bands – not 'poor people', least of all the *working-aged* 'poor' – who mobilized in favour of the Tories in 2019, and any simplistic conflation of the electorally decisive 'red-wallers' with the (economically) 'left behind' of popular folklore is therefore misjudged. Relatedly, while the most influential 'red-wall' demographic was to be found among its older voting segment, this was exactly the same story in historically 'true-blue' constituencies. To put it differently, though many older 'red-wall' voters might well have been more financially precarious than their retiree counterparts in the affluent shires, in terms of their 2019 *voting behaviour* (and, in many cases, enthusiasm for Brexit), these two superficially disparate groups had everything in common.

Moreover, while the levels of affluence enjoyed by Tory-leaning, older 'red-wallers' might well fall short of those of wealthy southerners, they tend to be *relatively* prosperous much more than younger and/or Labour-inclined 'red-wall' voters – akin to the influential 'squeezed middle' identified in a Brexit context by social policy scholar Lorenza Antonucci (2017). Indeed, just as misleading as conflating 'the red wall' with 'the left behind' in the *abstract* is any suggestion that most *individuals* in post-industrial constituencies who switched to the Tories were former 'proletarian traditionalists' (Goldthorpe et al., 1968: 74) who had finally been driven mad by *Labour's* slow-burn embourgeoisement. In fact, those who had previously identified with Labour were largely 'changers' (McKenzie & Silver, 1968), whom the Tories had slowly picked off over many years – by exploiting *their* growing affluence. As Sebastian Payne put it memorably in his 2021 travelogue through fallen 'red-wall' seats, *Broken Heartlands*, these aspirational successors to the solidaristic industrial workers of old were, by 2019, fast becoming just as much 'natural Tories' as the quintessential semi-owning, Mondeo-driving white-collar workers of the South-East commuter-belt: the same, 'satisfied' (but sometimes insecure) suburban voters, often living in 'new out-of-town estates' and 'dependent on their cars for transport' (Payne, 2021), that fellow journalist Duncan Weldon crystallized in a much-discussed 2021 *Economist* article as 'Barratt Britain' (Weldon, 2021).

For all the disparities in voting behaviour between different segments of the 'working-class' electorate(s), however, one consistent pattern to emerge from such analysis was the extent to which 'red-wall' seats had experienced greater degrees of economic *decline* since 2010 than other former Labour constituencies – fuelled by disproportionate exposure to benefit cuts and the fact that 'the performance of employment, pay, the sectoral mix and house prices' had all been 'relatively weaker than in other areas' (McCurdy et al., 2020: 65). Again, there is much in these findings that echoes analysis of the profile of *Brexit* voters by Antonucci and colleagues, who emphasized the impact on the referendum result of a 'squeezed middle' of 'intermediate' earners, who had *relatively* 'declined in economic terms' (2017: 212–13).

Returning to Baston's analysis, of the fifty ex-Labour constituencies the Tories gained in northern England, the Midlands and Wales, he could find only twenty conforming to the classic stereotype of long-time 'red-wall' areas that had suddenly succumbed to Conservative assault. And, though most of these were 'former mining seats and single industry towns along the line where the Midlands meets the North', many had been slowly yielding to Tory overtures for decades, reflecting long-standing patterns of working-class drift from Labour identified in the historical YouGov polling data – and, in effect, turning these areas into new marginals (Baston, 2020). Drawing on this critique, *Observer* columnist Kenan Malik has rightly observed that 'the red wall is deployed less as a demographic description' than 'a cypher for a certain set of values that working-class people supposedly hold' – that is, 'a social conservatism about issues such as immigration, crime, welfare and patriotism'. As a result, while the 'red-wall phenomenon' has left the post-Corbyn Left 'wary of appearing too socially liberal', in truth 'the conservatism' ascribed to working-class voters has been 'overplayed' – with differences '*within* the working class' being 'underestimated' (Malik, 2021; emphasis added).

One serious-minded, if controversial, conceptualization of this 'supposed' socially conservative working-class tradition is that proposed by the 'Blue Labour' advocacy group, whose most prominent advocate is social theorist Maurice Glasman. In its online manifesto, the group defines its ideological position as that of a form of 'socialism' that 'is both radical and conservative' – arguing for 'a politics about the work we do, the people we love, and the places to which we belong' (Glasman, 2020). Though widely criticized by some on the Left for apparently supporting reactionary positions on issues like immigration and crime – two (largely undisputed) commonalities identified by almost all explorations of small-c British working-class conservatism – Blue Labour's early positions on several issues now seem to have been somewhat prescient, and more nuanced than is sometimes recognized.

Chief among its broad underpinning principles has been an attempt to address tensions between the economic and cultural concerns of traditional working-class groups that would today be termed 'left behind': two distinct, but interlocking, issues that continue to confuse and confound contemporary debates around Brexit, the 'red wall' and moves by both Tories and Labour to promote their competing versions of 'Levelling Up' policies, particularly in the shadow of the COVID-19 pandemic. For Blue Labour, this began as 'a challenge to the liberal consensus of the capitalist order' – a quote that would not sound out of place in a stump speech by left-wing firebrands such as Corbyn – but one puzzlingly insistent that it did not favour 'a communitarian politics', and was less concerned about *overturning* capitalism than the ways in which Britain's cultural values had been colonized by the Left and its economic ones by the Right (ibid.). In other words, it sought to accommodate two ideological positions that had come to be seen as incompatible: a conservative attitude towards immigration, crime and some aspects of multiculturalism, paired with conventional socialist concerns about the 'the commodification of capitalism' and 'transactional culture of the market'(ibid.). If one term crystallized the Blue Labour approach more than any other, however, it was an appeal for a renewed recognition of the importance of promoting 'the common good' – which it defined as 'mutual loyalties binding human beings into families, groups and nations'; 'reciprocity' between individuals; and their consolidation through 'shared civic institutions' that could 'constrain the domination of both market and state' (ibid.).

Around the same time as Glasman was developing these ideas, a strikingly similar strand of argumentation was beginning to emerge from thinkers on the more communitarian wing of the Conservative Party. In his 2010 book *Red Tory*, Phillip Blond, director of centre-right think-tank ResPublica, advocated reviving the spirit of 'civil society', while deriding the idea that 'everything that ordinary citizens do' is 'reducible to the imposed traditions of the central state' or 'the compulsion and determination of the marketplace' (2010: 3). Though couched as a paean to the decline of individual autonomy (values championed by the libertarian Right) as much as a call-to-arms for new forms of collectivism, Blond's proposition was instrumental in shaping the discourse of the 'Big Society': a fuzzy amalgam of community-level voluntarism for the common good and the more individualistic Gladstonian virtue of self-help around which David Cameron initially shaped his vision as Tory leader.

If Blue Labour and Red Toryism's philosophical positions seemed too elusive for many when originally aired, in the aftermath of the 2007–08 financial crash and era-defining 2010 election, they have since found echoes in ongoing discussions about the plight of Britain's 'red-wall' communities. Though largely unacknowledged, much of the left-behind discourse promoted since the 2016 referendum draws on aspects of their analyses, although the rhetoric of many of those presuming to speak for the left-behind working class(es) – from Farage to Johnson – sits uncomfortably with aspects of their social and economic policies that are far removed from a Blue Labour (or even Red Tory) prospectus. While Johnson's administration may have committed vast sums of taxpayers' money and government borrowing to reducing the negative impacts of COVID-19 on low-income households, and has repeatedly (though, so far, emptily) promised to 'level up' through a post-pandemic pledge to 'Build Back Better', it remains committed to a neoliberal approach to running the economy, particularly in relation to post-Brexit overseas trade arrangements. Nonetheless, Glasman and Blond's common diagnoses of the forces responsible for the fracturing of civic bonds, and the challenges afflicting working-class communities, are widely echoed today – albeit in a pick-and-mix way – by politicians and pundits of both Left and Right. The latter's emotive tirades against 'governing elites in both Britain and America' – penned (like Glasman's) in the shadow of the crash – may have seemed like fringe thinking a decade ago, but nowadays they speak to a growing consensus, among mainstream and populist voices alike, that we need to be worried about widening disconnects between the governors and the governed.

While Blue Labour thinking may present ideological difficulties for those concerned to re-engage with working-class people from a liberal-Left political position, a more digestible (and perhaps palatable) adaptation of some of its arguments has been proposed by commentators such as *Guardian* associate editor Julian Coman. In a thoughtful 2020 article headlined 'Labour would do well to rediscover its Conservative side', he wrestled with the tortuous debates being held within Labour circles about how to reconnect with 'red-wall' voters without alienating the younger, metropolitan members it had gained by the million during the Corbyn years. Coman's proposal was for an alternative definition of working-class conservatism that cast both it and its supposed equal and opposite – social liberalism – as mindsets less diametrically opposed than previously assumed. Responding to trade unionist Paul Embery's then newly published polemic against the supposed 'woke' elitism of post-Corbyn Labour, *Despised*, Coman argued that 'throughout the history of capitalism, British working-class resistance to its disruptions and demands' had 'often taken the form of a conservative defence of threatened community' (Coman, 2020). In this insightful reconceptualization of social conservatism, Coman made a persuasive case for a progressive, solidaristic reconnection between Labour, the pursuit of 'individual freedoms' prized by its post-millennial middle-class adherents and the politics of 'stability, locality, honour, loyalty and patriotism' favoured by its historical working-class base. This might be achieved, he argued, by recognizing an 'honourable history on the British left' that embraces – and can make virtuous – this delicate balancing act. Coman concluded with this optimistic plea for bridge-building between these contrasting, but compatible, ideals:

> Equal rights and equal access to individual fulfilment are fundamental to any contemporary notion of the common good. But belonging, a sense of mutual dependency and the idea that

> individuals find meaning in something bigger than themselves contribute to it too. (Coman, 2020)

In considering what a grounded, more cohesive, less divided future might look like, this book's Conclusion consciously draws inspiration from Coman's argument.

STIGMATIZING DISADVANTAGE: FRAMING EXCLUSION AND THE RISE OF 'LEFT-BEHIND DISCOURSE'

Alongside the transformation and fragmentation of the 'traditional' working class, and the evolution of various forms of working-class conservatism, there sits a parallel history – a substantial part of which pre-dates the evolutionary developments on which we have so far focused. According to this alternate history, the social consequences of de-industrialization and other earlier and later structural economic upheavals and crises are cast not as the impoverishment or immiseration of the lower orders by external forces beyond their control – or even the transformation or dissolution of the industrial working class – but the emergence, resurgence and/or reproduction of a succession of *under*classes.

Though the historical separation of economically disadvantaged groups into the virtuous and the villainous dates back to the medieval period (if not earlier), we take up this tale in the industrial era – by which time it had crystallized into a moralistic narrative discriminating between the 'deserving' and 'undeserving' poor. In *Images of Welfare*, their seminal exploration of stigmatizing discourses around poverty and working-age social security (specifically, Britain's post-war benefits system), sociologists Peter Golding and Sue Middleton began by charting the evolution of deserving/undeserving oppositions through time, paying particular attention to the period since the (now first) Industrial Revolution: the term coined by economic historian Arnold Toynbee to describe the seismic transformations undergone by European and United States economies between 1760 and 1840, when they shifted away from relying on agriculture and handicrafts towards mechanized mass production.

Golding and Middleton's emphasis on the prominence of such discursive oppositions from the mid-eighteenth century reflects their wider thesis that the concept of 'undeserving poverty' has *repeatedly* been socially (re)constructed by elites as a political tool to displace blame for economic crises, such as slumps and recessions, and to mobilize popular consent for disruptive changes – from the process of industrialization itself to (more recent) moves to *de*-industrialize, deregulate and retrench the reach of the state, by cutting economic investment, public spending and social protections. By trading on an imagined in-group (the 'deserving *us*'), starkly juxtaposed with a deviant out-group (the 'undeserving *them*'), such discursive constructs are calculated to shame 'the poor' into falling into line – invariably by contributing their labour for even the most meagre reward – while often also blaming them for the economic difficulties that 'force' changes or cutbacks on society as a whole. In the context of the mass recruitment drive needed to kickstart Britain's move from a standing start to industrial production on a military scale, they argued that, from the mid-eighteenth century, 'poor law policy' had become 'more and more transparently the appendage of employment policy' – as 'the peasant economy dwindled, agrarian capitalism became more intensive and the industrial labour force, and indeed the overall population, increased' (1982: 13).

One key discursive turn Golding and Middleton noted around this time was a shift away from 'the correction of the idle poor' (driven by a moralistic Christian concern, with deep historical roots, about the 'blemished souls' of paupers) to more instrumentalist worries about the 'ever-quickening flow of taxation for poor relief' – as evidenced by figures from the period between 1784 and 1813 showing that the cost of providing for those unable to work or without employment had trebled due to 'dislocations of the industrial revolution, famines, war and an increasing population' (ibid.). In such circumstances, the (newly defined) 'unemployed' offered a convenient target for political opprobrium: a suitably abject other to be paraded as an article of shame facilitating the mass conscription of the 'deserving' poor into the service of the new national mission to attain industrial supremacy. Moreover, this objectification was twofold: not only were unemployed people cast as symbols of 'unused potential', or squandered national assets letting the side down: they were also 'a burden, a drain on hard-won wealth' (ibid.).

As has also been well documented elsewhere (for example, Morrison, 2019a), one of the most notorious developments to emerge from this new era of mass industrial conscription was the 1834 Poor Law Amendment Act: a statute that did more than any other before or since to criminalize indolence, by (in the words of E.P. Thompson) signalling 'the most sustained attempt to impose an ideological dogma, in defiance of the evidence of human need, in English history' (1968: 667). The ideology to which Thompson referred was multifaceted and sowed the seeds of ingrained forms of distrust in the nature and motives of 'the poor' which have repeatedly been invoked since. It encompassed a series of logically sequenced beliefs, enshrined in an 1834 report by the Royal Commission on the Poor Laws – beginning with the assumption that 'the poor' were, first and foremost, 'morally culpable' for their own poverty, through their 'excessive breeding, dependence on the ale-house and indolence', and, secondly, that they were invariably guilty of abusing and exploiting systems introduced to assist them (Golding & Middleton, 1982: 15–16). The next link in this sequence was the Commissioners' favoured solution: a new system of 'deterrence', based around a 'workhouse test' which made continued receipt of poor relief contingent on one's willingness to yield to a system of industrial servitude at the very bottom of the new mass-production food-chain. Finally, in an effort to deflect accusations of callousness from society's more stubbornly beneficent opinion-formers, the Commissioners embarked on the most systematic effort to date to 'classify the poor', to 'distinguish' – and publicly shame – the 'larger group of the "vicious" and indolent' from the 'small minority of blamelessly indigent' (ibid.: 16–17). Here, then, were the beginnings of the continuous process of (re)definition, categorization and problematization to which the unemployed, disabled people and other social security benefit recipients are subjected today (see, for example, Wiggan, 2012; Morrison, 2019a).

But what has all this to do with our (real or imagined) left behind? An enduring trait of stigmatizing discourses around 'the poor' – familiar from the outpourings of moral entrepreneurs of all kinds, from priests and politicians to journalists and campaigners – has been a persistent tendency to identify discrete social groupings, at times even entire communities, districts and places, as morally deviant. As historian John Welshman observed in *Underclass* – his authoritative 2013 'history of the excluded' – since the late Victorian period, economically disadvantaged groupings have been subjected to a succession of negative popular caricatures portraying them as the collective embodiments of endemic and pathological cultures of poverty (of both material and moral kinds). Between 1880 – when Welshman's survey commenced – and the early twenty-first century, there were numerous iterations of such discursively 'excluded' populations. These ranged from the 'dangerous classes' (a term imported from France, via the nineteenth-century writings of Balzac and Victor Hugo, and subsequently reconceptualized by Marx and Engels) to Britain's homegrown 'residuum' to the 'social problem group' pinpointed as the focus of putative moves to introduce state-directed welfare measures. They have also taken in the transatlantic concepts of 'underclass' (Biressi & Nunn 2013; Welshman, 2013: 6–7) and 'deplorables' (Clinton, quoted in Komlos, 2018) and the 'forgotten people' around whom the New Labour government constructed its 'social exclusion' agenda (bbc.co.uk, 1997).

What all these disparate confections have in common is their blanket construction of entire communities and neighbourhoods afflicted by unemployment, poor housing and other intersecting disadvantages as, at best, complex and unwelcome social problems and, at worst, retrograde rumps of economically burdensome and/or culturally backward non-contributors. One early prototype of this dehumanizing discourse is identifiable in the Marxian iteration of the 'dangerous class': a grouping Marx and Engels characterized, in *The Communist Manifesto*, as 'the social scum, that passively rotting mass thrown off by the lowest layers of old society' (1888 [1977]: 92). While it would be an argumentative stretch (not to say deeply demeaning) to draw any clear-cut discursive parallels between those Marx and Engels labelled the 'lumpenproletariat' and today's left behind, the *media-political* critiques applied to these groups share intriguing commonalities. Chief among these is the (dismissive) view, widely circulated among Remain-supporting politicians and commentators after the referendum, that left-behind communities voted against their own best interests – and that some have since compounded this error by backing UKIP, the Brexit Party and/or Tories in recent elections. How far removed are the more sweeping, scabrous criticisms of such working-class voters (particularly those framing them as ignorant and racist) from Marx and Engels' historical description of the 'dangerous class' as a grouping whose 'conditions of life' rendered it susceptible to becoming the 'bribed tool' of 'reactionary intrigue': in today's terms, that of elite-driven, if ostensibly common man-championing, right-wing populism?

Setting aside the lumpenproletariat, a perhaps more obvious starting-point for any attempt to locate the origins of latter-day left-behind discourse is the appropriation and repurposing, by UK politicians and media commentators, of a paradigm historically linked to media and sociological accounts of ghettoized Black urban communities in the United States: that of 'the underclass' (for example, Moynihan, 1967; Wilson, 1993). Britain's underclass debate owes its origins to a now-notorious 1989 *Sunday Times* article by the anti-welfare US political scientist Charles Murray, doyen of the 'New Right', in which he began a process (expanded on in later writings) of categorizing the latter-day 'poor' into one of two unsavoury lower orders. At the very lowest level lurked the 'underclass' itself – characterized as those 'who live in a different world from other Britons, who are raising their children to live in it, and whose values are now contaminating the life of entire neighbourhoods' (Murray, 1989: 26). Bobbing just above them, but in danger of sinking to the same depths if their problems remained untreated, were a 'new rabble' whose numerous deviancies were clinically itemized as including 'more crime, more widespread drug and alcohol addiction, fewer marriages, more dropout from work, more homelessness, more child neglect, fewer young people pulling themselves out of the slums, more young people tumbling in' (Murray, 1995: 115).

The role the New Right played in constructing and popularizing the concept of 'underclass' is of huge significance to this book's analysis, not least because many of the politicians and commentators most vocally claiming to speak up for today's 'left behind' – communities consistently framed as being blighted by similar social and economic problems to those listed above – are long-time ideological adherents of the scrounger-baiting, neoliberal worldview to which Murray subscribes. Moreover, many of these same actors continue to show little hesitation in rebooting and revitalizing scrounger (and underclass) discourse whenever it suits them to do so – albeit while strategically distinguishing the 'undeserving poor' from 'deserving' cases, such as low-waged 'strivers' and 'hardworking families' (Morrison, 2019a: 15). How credible was a July 2020 pledge by Equalities Minister Liz Truss reiterating her Conservative government's plans to 'level up' opportunities in 'deprived areas' by tackling inequalities relating to 'geography and social background' (Hansard, 2020b), given her track record of blaming a supposedly over-generous welfare system for rewarding 'laziness' and turning British workers into 'the worst idlers in the world' (quoted in www.bbc.co.uk, 2012)?

For all its similarities to its US antecedent, the UK incarnation of the underclass almost immediately distinguished itself from the 'original' in one crucial respect: its attachment not so much to ethnic minority groups as the (largely) white post-industrial working class. As social geographer Chris Haylett argued in an influential 2001 paper, Britain's white working class – increasingly problematized since the 1960s through tabloid accounts of mass industrial strikes, skirmishes between mods and rockers, neo-Nazi skinheads, football hooliganism and much more extreme crimes, such as the James Bulger murder – was constructed as 'a racialised and irredeemable "other"' (Haylett, 2001: 351).

Perhaps the most significant aspect of this analysis was Haylett's reading of the discursive reconceptualization this grouping underwent in the *aftermath* of this period. For Tony Blair's New Labour, entering power after an 18-year period of rapid de-industrialization, mass privatization of public assets and increasing socioeconomic (and cultural) atomization, the people formerly known as the underclass were at least a '*recuperable* "other"', rather than 'irredeemable' (ibid.; emphasis added). Nonetheless, from the point that Blair launched his social exclusion crusade on 2 June 1997, against the decaying Brutalist backdrop of south London's Aylesbury housing estate, they were symbolically marked as unmodern and atavistic, as 'an ugly contradiction: abject and white' (ibid.: 352). In this act of mass-stigmatization, masquerading (however well-meaningly) as social concern, dispossessed elements in the white working class were collectively portrayed as 'a mass of people, in mass housing', somehow 'falling out of the nation' and 'losing the material wherewithal and symbolic dignity traditionally associated with their colour and their class' (ibid.). This cast them in stark opposition to the (new) modernity the shiny 'New' Labour government sought to embrace and project, while also nodding to earlier historical conceptualizations of 'cultures' of welfare dependency (see Wiggan, 2012; Morrison, 2019a), 'cycles of deprivation' (Joseph, quoted in Welshman, 2007) and other dehumanizing explanatory frameworks for poverty which pathologized it as the result of deviant behavioural norms, rather than external societal forces. Here the deep-rooted discursive tradition of *blaming* 'the poor' for their poverty was repackaged as more than a poverty of income, housing, or education: it was a poverty of culture, imagination and ambition; of the white working-class's 'reluctance to "modernise"' and engage with the modern in all its forms, principally through multiculturalism (Haylett, 2001: 366).

Indeed, a fundamental tension addressed in Haylett's work – nearly two decades before discussion of the plight of left-behind working-class groups became common currency – was that between two opposing, mutually suspicious, cohorts of twenty-first-century British citizens. On the one hand, a then burgeoning middle class had found themselves in the educationally and materially privileged position of being able to 'extend their cultural capital' by 'cultivating liberal views on "ethnic" others and purchasing appropriate ethnic furnishings and foodstuffs as markers of how far they have come'. On the other, the 'white working-class poor' was confronted with the fact that 'the economic basis of their own citizenship' was 'often too insecure to be unthreatened by apparent competition (for jobs, housing, and other scarce social resources)' (ibid.: 365). The 'middle class' was, then, symbolically 'positioned at the vanguard' of 'the modern', which became 'a moral category' relating to 'liberal, cosmopolitan, work and consumption-based lifestyles and values', in binary opposition to 'the unmodern': the 'white working-class "other"' (ibid.). The most lasting contribution of this analysis was its contention that white working-class people were being interdiscursively reconceptualized through the prism of a multidimensional 'discourse of social division and decay' that spanned 'media, government, and academic fields'. This division – culturally crystallized in everything from TV sketch show *Little Britain*, comedy-drama *Shameless* and docusoap *Benefits Street* to daily scrounger-baiting tabloid headlines – arose from problems relating to 'the degraded state of families, communities, and the wider social space' and 'located' in 'people and places' refusing to conform to 'dominant cultural and economic visions of progress': throwbacks 'left behind' by 'modernity's forward march' (ibid.: 355). How far removed is this striking early iteration of 'the left behind' from that of a socially conservative working class repeatedly pitted against the similarly fabular 'metropolitan elite' in today's debates around the polarization of economic opportunities and cultural values?

LOCATING LEFT-BEHIND COMMUNITIES: FROM RACIALIZING TO SPATIALIZING DISADVANTAGE

Haylett's emphasis on the ways in which Britain's white working class had been racialized in the neoliberal era has since been developed by other sociologists, notably Bev Skeggs, Steph Lawler, Imogen Tyler, Tracey Jensen and Lisa McKenzie. Of particular note is the importance Skeggs attached to the 'spatial' dimensions of othering narratives directed against white working-class communities in a 2004 paper focusing on a specific strand of New Labour's social exclusion policy agenda: its focus on 'anti-social behaviour' and 'problem' parenting. In it, she argued that the construction of geographically situated 'zones' in which certain forms of behaviour (and, by extension, community) were closely policed and subject to tighter rules and reduced freedoms, from bans on congregating or drinking alcohol to curfews, discursively constructed a 'spatializing of difference' – by drawing 'boundaries' around those who 'need policing and containing' and protecting 'the rest of respectable society' from their 'potentially disruptive, contagious and dangerous impact' (2004: 89).

This concept of the 'spatializing of difference' – and its relationship to that of 'territorial stigmatization' (Wacquant, 2008) – have clear parallels with the visualizable geographic ways in which left-behind communities are frequently discussed today: for example, as 'post-industrial northern towns' or 'declining coastal resorts'. Jensen also touches on the use of territorially stigmatizing imagery, by focusing on the ways in which 'new forms of "commonsense" about welfare and worklessness' during the period of sustained 'welfare reform' and benefit cuts pursued by the 2010–15 UK Coalition government in its mission to drive down Britain's post-crash budget deficit was embedded through a 'meeting of minds' not only between mainstream political and news discourses but also a new breed of reality television show, popularly known as 'poverty porn' (Jensen, 2014). In Channel 4's *Benefits Street*, the receipt of state welfare (and poverty itself) was both sensationalized and 'episodically framed' (Iyengar, 1991), through the person of classic tabloid archetypes such as single mother 'White Dee', while also being projected onto specific locales, neighbourhoods, towns, regions and – by extrapolation – *analogous* communities (or *types* of community).

More recently, McKenzie, an LSE-based ethnographer, drew on her own experience of growing up on Nottingham's economically disadvantaged St Ann's estate – where Coates and Silburn once sought out their 'forgotten Englishmen' – to explore how territorially stigmatizing tropes had been used to other such groups specifically in the context of the left-behind debate. In a subsequent commentary for the IPPR's *Progressive Review*, McKenzie critiqued a succession of elite media-political policy prescriptions that, she argued, had tried 'to "fix" working-class people' – from 'New Labour's concept of social exclusion' to the Coalition's 'broken Britain' narrative to the post-Brexit imaginary of the 'left behind' (2019: 233). These successive reinventions of a problematized white working-class 'other' symbolized, she argued, how the working class had continually 'been squeezed, divided and encouraged to blame itself for its experience of poverty and exclusion' (ibid.: 235).

In this and a series of other recent contributions, McKenzie has framed her defence of working-class communities around two central arguments: a rejection of charges that they were stupid, selfish, or both to vote for Brexit, and, underpinning this, a linkage of such narratives to the continuum of discourses preceding it that consistently othered such groups as backward and deviant. In her introduction to a 2017 article drawing on a comparative ethnographic study of working-class communities in former Nottinghamshire and Derbyshire mining towns and an East London estate, she recalled how the 'surprise and disappointment of the [referendum] result' among mainstream media and politicians had been 'accompanied by a tone of anger and indignation', as they sought to identify those 'whose fault it was' that this 'seemingly tragic and self-defeating decision had been taken' – with blame falling squarely on 'working-class voters' (2017: 200). McKenzie argued that, in truth, 'the marginalization of these groups' was 'so significant' that 'their democratic rejection of the UK's membership of the EU' was 'entirely understandable'. Dismissing their views as 'irrational' or 'xenophobic' betrayed 'a lack of sociological understanding of the long-term progression of narratives and markers' about 'class as a social formation' over recent decades (ibid.). Most powerfully, she condemned 'patronizing "left-behind" rhetoric', which, she argued (citing Haylett), 'actively supports' the 'devalued identity of the deindustrialized working class' familiar from long-standing discourses framing them as 'not only economically impoverished but also culturally impoverished'. Instead of trying to 'genuinely understand the structural nature of deindustrialization, of class inequality and of class prejudice', she argued, '"left-behind" rhetoric relies on the stereotypes and prejudices that the poor white working class are "old fashioned", un-modern, have no mobility and long for the past' (ibid.).

Nonetheless, while McKenzie rightly criticized the ways the left-behind concept had been narratively mobilized, particularly by some Remainer politicians and media commentators, much of the testimony she quoted did reflect feelings of abandonment – sentiments commensurate with a sense of being, at the very least, left *out*. Responding to social media comments published in *The Guardian*, one of her subjects remarked that 'we don't exist to them' (the paper's journalists and readers). Others described a sense that elite political and media actors thought their views and feelings 'didn't matter' before the referendum, while one ex-miner indignantly rejected any suggestion that his Leave vote had been driven by anti-immigrant, 'racialist' feelings – insisting he 'didn't really know anyone that had come from "somewhere else"', but had instead been motivated by watching 'the community where his family had lived for generations being devastated' (ibid.: 205–7).

Through the work of Skeggs, Jensen, McKenzie and others, then, we can glimpse the impact and implications of discourses that have repeatedly othered white working-class communities as the domains of feckless and amoral 'scroungers', uneducated, ill-informed and/or xenophobic nativists, and (at their worst) ignorant, backward savages. It is this latter framing to which critics have alluded in condemning popular discourses that objectify and dehumanize 'the poor', constructing them as 'abject figures' (Tyler, 2013: 9) or 'outlandish circus animals' (Morrison, 2019a: 37) – often with the ostensible aim of introducing relatable 'human interest' to discussions about widespread societal issues (poverty, inequality, the benefits system). Moreover, in extending such frames to encompass the working class as a whole – or, more often, specific communities, areas and/or regions designated (however inaccurately) as being somehow typical or emblematic of the 'white working class' – such imaginaries build on a deep-rooted historical tradition of 'Orientalizing' the poor (Said, 1978).

The agendas motivating the producers of prime-time poverty porn shows and the 'human bear-baiting' of ITV's (now axed) *Jeremy Kyle Show* might well have owed more to commercial concerns about maximizing audiences than any conscious ideological interest in bolstering incumbent governments' welfare reform agendas, but, in cynically spotlighting individuals and incidents closely conforming to tabloid archetypes, such shows had the *effect* of reviving and amplifying a litany of portrayals of backward underclass tribes dating back to the (often well-intentioned but uncomfortably colonialism-tinged) ethnographies of Victorian social explorers. Among the most widely cited of these historical accounts was William Booth's *In Darkest England and the Way Out*, in which he ventured, with the moralizing fervour of a Christian missionary, into the sepulchral domain of 'the submerged tenth' of the British population. There he encountered 'the Lost, the Outcast and the Disinherited of the world' and

> those who have gone under, who have lost their foothold in Society, those to whom the prayer to our Heavenly Father, 'Give us day by day our daily bread,' is either unfulfilled, or only fulfilled by the Devil's agency: by the earnings of vice, the proceeds of crime, or the contribution enforced by the threat of law. (2014: 18)

Booth's peculiar blend of charitable concern, moralism and disgust would find echoes through the writings and pronouncements of countless commentators in later generations, while infusing the 'moral missions' of welfare reformers ranging from Conservatives Keith Joseph and Iain Duncan Smith to Labour's Tony Blair, Gordon Brown and Frank Field (Morrison, 2019a: 84–5).

In Field's provocative 1989 book *Losing Out? The Emergence of Britain's Underclass*, the former director of the Child Poverty Action Group and soon-to-be Labour Minister posited a provocative (if, at times, insightful) diagnosis of the impact of rising aspirationalism among sections of the post-Thatcher working class on their conceptions of their less upwardly mobile neighbours. In highlighting then growing evidence of these heterogeneous tensions *within* the working class, Field identified discernible changes in the attitudes of 'mainstream society' towards people who had 'failed to "make it"', or the 'very poor': a sub-grouping encompassing single parents, the unemployed and elderly people who were entirely reliant on the basic state pension, whom New Labour would later redefine as 'the workless class' (Blair, 1997). Though aspects of Field's reasoning have since been questioned by critics puzzled by its 'confused right-wing labourism' (Robinson & Gregson, 1992: 43), his warnings of 'deepening social divisions' were prescient – especially his prediction that the 'very poor' would be consigned, discursively and materially, to a 'subtle form of political, social and economic apartheid', set apart from the (true) 'working-class' (Field, 1989: 4).

Indeed, the 'deepening social divisions' Field predicted have been ever more exposed by contemporary debates around the status and position of left-behind groups – often in toxic and intolerant terms. Most obviously, the concept of the left behind speaks to an implicit recognition of the deepening *economic* divide(s) between (in the words of Mattinson's 'red-wallers') 'the haves' and 'the have-nots', particularly when the former were aligned with more prosperous places than *their own*, notably London (2020: 110). Viewed through one lens at least, it is a term that connotes a sense of neglect and abandonment, especially when allied (as it so often is) to increasingly normative examples of left-behind places, notably the post-industrial towns and faded coastal resorts of lore. In this respect, the discourse recognizes, and at times aggravates, divisions that are primarily seen to exist in the material, financial and infrastructural sense – as historically conceptualized through timeworn binary oppositions such as 'the North–South divide'. While researching her book, Mattinson encountered numerous people who alluded to this divide through the lens of their disaffection with the Labour Party, which they said had 'moved away' from them to become a 'party of losers and scroungers' and, crucially, the middle-class 'south', as opposed to the working-class 'north'. In expressing this binary disconnect (real or imagined) in such stark geographic terms, they gave voice to a conceptualization of 'the North' that Tom Hazeldine, author of *The Northern Question*, describes as 'a *subjective* category of widely received social or political significance' (2021: 14; original emphasis) and literary scholar Milada Frankova has crystallized as a 'North and South of the mind' (Frankova, 2000). Reality is, as ever, more complicated, given the recent resurgence of prosperous metropolitan economies in cities like Manchester and Leeds – though the spectre of a more tangible North–South divide lives on through recent governments' pledges to *correct* it by reviving former industrial heartlands in the service of Britain's post-crash economic recovery, whether via Coalition Chancellor George Osborne's short-lived 'Northern Powerhouse' agenda or, latterly, Johnsonian 'Levelling Up'.

INTERNALIZING STIGMA: FROM INTER-CLASS TO INTRA-CLASS DIVISIONS

As we have already seen, the sense of societal division between 'haves' and 'have-nots' – between the 'North and South of the mind'

– has been complicated and exacerbated by the infiltration (and exposure) of other fault-lines intersecting with those of economic inequality. Chief among these are the multifarious tensions collectively categorized – by politicians, journalists and academics alike – as 'culture-war' issues, such as immigration, multiculturalism, race and gender (for example, Ford & Goodwin, 2014; Goodwin & Heath, 2016; Virdee & McGeever, 2017; Lind, 2020). Conflicting priorities, values and worldviews have repeatedly been ascribed to blue-collar, non-graduate, socially conservative (and predominantly white) *older post-industrial* working-class voters on the one hand, and white-collar, university-educated, socially liberal (more multi-ethnic) middle- and *younger urban* working-class voters on the other. But, as Frank Field rightly recognized, the sites of societal conflict and division are often more invidious even than this; where discourses of difference are at their most corrosive is when they are *internalized* by those suffering from economic and other disadvantages, fuelling internecine resentments between people *within* the most disadvantaged groups. The internalization of such divide-and-rule discourses, and the acceptance of normalized conditions of subjugation to which this leads, are examples of what Bourdieu and Wacquant have termed 'symbolic violence': routine, day-to-day forms of oppression that are 'exercised upon a social agent with his or her complicity' (2002: 167).

Indeed, analysis of discourses around conventional topics relating to marginalized economic groupings – whether conceptualized as 'the residuum', 'the underclass', or 'the left behind' – has repeatedly identified enduring intra-group tensions and prejudices, often manifesting in terms strongly redolent of dominant media-political distinctions between a deserving and undeserving poor. That some of the most materially disadvantaged, even impoverished, people – including those *themselves* framed as 'undeserving' – should be stigmatizing *each other* in such ways may be profoundly ironic. However, as several studies have rightly argued, an enduring function of popular discourses about 'welfare' has been to displace blame for the causes of poverty and justify cuts to the social security safety-net by directing resentments away from government, the neoliberal economic order and/or 'undeserving' *elite* groups (for example, casino stock-brokers or tax-dodging corporations) towards more proximate 'familiar strangers', most obviously 'scroungers' (Morrison, 2019a).

True to form, the twin imaginaries of 'the scrounger' and the foreign 'benefit tourist' repeatedly resurfaced, often with little prompting, in Mattinson's interviews with disaffected Labour red-wall voters. She wrote of a Darlington woman who conflated her disdain for the ever-coarsening behaviour of today's youth with the sweeping assertion that 'lots of single mums [are] bringing up their kids quite happily to live on benefits', and observed how 'familiar, visible' but 'poorly understood' immigrant families were often 'offered up' as answers to the 'misfortunes' that left red-wall voters 'aggrieved' (2020: 74–5). In a chapter devoted to reasons for 'red-wallers' having abandoned Labour, she identified a strand of opinion among voters in Accrington that it suited the party to *keep* 'the poor poor' and 'dependent on them': perpetuating poverty and (perceived) benefit dependency as tools for preserving its voter-base (ibid.: 131). One care worker crystallized the heterogeneous intra-class oppositions these self-identifying grafters – the 'hard-working taxpayers' beloved of both Left and Right politicians – perceived between themselves and the unemployed, by characterizing Labour as a party 'for the poor' but *not* 'the poorly paid like us' (Mattinson, 2020: 131). Elsewhere, interviewee after interviewee – including people claiming benefits themselves to supplement low incomes – lined up to criticize those they considered 'undeserving' and 'milking the system' (ibid.: 26). Unpacking the factors driving these internecine tensions, Mattinson's most useful insight was her (deceptively simple) suggestion that it was precisely *because* many of her interviewees were 'recipients of benefits' themselves that they felt so strongly about 'people who simply didn't want to work' (ibid.: 171). Not only were these individuals working long hours for comparatively little reward – in low-waged, precarious occupations like care, security and retail – but the fact that they still had to at least partly rely on 'welfare' left them particularly sensitized to media-political narratives about 'scroungers', and all the more determined to 'distinguish their position' from 'those they would dismiss as work-shy' (ibid.).

Mattinson's findings carry uncomfortable echoes not only of the heterogeneous 'social divisions' predicted by Field but earlier analyses of the apparent effectiveness of divide-and-rule discourses in driving wedges between disadvantaged groups who might otherwise be in danger of recognizing their common economic (and class) interests – and, potentially, rising up to challenge the status quo. It also recalls anecdotes from low-income interviewees quoted in *Images of Welfare*, including claims by a low-paid slaughterhouse-worker to have spotted '40 or 50' fraudulent claimants 'in the pub' and a fitter's wife's insistence that 80 per cent of unemployed people were 'scroungers' who 'bleed the country dry' (Golding & Middleton, 1982: 172–3). More significantly, it suggests that decades of neoliberalism have bequeathed not only unacceptable levels of inequality but a persistent belief among many British people (including those struggling themselves) that unemployment and poverty are largely down to the failings of lazy, inadequate individuals, rather than structural imbalances in society and economy.

At time of writing, this depressing conclusion appeared to be supported by the then latest public attitudes research. According to *Unequal Britain*, a 2021 study published by King's College London and UK in a Changing Europe, a stark disconnect was emerging between public perceptions of the causes of economic inequality at the national (inter-regional) and local (inter-neighbourhood or inter-household) levels. While researchers identified growing public support for 'Levelling Up' to address the widening disparities in wealth and investment *between* deprived and better-off regions of the country – the *macro-level* 'haves' and 'have-nots' Mattinson's 'red-wallers' identified – this was not matched by any commensurate compassion towards disadvantaged households within *their own* neighbourhoods. By contrast, although the research was conducted at a time when unemployment was rising, following the enforced closure of much of Britain's economy due to COVID-19, nearly half those surveyed said people who had lost jobs during the pandemic had themselves to blame. Disturbingly, discrimination between 'deserving' areas/regions and 'undeserving' individuals/households – an intriguing latter-day expression of age-old dichotomies – was also heavily racialized, with one in eight respondents saying they thought Black people were likely to be unemployed due to 'lack' of 'motivation and willpower'. Summarizing their findings, the researchers noted that Britons were 'more likely to think' that job losses 'caused by the crisis' were 'the result of personal failure than chance', even during 'exceptional circumstances' – pointing to the persistence of a hardwired post-Thatcher 'belief in meritocracy' and the notion that 'hard work and ambition' were 'key drivers of success' (Duffy et al., 2021: 7).

Similarly dispiriting data would later emerge from a COVID-focused University of Salford-led study, *Welfare at a Social Distance*. While interviews conducted at an early point in the pandemic suggested social attitudes towards 'welfare' were becoming 'slightly more generous' than previously, by September 2021 they had reverted to harsh pre-COVID norms. The study's standout finding was the stark distinction between the degrees of 'deservingness' respondents ascribed to people who had already been claiming working-age benefits *before* the pandemic compared to those forced to seek state help *because* of it. Half of interviewees said 'COVID-19 claimants' were 'more likely than pre-pandemic' recipients to be 'deserving', while respondents were more than twice as likely to blame 'pre-pandemic claimants (vs. COVID-19 claimants)' for their inability to find jobs (de Vries et al., 2021: 2).

We end this chapter, then, on a note that is as unsettling as it is intriguing. Although much of the discursive underpinning of the left-behind concept relates to issues around the evolution and fragmentation of the 'traditional' working class, its social attitudes and political sympathies, a secondary strand of discourse, with deeper historical roots, repeatedly reconstructs *elements* of this class as undeserving – normally through the prism of debates around poverty and 'welfare'. Where discourses of 'underclass', 'shirkers' and 'scroungers' are most relevant to discussion of the nature and composition of the left behind is in the context of generalized, negative framings of those with which such tropes are associated – particularly ones that homogenize them as primitive, uncultured, unenterprising and economically burdensome. It is *this* discursive strand that has arguably been invoked, at times, by those struggling to understand the (to their eyes) counter-intuitive behaviours of working-class Brexit supporters and Tory converts, with more sympathetic commentators conceptualizing their value-systems through the framework of 'social conservatism' while the most disparaging dismiss them as ignorant and/or racist. The next two chapters unpack the ways in which left-behind discourse has been constructed and contested in the mainstream UK press and political arenas around a succession of pinch-points – or 'discursive events' (Wodak, 2001: 48) – over the years since the 2016 EU referendum. We then examine how the public responded and contributed to this discourse, before turning to the most important measure of its accuracy and representativeness: the extent to which terms like 'left behind' accord with the experiences and perspectives of people from economically disadvantaged groups *themselves*, including those to whom they are seldom applied but perhaps should be.

2

Politics, the press and the construction of the post-Brexit left behind

During the weeks running up to the 2016 European Union referendum, and the months and years succeeding it, the British working class became a subject of conspicuous anthropological curiosity. 'Left behind, ignored, irrelevant to Britain's London-centric economy, and harboring a rose-tinted nostalgia for a prouder past, many who would identify as traditional working class, particularly in England, are in open revolt', observed American news-site *cnn.com* on the eve of the historic vote (Wismayer, 2016). Days later, as pundits far and wide struggled to process the scale of the Leave vote in Britain's onetime industrial heartlands, a row erupted over a colour piece about Sunderland that appeared in the *New York Times.* The offending article described the city's 'once-robust shipyards' lying 'silent and dead' and a pub that 'still had "Vote Leave" posters on its walls', before dismissing its citizens – 'leery of both London and Brussels' – with the soon-to-be-familiar refrain that they had 'voted against their own interests' (Freyas-Tamure, 2016). This (supposedly) 'biased, patronising and grossly distorted' reportage so enraged the city's paper of record, the *Sunderland Echo*, that it ran an editorial demanding a formal apology (sunderlandecho.com, 2016).

Meanwhile, in the run-up to the 2019 general election, another US-based site *cnbc.com* parachuted a correspondent into 'Britain's most pro-Brexit town' (Boston, Lincolnshire) to explore the views of locals sweepingly characterized as 'still angry and disillusioned' (Smith, 2019). Though writer Elliot Smith strained to contrast his kinder observations of a 'typical sleepy, post-industrial East

Midlands town' with the 'dystopian' images of a 'wasteland of boarded up windows' evoked by locals, his piece otherwise read like a greatest hits compilation of disparaging left-behind tropes. Bostonians were defined by their 'blunt local parlance' and nativist grievances – with Smith remarking that 'the first word out of the mouth' of 'every local' when asked about the problems facing their town was 'immigration'.

Two years earlier, in a move that might have been calculated to conform to all the clichés of metropolitan elitism, business intelligence platform *Stratfor.com* had marked the first anniversary of the Leave vote in similarly Orientalizing vein – commissioning writer Ian Morris to emulate Harvard professor Robert Kaplan's recent road-trip through 'the America that exists beyond the reductions of television cameras and reporters' questions' for his widely reviewed travelogue *Earning the Rockies*. Morris framed his homage to this picaresque odyssey as a return (after many years) to his 'hometown', Stoke-on-Trent – into which he edgily ventured, like a Victorian explorer, for a feature bearing the provocative headline, 'Left Behind in the Brexit Capital?'. Though his piece (later republished in elite business journal *Forbes.com*) went on to paint a more balanced picture than its title intimated, it opened with passages every bit as bleak as the observations of Jacob Riis (2009), William Booth (2014) and other chroniclers of 'how the other half lives' and 'darkest England'. The 'depressing' sights Morris encountered included 'climbing' rows of 'modest terraced houses', 'shuttered' and 'tagged with graffiti'; faded high streets where police 'seemed to outnumber' shoppers and 'every other store was a bargain-basement outlet', and locals rendered in terms hauntingly redolent of earlier iterations of 'abject figures' like 'the chav' (Tyler, 2013: 9):

> On his American journey, Kaplan noticed that exchanging the East Coast's 'world of slim people on low-carb diets with stylish clothes ... where both skin tone and sexual orientation are not singular but multiple, and celebrated for that' for Middle America's smaller cities meant entering 'a vast and alternative universe' unto itself. The locals, he writes, are 'downtrodden, unpretty, unprogressive, often obese people, but there all the

> same'. That would overstate what I saw in England, yet the similarities (like the people) are there … The body shapes, the baseball caps and ill-fitting sweatpants, the cigarettes, and the sheer number of people who apparently had nothing to do were a world apart from London. (Morris, 2017)

Indeed, of all Brexit-voting post-industrial areas, it was Stoke – the scattering of five Staffordshire pottery towns collectively comprising Britain's most disembodied city – that captured writerly imaginations most vividly. It was to here that even self-styled alternative news site *UnHerd.com* despatched ex-*Independent* foreign correspondent John Lichfield three years after the referendum to reappraise his birthplace under the headline 'Stoke, the city that Britain forgot' (Lichfield, 2019). His bittersweet account described colourful encounters in otherwise 'deserted' town-centres – depicting Stoke as 'the victim of a triple economic crisis and a triple identity crisis', buffeted by a perfect storm of de-industrialization, austerity and (through the mass take-up of online retail) 'the collapse of traditional shopping habits'. As the *Guardian*'s John Domokos had self-consciously reflected the previous year, recalling the frosty reception he and other journalists received as they 'descended on the former industrial powerhouse' to cover a lazily labelled 'Brexit by-election', 'the national media only tells one kind of story about places like Stoke-on-Trent: that of the post-industrial, broken-Britain, Brexit-voting heartlands. The left behind' (Domokos, 2018).

The left-behind narrative has, then, been a recurring feature of UK popular discourse since at least 2016. But how *pervasive* has this narrative been in the British press at key pinch-points during the unfolding socio-political history of the post-Brexit period? Precisely how have conceptualizations of left-behind peoples and places shifted and evolved over time? And, above all, what has the overall balance been between economic, cultural, political and other representations of the drivers and characteristics of the left-behind 'condition'? This chapter attempts to address these questions through a framing analysis of two core sites of media and political discourse around the relationship between the left behind and recent democratic events: coverage in the print and online national and regional press, and extracts from speeches, debates and other proceedings in the British Parliament. Framing analysis involves analysing the 'principles of selection, emphasis and presentation' underpinning texts (Gitlin 1980: 6) and how this process is used to present a specific 'aspect of a perceived reality' as 'more salient' than others and/or promote a particular 'definition, causal interpretation, moral evaluation and/or treatment' for a 'problem' (Entman, 1993: 53). In this case, analysed texts were obtained from two key sources: the Lexis Library database of UK newspaper articles and the online Hansard record of parliamentary proceedings.

FROM ECONOMIC CASUALTIES TO CULTURE WARRIORS: FRAMING THE LEFT BEHIND

The focus of both this chapter and the next is on deconstructing how the left-behind imaginary has been discursively mobilized in media coverage, political debate and wider public discourse – both as a denotive descriptor and a connotative, value-based label. As we have established, in the UK context the term has generally been applied to communities, regions and/or groups with particular socioeconomic and/or cultural characteristics. Specifically, it has often (though not exclusively) been ascribed to working-class areas whose identities and traditions are intertwined with their histories as one-time industrial centres or tourist resorts, but which have latterly endured declining prosperity, significant changes in cultural and ethnic compositions and/or political marginalization relating to inadequate representation and accountability by local, regional, national and European institutions. But to what extent have such (assumed) *empirical* characteristics dictated how the left behind have been conceptualized and discussed in the public sphere? And what balance have popular framings of the left behind struck between the economic, the cultural and the political?

Given that the left-behind concept (though far from new) rose to prominence in the context of the 2016 EU referendum, the chosen keyword combination used for both Lexis and Hansard searches was 'left behind' and 'Brexit'. An initial search of the Lexis database was carried out for the three-and-a-half-year period commencing with the start of the referendum month (June 2016) and finishing at the end of the month encompassing the 2019 general election (December 2019). As this produced a huge corpus of 4,847 results, the search was then narrowed, to focus on articles and parliamentary proceedings addressing the left behind in and around a series of five key 'discursive "events"' (Wodak, 2001: 65) during the overall life-cycle of the Brexit vote.

The first of these was the two-month period between 23 June and 22 August 2016, commencing with the date of the referendum and encompassing the resignation of then Prime Minister David Cameron, the appointment of his successor Theresa May, and an attempted internal Labour Party coup against then Leader of the Opposition Jeremy Corbyn.

The second was the three-month period beginning with the activation of Article 50 of the Treaty of Lisbon (which initiated the formal process of Britain's withdrawal from the European Union). This encompassed both the 2017 general election campaign and Mrs May's subsequent loss of her House of Commons majority.

Period three covered the eventful two months between 4 December 2018 and 3 February 2019, during which Mrs May's government failed to pass its EU Withdrawal Agreement through the Commons; former UKIP leader Nigel Farage launched the Brexit Party, and the prime minister survived not one but two votes of confidence – the first initiated by her own Conservative Party and the other by Her Majesty's Opposition in the Commons.

The fourth period (3 May–2 June 2019) was the month encapsulating the UK's final elections to the European Parliament, at which Mr Farage's new party triumphed and the ruling Tories were relegated to third place.

The final discursive event was the two-month period commencing with the passage (on 28 October 2019) of a government Bill bypassing the 2011 Fixed Term Parliaments Act to enable a 'snap' election. It encompassed the Conservatives' victory and Boris Johnson's Queen's Speech setting out his legislative agenda for the ensuing Parliament. As MPs were not sitting for substantial chunks of these periods – notably the two months succeeding the referendum and the duration of the 2017 and 2019 election campaigns – Hansard searches were combined into a single overarching dataset, rather than split into discrete snapshots.

Taken together, Lexis searches produced a total corpus of 662 print and online articles spread over the five discursive events. Hansard searches generated 270 relevant records – though these were confined to the first four periods only, as Parliament was dissolved throughout the fifth. Newspaper articles were eventually coded into six broad categories identified during an initial process of immersion in the material:

- those framing the left behind as a primarily *economic* phenomenon relating to decline, disadvantage and underinvestment;
- those defining it principally in *cultural* terms, as a condition relating to concerns about threatened values/group identities and the disconnection between the worldviews of traditional, older and/or less educated working-class voters and other groups (principally middle-class and/or metropolitan graduates);
- pieces presenting it as a *political* concept relating to exclusion from democratic processes;
- a 'hybrid' category framing it as a combination of two or more of these factors;
- a small number of pieces exploring the left-behind concept through the words of those described as such (coded as 'voices of the left behind'), and
- and an 'incidental' category, comprising articles referring to the term only in passing, without defining or debating it.

Only the first four categories were found to apply to Hansard records. Full breakdowns of the number of articles and parliamentary records coded under each heading are given in Tables 2.1 and 2.2, with the former further subdivided by snapshot period. A more detailed explanation of methodology is given in the Appendix.

Table 2.1 Detailed breakdown of frames for five article datasets

Frame	*Snapshot 1*	*Snapshot 2*	*Snapshot 3*	*Snapshot 4*	*Snapshot 5*	*Total*
Economic	132 (75.9%)	124 (72.9%)	57 (68.7%)	42 (71.2%)	137 (74.1%)	492 (74.3%)
Cultural	3 (1.7%)	13 (8.1%)	9 (10.8%)	3 (5.1%)	11 (5.9%)	39 (5.9%)
Political	6 (3.4%)	0	2 (2.4%)	3 (5.1%)	2 (1.1%)	13 (2%)
Hybrid	30 (17.2%)	21 (13%)	2 (2.4%)	3 (5.1%)	19 (10.3%)	75 (11.3%)
'Voices of the left behind'	3 (1.7%)	2 (1.2%)	3 (3.6%)	3 (5.1%)	3 (1.6%)	14 (2.1%)
Incidental	0	1 (0.6%)	10 (12%)	5 (8.5%)	13 (7%)	29 (4.4%)
Total	174	161	83	59	185	662

Table 2.2 Detailed breakdown of frames for four parliamentary record datasets

Prevalence of frame over period	*Economic*	*Cultural*	*Political*	*Hybrid*	*Total*
	245 (90.7%)	5 (1.9%)	7 (2.6%)	13 (4.8%)	270

MATERIAL DISADVANTAGE OR STATE OF MIND? COMPETING FRAMINGS OF THE LEFT BEHIND

The overwhelmingly dominant framing of the left behind to emerge from analysis of both newspapers and parliamentary proceedings associated it with the *economic* decline and disadvantage experienced by certain communities, regions and/or groups. Nearly three-quarters of all articles analysed across the three-and-a-half-year timeframe (492 out of 662) adopted this reading of the left-behind condition. Moreover, the economic frame was even more dominant in parliamentary debates, appearing in nearly 91 per cent of all contributions (245 out of 270). This suggests that, throughout the short- to medium-term post-referendum period – when prime ministers May then Johnson were battling to persuade Parliament to pass their various EU withdrawal Bills – MPs and peers were almost exclusively preoccupied with the *economic* drivers and implications of Brexit.

Though dwarfed by the number of articles and parliamentary mentions framing the left behind in economic terms, the second most commonplace frame (excluding the 'hybrid' category) was *cultural*: portrayals of left-behind areas and communities focusing not on their material or infrastructural characteristics but their distinctive and/or threatened values and traditions. Across the overall newspaper corpus, this amounted to a mere 39 out of 662 articles (5.9 per cent of the total). However, the periods during which they were most prominent in the press were snapshots 2 and 5: intriguingly, protracted discursive events both encompassing general elections. This suggests that culturalist representations tended to become more prominent during political campaigns (and media reporting of them), when parties were vying for government in the shadow of Brexit – a correlation we unpack in the coming analysis. In terms of their appearance in parliamentary discourse, culturalist frames applied to just five out of all 270 Hansard comments about the left behind (fewer than 2 per cent).

Of the three categories of frame identified across both press and parliamentary datasets, occurrences of those positioning left-behind groups as a *political* concept – as communities marginalized by democratic institutions/processes – were in the minority, with just 2 per cent of articles and 2.6 per cent of parliamentary references applying them (13 out of 662, and 7 out of 270 results respectively). However, although this frame was consistently low profile across the whole period, making it difficult to discern clear correlations between its relative prominence at particular times and external, real-world events, it is intriguing to note that nearly half of all such articles appeared in snapshot 1 – indicating that, in the immediate shadow of the referendum, there existed a clear current of debate conceptualizing the left behind as agents of a *political* (rather than purely economic and/or cultural) backlash.

Also noteworthy were the numerically few instances of articles prioritizing the 'voices of the left behind' – that is, opinions of people from left-behind areas/communities themselves – and a creeping increase, over time, in newspaper coverage featuring normative 'incidental' references to this term. The former demonstrates a consistent pattern of excluding or sidelining the voices and lived experiences of groups and individuals *identified* as left behind: a practice which had the effect (if not intention) of discursively othering them. This tendency to objectify socially excluded groups echoes a long tradition of stigmatizing discursive practices in the press (see, for example, Golding & Middleton, 1982; Morrison, 2019) and is one to which coming sections return, in detailing the tropes that emerged from more in-depth qualitative analysis of the framing of left-behind communities, both by press and Parliament.

As for the growing prominence of articles mentioning the left behind incidentally – rising from zero to 13 (7 per cent) between snapshots 1 and 5 – this indicated an increasing recognition of the *existence* of the left-behind phenomenon alongside a creeping normalization of taken-for-granted assumptions about what the term denoted. In other words, by the time of the 2019 election campaign, the left-behind imaginary had become such a routine, normative term of reference that it increasingly insinuated itself into media discourse, even in articles that were nominally about other subjects entirely.

The final pattern to be considered is the fluctuating prevalence of the second most prominent category of newspaper and political frame: the hybrid one. Of all frames, this one's trajectory oscillated the most, as it was highly visible during snapshots 1 and 2 – at 30 out of 174 (or 17.2 per cent) and 21 out of 161 (13 per cent) articles respectively – before plummeting in snapshot 3, to just 2 out of 83 (2.4 per cent), and edging slightly upwards again in snapshot 4, to 3 out of 59 (5.1 per cent). However, another dramatic shift occurred between snapshots 4 and 5, when the incidence of this frame more than doubled – rising to 19 out of 185 (10.3 per cent). Precisely what happened, then, at various stages to drive such visible upturns in the prominence of frames defining the left behind in more nuanced (or confused) terms?

One obvious interpretation of the early prevalence of hybrid framing was an initial haziness among editors, journalists and their sources around the precise meanings that should be attached to the term 'left behind', as they struggled to absorb the significance of the UK's decision to leave the EU and, thereafter, scrambled to identify a typology of Brexit voters. In an age of social media-friendly 24/7 news coverage, it is easy to understand how a 'working terminology' might rapidly have emerged to associate strong support for Leave among working-class communities with the pre-existing concept of the post-industrial left behind: one crystallized as a fusion of economic and cultural traits in the writings of political scientists like Robert Ford and Matthew Goodwin. The continuing prominence of hybrid frames during snapshot 2, meanwhile, arguably reflects the ongoing public *negotiation* of what the 'condition' of being (or feeling) left behind amounted to in a post-referendum context. But while distinctly cultural, political and (especially) economic definitions of the left behind became dominant during snapshots 3 and 4, period 5 saw the resurgence of a more nebulous, multifaceted conceptualization. This was the phase encompassing the 2019 election campaign, during which a feverish rhetorical and policy battle was under way to win the hearts and minds of constituents in the newly dubbed 'red wall' – and politicians of both Right and Left sought to weaponize the floating signification of the left-behind concept in an effort to appropriate working-class, post-industrial voters as their own.

If there is any kind of 'big picture', then, that typifies the ebb and flow of media-political discourses around the left behind between June 2016 and December 2019, it is that the most widely accepted definition of this term has consistently focused on economic factors – casting left-behind communities as those that had missed out on the fruits of globalization and/or suffered from inequalities caused or worsened by structural forces such as neoliberal market reforms and de-industrialization. Feeling left behind in this context was treated as a simple matter of being – or considering oneself – left out of the benefits of technological, infrastructural and wider economic changes enabling *other* areas to prosper.

A competing reading was the idea that being left behind was as much a cultural or ideological phenomenon as one relating to nuts and bolts or pounds and pence. In other words, the left-behind condition was (or is) a state of *mind*, not just a state of *being*: a perspective relating to everything from a community's collective sense of place, identity, tradition and self-worth to its views about *other* communities and cultures, and the desirable extents and limits of 'opening itself up to' those groups. Viewed through this lens, the idea of being left behind is best understood as a generational and/or attitudinal concept with strong echoes of the situated worldview Goodhart ascribes to 'Somewheres' (2017): a sense of falling behind, or being unable (or unwilling) to 'keep up with', the shifting political priorities, worldviews and social mores championed by younger, more cosmopolitan generations than one's own. While public discourse about the left behind throughout the sample period was dominated by the economic frame, the third and fourth snapshots saw a marked upturn in the prominence of articles defining it in relation to culture, values and identity.

However, such culturalist framings were largely absent from the parliamentary arena, other than as one strand of a more hybrid discourse conceptualizing the left behind as a combined economic, cultural and/or political phenomenon. This also applied to the third characterization of what it meant to be left behind: that of imagining this condition as a *political* issue arising from disengagement with and (perceived or actual) exclusion from democratic processes. This final variation on the left-behind imaginary – a common preoccupation of political scientists, though not (it seems) media-political actors – relates to marginalization, and the sense that certain groups of citizens are ignored, taken for granted and/or treated as less worthy of attention or being consulted than other segments of the electorate. As we shall see, these three competing aspects of what it means to be left behind are far from mutually exclusive, and at times two or more have been discursively at play concurrently. In the following sections we examine the intersectionality of these aspects, while also considering them as discrete forms of economic, cultural and political exclusion.

ECONOMIC, CULTURAL OR POLITICAL? THE LEFT BEHIND AS FLOATING SIGNIFIER

As previously indicated, the fluid and malleable nature of the left-behind imaginary is consistent with what semioticians would term an 'empty' or 'floating signifier': a word or other form of sign (signifier) for which 'there are multiple referents', allowing 'different political groups' to 'compete to assign their desired signified' (Dabirimehr & Fatmi, 2014). Viewing the term as a floating signifier offers a useful explanatory tool for considering how politicians and pundits on both Left and Right – and, indeed, other primary and secondary definers of 'the left-behind problem' – have repeatedly (re)framed and operationalized it, invariably for their own ideological ends. For example, as we shall see, liberal-Left actors have *generally* applied economic diagnoses and prescriptions to the left-behind condition – drawing on class-based Marxist thinking and/or redistributionist Keynesian solutions to conceptualize it, primarily, as symbolizing a crisis of capitalism and economic inequality. By contrast, right-wing commentators often define it in cultural terms: relating it to inequalities of values, identity and *status*, rather than income or wealth. However, as we shall see, the quality of floating signifier renders the left-behind concept susceptible to redefinition and (re)appropriation by actors on both Left *and* Right, often at short notice and whenever it suits them to reframe it. For example, while both mainstream and radical Left have generally privileged economic framings, they have also acknowledged *cultural* factors (at least rhetorically). Moreover, ardent liberal-Left Remainers have, at times, mobilized negative cultural stereotypes, to discredit or counteract the left behind's supposedly retrograde tendencies. Conversely, certain right-wing actors – among them MPs elected to former 'red-wall' areas – have adopted pointed (if performative) positions emphasizing the economic precariousness of left-behind communities, while also stressing their proud *identities*.

So precisely *how* did this floating signification resolve itself at specific points in the life-cycle of this first post-referendum epoch: the period between the historic vote itself and the decisive election that finally made Brexit a certainty? At what precise points in this life-cycle did economic, cultural, political and hybrid framings of the left behind become more or less dominant – and why might this have happened? Most importantly, what was the *overarching* narrative to emerge about the left behind over this three-and-a-half-year life-cycle – taking in all the peaks, troughs and ruts in the road on the way?

Even as referendum-night ballot-papers were still being counted, there was already widespread agreement that it would largely be decided by a category of working-class voter often (though not always) characterized as left behind. Nonetheless, an enduring question that was to preoccupy media and political debates about the societal fault-lines that had 'caused' (and been exposed by) Brexit in the weeks and months following the vote was this: to whom, or what, *exactly* did this term relate? As politicians, journalists and experts offered competing interpretations of why working-class communities had voted in such numbers to reject the European Union – and, with it, the decades of structural economic support it had offered many of their areas – media-political narratives increasingly coalesced around a nexus of popular imaginaries. The following sections unpack the ways in which these imaginaries were negotiated and articulated, by focusing on three archetypal versions of the left-behind condition: the *economically* left behind (here termed 'casualties of capitalism'); those left behind by shifting socio-cultural currents of the times ('cultural throwbacks'); and *politically* left-behind groups ('political rejects') who only featured in national conversations at times when parties competing for government were trying to mobilize their votes to ensure victory.

Casualties of capitalism: the 'left behind', the 'held back' and the 'forgotten'

Perhaps the most quintessential economic representation of the left behind was to be found in the headline of a *Guardian* opinion piece by human rights campaigner Deborah Doane published on 26 June 2016, three days after the referendum. In it, Brexit was unhesitatingly described as 'a backlash against globalisation' by 'the poorest', who were being 'left behind everywhere' – a theme Doane took up by asserting that Leave voters had rebelled 'against free markets and free labour, against winner takes all capitalism that pits worker against worker; marginalised against marginalised' and 'neoliberal economics that beats a drum to the mantra of keeping wages low and work insecure' (Doane, 2016). But perhaps the most significant aspect of this early salvo in what was to become an ever-testier economics versus values/sovereignty debate was Doane's implicit rejection of both 'culture-war' and 'democratic deficit' theses; these were the notions that the main drivers of Brexit were not economic disadvantage but a growing ideological schism separating older, socially conservative working-class voters in areas remote from Britain's and Europe's cultural and political epicentres both from those who were younger, more cosmopolitan and socially liberal and from metropolitan elites who supposedly lorded it over them from afar. 'The historic "Brexit" vote' was less about 'a small island's fear of immigration and a remote European government' than 'the outcome of years of austerity that saw people jobless, threatened and insecure' (ibid.).

Blunter still was the assessment of James Reed, political editor of the *Yorkshire Evening Post*. 'The disconnected, the forgotten, the disillusioned, the left behind', read the evocative opening to his column on 4 July (coincidentally, Independence Day in the US). It was 'this group', he argued, 'which won or lost the referendum, depending on your point of view', by rebelling, 'loudly and in huge numbers', at what had 'happened to them and their communities' over decades (Reed, 2016). A similar diagnosis was made the same day by Mike Kelly, social affairs correspondent of the *Newcastle Chronicle, Journal* and *Sunday Sun*. Reasoning that, as the 'place in the economy' for 'a large swathe of the North East' was 'not a great one', it was unsurprising voters felt they 'had nothing to lose by voting for a change', he quoted Sunderland-based Labour MP Bridget Philipson's identification with 'people in the North East' who 'feel that time and time again we're left behind' (Kelly, 2016a).

Elsewhere, the regional commentariat's assessments of the inequities of the economic system were more unforgiving. 'Brexit reveals the stark contrasts of a divided nation' roared the headline on a think-piece by Andrew Vine in the Leeds-based *Yorkshire Post* (Vine, 2016). Recalling how some 'former industrial heartlands of Yorkshire' had 'registered protest votes' a decade earlier by 'giving the odious British National Party its mercifully brief place in the sun', he argued that, just as that rebellion had represented 'less an embrace of the politics of hatred' than 'an attempt to send a message' about immigration, Brexit voters were protesting that 'too much attention' was paid to 'well-heeled metropolitan voters for whom globalisation and mass immigration meant chic holiday homes and cleaners willing to work for below minimum wage'. Ten days earlier, picking up a similar 'two-nations' theme, an editorial in the first *Observer* edition published since the referendum had situated the vote as a long-term consequence of Margaret Thatcher's legacy. Recalling her notorious declaration 'that society did not exist' and her 'discriminatory brand of class warfare' that had left many industrial regions 'lacking a living, a future and self-respect', the paper concluded:

> For 30 years, the 'left-behind' (the working poor, the 'strivers', the zero-hours workers) have waited for a new economic reality based on fairness and equality to rebalance the effects of late capitalism as it advantaged a smaller and smaller number of people with grotesque income inequalities. This time, they were led to believe that a correction was at hand. (*Observer*, 2016)

The referendum's initial aftershock also saw widespread agreement with this economic thesis in *news* reports. 'Northern uproar' screamed the front-page headline on the left-leaning, Remain-supporting *Daily Mirror* on the morning after the referendum. It quoted outspoken Brexit-backing Labour MP John Mann's condemnation of his own party for losing 'touch with its voters' over immigration and the largely Remain-supporting Conservative-led government for offering nothing but 'zero-hours contracts' and 'agency work' – leaving 'working-class people' feeling 'sick to death' (Blanchard, 2016). Near-identical images would surface over ensuing months in numerous reports, including a July *Western Mail* story in which Geraint Talfan Davies, leader of Wales's Remain campaign, described the country's Brexit vote as a 'cry of rage' partly attributable to 'the decimation of the Welsh economy during the Thatcher years' (*Western Mail*, 2016). And, amid growing calls from the Opposition for the Government to put the question of who should succeed outgoing Prime Minister David Cameron to the public, rather than Tory members, numerous papers were soon reproducing quotes from Labour's election coordinator, Jon Trickett, in which he sought to distract attention from a simmering leadership challenge against his ally, Jeremy Corbyn, by redirecting colleagues' fire towards their common enemy, with a rallying cry to 'unite' to ensure 'the millions of people in the country left behind by the Tories' failed economic policies' had 'the opportunity to elect a Labour government' (quoted in Stone, 2016b).

Though couched somewhat differently, economic frames were also embraced by elite conservative actors, including Carolyn

Fairbairn, director-general of leading business lobby group the Confederation of British Industry (CBI), and one-time adviser to Tory premier John Major during his own battle to preserve Britain's EU membership. Fairbairn was quoted in an *Evening Standard* report reflecting that the referendum signified 'the feeling' in 'the regions' that people had been 'left behind by the success of London's economy' (Armitage, 2016). Previewing her speech to the paper's inaugural business awards, she proposed a new economic settlement redolent of then Chancellor (and soon-to-be *Standard* editor) George Osborne's 'Northern Powerhouse' initiative and the inter-regional 'Levelling Up' agenda later espoused by Boris Johnson – arguing for policies to 'kickstart' regional growth, by investing in infrastructure, skills and moving company headquarters outside London.

Through endless repetition, this economic framing of the left behind became progressively more accepted over the course of the five snapshots – and, by the end of 2019, could be described as the taken-for-granted, go-to newspaper explanation for their grievances. The position of the economically left behind also presented a useful locus for political campaigns during this year of multiple electoral events. In widely reported quotes published to coincide with her return to work from maternity leave that May, then Scottish Conservative leader Ruth Davidson promised a 'blue-collar revolution' if elected at Holyrood (Ferguson, 2019). Later that month, the *Western Mail* quoted Welsh First Minister Mark Drakeford's recognition that the country's 'regional communities' were 'telling us' they felt 'left behind' by 'uneven' economic development, as he pledged to harmonize public investment across Wales (Pyke, 2019).

Indeed, during this one month alone, pitches to the economically left behind were made by everyone from the chief executive of Northern Irish trade body Retail NI, in a *Belfast Telegraph* opinion-piece appealing for infrastructural investment in the province's 'rural towns and villages' (Roberts, 2019), to soon-to-be British premier Johnson. During a brief absence from the government frontbench (following his resignation as foreign secretary), the latter used his weekly *Telegraph* column to criticize Britain's 'miserable' final European Parliament election while previewing his impending leadership bid with a policy wish-list including investment in 'transport infrastructure and broadband' and the 'championing' of start-ups and apprenticeships, to 'bring growth and dynamism' to areas that 'for too long have felt left behind' (Johnson, 2019). Not to be outdone, ex-Prime Minister Tony Blair used a tribute to the recipient of a regional business award to praise him for ensuring rural areas were 'not left behind' during his time as New Labour's 'rural tsar' (Winter, 2019).

Intriguingly, the adoption of a predominantly economic framing of left-behind voters, not only by journalists but key actors they quoted, had initially been as prevalent on the political Right as the Left – with Cameron's instant post-referendum resignation signalling the start of feverish campaigns by several senior Tories to succeed him. Prior to then Home Secretary Theresa May's emergence as frontrunner, all candidates for the top job – from Business Secretary Andrea Leadsom to Justice Secretary Michael Gove, via short-lived hopeful Johnson – had sought to appropriate the disaffected post-industrial working class in their frantic appeals for support from grassroots party members. In a 4 July *Newcastle Chronicle* story angled around outgoing Chancellor Osborne's 'restated … commitment to the Northern Powerhouse', Leadsom was quoted arguing that it should be 'supercharged' after Brexit (quoted in Kelly, 2016b). The same day saw several newspapers, including *The Times*, report Gove's pledge to represent '"two Britains" – one 'doing "very nicely"' and the other 'left behind' (quoted on conservativehome.com, 2016). The following day, May sought to crystallize the plight of the left behind, by conjuring up the memorable montage of 'burning injustices' she would seek to address as prime minister – from 'extreme variations in life expectancy and educational chances' to 'the gender pay gap' and 'job insecurity' (Butler, 2016). This singular evocation of the left-behind condition would haunt her tenure in Downing Street, repeatedly resurfacing in articles throughout that period. Most notable were those marking her eventual downfall, which saw commentators both Left and Right reflect on the missed opportunities in her domestic agenda caused by three years of Brexit paralysis. Writing in the *Sunday Express* on 26 March 2019, the day after May's tearful resignation on live TV from the same spot outside Number Ten where she had delivered a victory speech three years earlier promising to help people who were 'just about managing', Nick Ferrari insisted she had 'totally meant it' when she set out to liberate 'those who had been left behind' – adding that 'copies of that speech' had been 'put up on the walls' of her offices (Ferrari, 2019).

Beyond the realms of the media, the left behind were also consistently framed as an economic phenomenon in the narratives Parliament constructed to characterize Leave-voting working-class communities. The earliest post-referendum parliamentary reference came during a House of Lords debate about the European Council on Wednesday, 29 June 2016 – less than a week after the vote. During a lengthy speech, Remain-supporting Liberal Democrat peer Lord Wallace of Tankerness implicitly acknowledged the 'democratic deficit' undermining public trust in EU institutions – an interdiscursive allusion harking back to a famous critique of the Union by another Lib Dem, Bill Newton Dunn, three decades earlier (Newton Dunn, 1988). Arguing that 'many people' in English regions and Wales 'felt let down and left behind', both by Europe and politicians at home, the peer predicted 'growing dissatisfaction and frustration' as they realized that 'much of what they have been promised' would 'not be possible' and 'the alternatives offered by the leave campaign' would not 'help those in England's poorer regions' (Hansard, 2016a).

Six days later, the term 'left behind' resurfaced in a debate explicitly focused on the referendum outcome. In a passing reference presaging the increasingly self-explanatory ways in which it would be used in coming months, Labour peer Baroness Royall proposed that local councils be given a central role in negotiating Brexit, because they understood its likely impact in areas where people 'already feel left behind' (Hansard, 2016b). As with other such normative references, this speech avoided overtly diagnosing the causes of the left-behind condition – though, like similar allusions elsewhere, it implicitly framed it as an economic phenomenon. Describing working-class Leavers as people 'using the referendum' to 'vent their anger about a system which does not respond to their needs', it conjured up a montage of precarious, low-paid work, austerity and overstrained public services that had left them 'constantly worried about their jobs, the roof over their head, problems getting their kids to school, and the long wait to see the GP'.

Analogous depictions were also routinized in the House of Commons – particularly by Labour MPs representing northern constituencies, who (apparently anticipating the coming 'red-wall' rout) eagerly emphasized regional inequalities that had left their constituencies behind under successive recent governments. During a January 2017 debate on the May government's plans for a Charter for Budget Responsibility, then Shadow Chief Secretary to the Treasury Rebecca Long-Bailey spoke of the 'need to rebuild' areas that had 'been left behind for far too long' – describing 'communities up and down Britain' as having been 'starved of investment for decades' (Hansard, 2017b). Six months on, after his party had deprived the Tories of their Commons majority in a 'snap' election, Peter Dowd, Labour MP for Bootle in Merseyside, observed accusingly that, while 'the global economy' was 'on the move', 'Britain under the Tories' was 'being left behind' (Hansard, 2017i).

At times, sentiments such as these were bound up with more specific references to manifestly 'deserving' left-behind groups *within* regions and communities that had been short-changed by the unequal spread of prosperity under the present settlement. Adopting a blanket, regionally focused purview, John Mann, then Brexit-backing Labour MP for Bassetlaw, used a January 2019 debate on the still gridlocked EU (Withdrawal) Act to demand (on behalf of northern England) that 'whoever' was in government over the next five years deliver 'the real Brexit dividend – our fair share – to areas like mine'. This necessarily meant 'that other areas would get less', he added, because 'that is what "left behind" actually means' (Hansard, 2019a). The substance of Mann's intervention was significant, in that it mobilized the 'North and South of the mind' to construct an idea that specific (hitherto left-behind) regions were *deserving* of redistributive economic and infrastructural investment – in implicit opposition to *undeserving* ones already enjoying more than their 'fair share' of Britain's economic spoils. In doing so, it echoed grievances about regional 'haves' versus 'have-nots' aired by Mattinson's 'red-wallers' and offered a macro-economic expression of a political (and media) discourse of 'fairness' that had become deeply embedded over the previous decade, since the Coalition government had sought to win public support for its sweeping 'welfare reform' programme by discursively segmenting society into 'deserving' and 'undeserving' groups (see Morrison, 2019a: 14–18). While Mann *inverted* this discourse – casting *disadvantaged* communities as deserving and *affluent* ones as undeserving – he adopted an 'us-and-them'/'in-versus-out-group' frame redolent of this divisive rhetoric.

We will return periodically to considering the pervasiveness of rhetorical tropes constructing the left behind as geographical or territorial imaginaries – for example, towns versus cities, rural versus urban, and (of course) North versus South. Beginning here, one key characteristic of parliamentary references to the left behind that emerged over time was the increasing prevalence of competitive posturing, even virtue signalling – as MPs vied to be caught on record sticking up for disadvantaged communities generally and their own constituents specifically. The numerous regions and areas identified at various stages of the sample period as being economically left behind ranged from the sweepingly all-encompassing – Yorkshire, Cornwall, Wales, 'much of rural England', 'half or more of the country' and (of course) 'the North of England' – to highly specific localities, such as Stoke-on-Trent, Great Yarmouth, Hull and even a single small Scottish coastal port (Cairnryan).

Many such namechecks occurred in debates during the lead-up to electoral events – though, conversely, some took place in the *wake* of elections, as MPs reflected on 'messages' voters were felt to have conveyed to their parties (and Westminster) at the ballot-box. It can hardly have been coincidence, for example, that during a topical question to then Chancellor Sajid Javid in October 2019 – weeks before Johnson's government introduced a one-line Bill prompting the second snap election in just over two years – Grahame Morris, Labour MP for the party's emblematic heartland constituency of Easington, County Durham (once represented by its first prime minister, James Ramsay Macdonald), asked what 'fiscal policy steps' ministers were planning to rectify economic imbalances affecting 'coalfield communities', like his, that were 'left-behind areas' (Hansard, 2019h). Three weeks later, during a debate on what she dubbed a 'Queen's Speech for a parallel universe' designed by Ministers purely to 'set out an electioneering position', Redcar's soon-to-be defeated Labour MP, Anna Turley, warned that a 'hard Brexit' would punish constituents who had endured 'decades of being left behind' in an 'unequal, loaded economy' (Hansard, 2019i).

Moreover, as more and more post-industrial areas became other parties' electoral targets (and, in time, newly prized post-election assets), competitive championing of the left behind seemed to become ever more contagious beyond Labour's ranks. In a lengthy speech during a September 2017 debate on the then European Union (Withdrawal) Bill extolling the virtues of his newly secured Stoke-on-Trent seat, Jack Brereton spoke of how his 'left-behind' constituents had voted Tory for the first time in 82 years 'because we demonstrated our trust in the public's judgment in voting to leave' (Hansard, 2017j). By contrast, a humbler, more poignant reading of the newly assembled 'blue wall' was offered in December 2019 by ex-premier May, who used an intervention in the Queen's Speech debate to urge colleagues to 'deliver' on 'good trade deals' and an employment Bill which would 'not only enshrine but enhance workers' rights' (Hansard, 2019j). These she cast as key issues for communities that had 'lent us their vote': those who had felt 'most left behind by globalisation' when their rights had 'not been protected'.

Left-behind values: Cultural custodianship/backwardness and 'identity politics'

Elsewhere in the discourse, the days immediately after the referendum saw the earliest stirrings of a *culturalist* interpretation of the result. In two strikingly similar readings published during the initial post-mortem period, both Matthew Goodwin, co-author of *Revolt on the Right*, and Scottish historian-cum-political journalist David Torrance addressed the role of one of Brexit's chief architects, then UKIP leader Nigel Farage – and the pre-referendum fallacy that his appeal was confined to right-wing 'little Englanders' and nostalgists for empire in the wealthy shires. In a *Guardian* article reducing the argument of his 2014 book to one emphasizing the cultural and identity-based drivers of Brexit over those relating to economic disadvantage, Goodwin recalled how, though UKIP had once been 'a party of the Tory shires', it had begun to 'emerge as a serious force in many traditional Labour areas' some years back – by moving into space vacated by more rampantly right-wing populists, such as the neo-Nazi British National Party (BNP). In so doing, it had increasingly attracted 'Britain's left-behind voters': people 'intensely anxious over immigration', who 'saw the cause of it as Britain's EU membership', and 'loathed a Westminster elite that appeared uninterested in their concerns' (Goodwin, 2016).

Three days later, writing in Glasgow's *Herald*, Torrance allied himself to 'anyone who's bothered reading proper analysis about where UKIP's support came from', dismissing 'the stereotype of corduroy-wearing, cigar-smoking hang-em-and-flog-em Tories' as 'an escapist fantasy' (Torrance, 2016). In reality, 'just as many former Labour voters' were 'attracted by populist Faragist patter': 'working-class men and women who feel left behind and ignored'. If any subtle emphasis distinguished these twin readings, this related to the length of time over which Labour had quietly lost ground to UKIP. Torrance focused exclusively on recent rumblings of discontent among Labour's former working-class base, arguing that voters had not deserted it because, 'as the SNP and Corbynistas would have us believe', it had 'drifted to the Right', but due to its emphasis on metropolitan woke concerns, such as 'wind farms, equal marriage and a *laissez faire* approach to migration'. By contrast, Goodwin dated the start of this decline to much earlier, opening with a paragraph recalling how 'some Labour insiders' had started noticing 'economically disaffected working-class voters … drifting into political apathy' as far back as 'the end of the 1990s' – and that Labour's vote had dropped by 3 million in 2001 and another million in 2005 'after the high of Tony Blair's landslide election in 1997' (Goodwin, 2016).

A key strand of culturalist framing particularly visible in articles penned by Right-leaning commentators was that emphasizing the patriotic, place-centred aspects of the 'left-behind mindset' – in essence, framing them less as throwbacks than cultural *custodians* of a valued, under-threat past. In a highly partisan intervention during the 2017 election campaign in his former newspaper,

The Times, ex-journalist Michael Gove drew on a melange of intertextual references to locate then Prime Minister May's philosophy – which he scrupulously aligned with that ascribed to working-class, left-behind voters. Likening her worldview to those of Scottish-American philosopher Alasdair MacIntyre and Blue Labour's Lord Glasman, he said the upcoming Conservative manifesto would be 'rooted in the concerns' of David Goodhart's 'citizens of Somewhere' (Gove, 2017). Gove's definition of 'Somewheres' was both selective and all-encompassing – judiciously downplaying the role of the more well-heeled segments of Goodhart's (socially diverse) concept to focus mostly on those 'overlooked, ignored or side-lined in our national conversation', who 'don't have the reserves of capital, or connections' to 'chase every new opportunity globalisation might provide'. Elsewhere, he reverted to terms reflective of Goodhart's own – conceiving of 'Somewheres' as a much wider popular imaginary, by describing them as 'the unflashy, the unmetropolitan, the under-appreciated majority', and their act of Brexit-backing defiance as 'a counter-revolution'. This engaged with an emerging current of discourse which implicitly re-imagined the (or *a*) left behind as a more expansive, *cross-class* mass of rebelling people: the idea of a hitherto silent majority that was, by this stage, rapidly gaining traction on social media (as Chapter 4 will show).

Two days later, in the *Observer*, it fell to another writer preoccupied with the emerging 'culture-war' thesis to predict how the distribution of votes might pan out on polling-day, based on the fragmentation of traditional party loyalties along 'Anywhere' or 'Somewhere'-style lines. 'The two-party swing' was 'only part of the story' in a country where 'vote choices' were 'fragmented' and might be 'further disrupted by the new divides over Brexit', argued Robert Ford, Goodwin's co-author of *Revolt on the Right*. Labour could be squeezed from both sides, he suggested, as some 'socially conservative, "left-behind" traditional' voters drifted towards UKIP 'as an outlet for protest votes against [Jeremy] Corbyn', while 'angry and energised Remain voters' were picked off by Liberal Democrats in seats where that party had 'little chance of victory' (Ford, 2017).

While Ford's prediction proved to be premature, by the time the red-wall collapse finally loomed two years later, a more literary depiction of left-behind 'Somewheres' was being drawn by novelist and travel-writer Martin Hesp. Writing in Bristol's *Evening Press*, he evoked the poetic image of a 'person walking alone down a leafy valley in the warm breeze, on their way to vote in the EU elections at the village hall' – speculating that they were musing, 'how can my one little vote change anything in a place that plays home to 741 million people?' (Hesp, 2019). The reason people wanted 'out of Europe', he posited, was because 'it's just too big' and 'we citizens – we country folk – are being left behind', with 'our voices, opinions, needs and desires' unheard 'in the great morass of humanity' stretching 'west from the Caucasian steppes'. Describing how 'the person in the valley – like every person strolling over every hill or down every valley either west or east of the Ural Mountains' was 'programmed to think first in terms of themselves', then 'within the circle of their family or immediate community', Hesp recalled the mindsets ascribed to Goodhart's 'Somewheres' and Mattinson's hyper-localist red-wallers.

Though unambiguously culturalist definitions of the left behind were only applied by a handful of MPs and peers, patriotism and pride in place also surfaced repeatedly in economically framed and hybrid remarks. In one of few unapologetically culturalist parliamentary interventions, staunch Tory Brexiteer Nigel Evans used a February 2017 debate about Donald Trump's putative state visit to take aim at the fabled metropolitan elite – condemning arch-Remainer Tony Blair for 'visiting TV and radio stations' to try to 'reverse the democratic decision' of 'the British people' (Hansard, 2017d). Directly likening working-class Brexiteers to blue-collar Trumpists, he accused liberals of failing to 'come to terms with the fact' that 61 million people had voted for Donald Trump 'because they felt left behind'. Labour peer Lord Bassam would also draw on patriotic imagery during a July 2019 'Future of seaside towns' debate – demanding urgent action 'to reverse the decline' of coastal resorts 'left out and left behind' in 'our nation's story' (Hansard, 2019g). And, adopting a more focused form of patriotism, Drew Hendry, SNP MP for Inverness, had used a 'Shared Prosperity Fund' debate that May to demand (on behalf of Scotland) that 'our people' were not 'left behind' by a UK government 'too chaotic' to come up with a plan for communities (Hansard, 2019f).

But while patriotic imagery was often mobilized to emphasize *disparities* in prosperity levels between one region/nation and another, such tropes were also used in more unifying ways – for example, to conjure up images of how a fairer, less divided Britain might look if wiser future policy choices were made. It was in this vein that, during a January 2020 debate entitled 'Productivity', then Chancellor Javid promoted his government's fledgling 'Levelling Up' agenda, promising to invest 'billions more in infrastructure', a new national skills fund and research and development, to 'unleash the potential of the whole country' – ensuring 'no place' was 'left behind' (Hansard, 2020a). A year earlier, then Parliamentary Under-Secretary for Education Nadim Zarhawi had used a near-identical turn of phrase to frame the previous government's industrial strategy as a 'comprehensive plan' to ensure 'no place' was 'left behind'. Shortly afterwards, in a culturally tinged call-out to the left behind during a March 2019 debate on a newly launched 'Stronger Towns Fund', Housing Secretary James Brokenshire congratulated fellow Tory minister Robert Halfon for 'spearheading plans' to boost local economies in his own constituency and 'other towns, such as Blackpool' that were 'bursting with ideas'. Evoking images of grassroots entrepreneurship reminiscent of the 'Big Society' spirit championed by Cameron's government, he spoke of 'people who care so much about the towns in which they live' coming together to harness their 'strength of place and identity' and unlock the potential of 'all parts of our proud United Kingdom' – so 'no-one is left behind' (Hansard, 2019e).

Such patriotic calls-to-arms also featured in debates focused on issues affecting more specific groups considered to be economically left behind. In a November 2017 Commons debate entitled 'Deafness and hearing loss', ex-Disabilities Minister Sir Mike Penning appropriated left-behind discourse to stand up for disabled people struggling to overcome barriers to entering the workplace, while promoting his government's Access to Work initiative in flag-waving terms – as a 'great' scheme for people 'across this great nation' who had previously been 'left behind, ignored and told that they could not work' (Hansard, 2017l). Even when the main definition applied to left-behind groups carried an *economic*, rather than culturalist, emphasis, then the patriotic language and imagery of 'new deals', 'united efforts' and 'national renewal' – familiar today from rhetoric popularized in the context of the 'save lives', 'save our NHS', 'new normal' and 'Build back better' messaging of the pandemic – insinuated themselves into almost all variations of the left-behind debate.

The left behind as political rejects: Marginalization, exclusion and democratic deficits

The final framing of the left behind – defining the concept principally in *political* terms – emerged as its own discrete category from fewer newspaper articles than either economistic or culturalist frames. Nonetheless, it *was* visible in discourse from almost immediately after the referendum. On the very morning the Leave victory was confirmed, Iain Macwhirter, Remainer political commentator of Glasgow's *Herald*, argued that one virtue of the vote had been to focus attention on previously under-examined 'aspects of the EU' – including the fact that 'the institutions of Europe' were 'unacceptably bureaucratic' and prone to 'capture by corporate lobby groups', while many decisions were taken by 'a remote banking elite' that prioritized debt reduction 'above the welfare of EU citizens' (Macwhirter, 2016). While critiquing more neoliberal aspects of EU governance, Macwhirter stressed that there was 'too little democratic accountability in Brussels' – and 'above all, there needs to be democratisation', because 'there is no community unless everyone is part of it.' The following day, a *Guardian* opinion-piece by Leave-backing commentator Giles Fraser was headlined 'Brexit brought democracy back – now we need to start listening to each other' (Fraser, 2016a). In the same paper, Remainer Rafael Behr's analysis carried a heading declaring both 'Westminster' and 'Brussels' the 'target' of the referendum, and reflecting on the 'demand' it had exposed for 'all of politics' to be 'conducted on different terms', following voters' 'flat refusal to take any kind of instruction from party leaders, expert opinion' or 'celebrities' (Behr, 2016). Three years on, this democratic deficit framing resurfaced prominently in Scotland (significantly, given the ongoing independence debate). In a May 2019 opinion piece in the *Scotsman* headlined 'Brexit-induced contempt for politicians is risk for democracy', SNP MP Kenny MacAskill argued that growing 'contempt' for Britain's parliamentary system was a 'real concern for the established parties' and 'a worry for democracy', because 'an entire political class' was 'being blamed' and 'alternatives' sought (MacAskill, 2019).

Parliamentary interventions defining the left behind primarily in political terms were scarcely more commonplace, but those that did emerge were primed by specific democratic events – including (but not confined to) the referendum. During an October 2016 debate entitled 'Parliamentary scrutiny of leaving the EU' – barely four months after the vote – then Labour backbencher Gisela Stewart, ex-chair of the Vote Leave campaign, urged parliamentary colleagues to heed the 'deep disillusionment with the political processes' it had exposed, by 'listening' to 'areas that feel they have been left behind' in a 'non-partisan' and 'non-judgmental way'. Others foregrounding the issue of democratic accountability included Dan Jarvis, MP for Barnsley Central and soon-to-be mayor of Sheffield City Region, who used a contribution to a January 2018 debate on 'Yorkshire devolution' (Hansard, 2018a) to celebrate the then recent mandate delivered by regional voters supporting a devolution deal granting local council leaders direct control of spending on economic development, regeneration and public transport. Though he later diverged into wider reasons why much of South Yorkshire's population qualified as left behind – including the fact their wages were 20 per cent lower than the national average and they had worse health and education outcomes – Jarvis primarily framed the devolution vote as a triumph of democracy in action, relating it to the disenchantment with distant, unaccountable UK and EU politicians many of the same people had expressed 18 months earlier. People were 'disillusioned' and had 'a right to feel that way', he argued, in terms foreshadowing emerging academic theses like that of social scientist Michael Lind, who emphasizes the battle over 'power' as a key site of the 'new class war' – and 'demagogic populism' as a 'symptom' of a 'disease' of 'technocratic neoliberalism' which only 'democratic pluralism' could cure (Lind, 2020: xv). To Jarvis, Barnsley and Doncaster voters had 'overwhelmingly' backed Brexit, and now supported devolution, because 'they felt powerless' – and were 'tired of being left behind', unable 'to do anything about it'.

Perhaps the most significant strand of the political framing of left-behind voters, however, emerged two or three years after the referendum, as a protracted Westminster deadlock over how (or whether) to implement Brexit led to pro-Leave voices framing this intransigence as a classic establishment stitch-up designed to deny the democratically expressed wishes of 'the people' – a populist imaginary increasingly debated on social media (as we shall see). Not only had the Brexit vote exposed deep-seated resentments about the EU's lack of transparency and accountability that could only be answered by leaving it; now MPs and peers were conspiring to ignore the public verdict they had solicited, thereby compounding the sense that people were being ignored and short-changed. Thus, in a January 2019 contribution to the debate on the European Union (Withdrawal) Act by Stoke MP Brereton, the demands of 'supporters of a second referendum' were characterized as 'asking us' to 'hold the electorate and our democracy in total contempt' (Hansard, 2019b). By further delaying Brexit, they would be 'deepening divisions instead of healing them' by failing to respect 'the people's choice' – potentially reviving support for 'extremist' parties, such as the BNP, which he 'would not be so cavalier as to assume' had 'gone away'. Two years earlier, Tory peer Baroness Pidding had made a strikingly similar appeal during a Lords debate on the European Union (Notification of Withdrawal) Bill, quoting the government leaflet sent to voters before the referendum, which had promised to 'honour' its result – 'whatever the outcome' (Hansard, 2017e). 'Trust in British politics and politicians is at a terrible low', she had warned, defining 'those who felt left behind' as people feeling 'looked down upon by distant elites, sitting in high, lofty chambers and deaf to their concerns'.

The left-behind hybrid: Economics-culture-democracy interfaces

While economistic definitions of the left behind dominated press coverage around all five discursive events, in more thoughtful op-ed articles there were early signs of an emerging recognition that other, more complex, factors might also have contributed to Brexit. One notable trend from almost immediately after the referendum was a leaning towards hybrid readings of its outcome in liberal-Left quality papers – with both their own columnists and invited academics beginning the slow process of unpacking deeper patterns to emerge from analysis of the demographic profile(s) of Leave-voting populations. In a punctual think-piece published in the *Independent* just hours after the result was declared, Sir John Curtice, one of Britain's leading psephologists and director of the National Centre for Social Research, had already arrived at the diagnosis (long-rehearsed before the vote by Goodwin, Goodhart and others) that Brexit could be attributed to 'a serious social divide' between 'a highly-qualified Britain that feels able to compete in an international labour market' and is 'comfortable with' cultural diversity and immigration, and 'a left-behind Britain' that had 'not enjoyed the privilege of an advanced education, feels economically squeezed, and is challenged by the social changes that come with immigration' (Curtice, 2016).

Within three days, the same paper published an early analysis by social scientists Paul Whiteley and Harold D. Clarke, under the headline 'Brexit: why did older voters choose to Leave [*sic*] the EU?' (Whiteley & Clarke, 2016). Based on an Internet survey of 2,100 British voters conducted immediately before the referendum, it examined factors contributing to high Leave support both in specific parts of the UK and, within them, particular social groupings. It noted that, while backlashes against the disproportionate impact of austerity on northern areas played a part, so too did the types of jobs people did and their conceptions of both self- and national identity. The survey was significant in that it offered early indications of an emerging identity divide, partially related to income, occupational status and social class, between a European and/or internationalist worldview on one hand and a more nativist one on the other. While 58 per cent of professional and managerial respondents voted to stay in the EU, this only applied to 27 per cent of those in 'unskilled' jobs – significantly, most people identifying as 'British' voted Remain, while those who identified as 'English' backed Leave. However, as with the generational compositions of the 2019 Tory/Labour votes (Fieldhouse et al., 2021), the *age* divide between Leave–Remain voters was crucial: more than 44 per cent of those over age 65 said they considered themselves English (not British – or European), compared to 21 per cent of those aged 26 or under. Illustrating the *Independent*'s online report was a large photo of a smiling older voter brandishing a mobile smartphone bearing the legend 'Vote Leave'.

A similarly multidimensional assessment of the nature and composition of the Leave-voting majority was offered by Andrew Rawnsley, chief political commentator for the *Observer*. He used his first column since the result to describe the vote as 'an x-ray of the body politic of the nation' that exposed 'multiple fractures in this disunited kingdom', both 'about class' and 'generation', as 'the young, overwhelmingly for In', were 'defeated by Out-voting pensioners', who 'felt politics had let them down'. In his most insightful passage, he described the fissures in this 'disunited kingdom':

> Two of its constituent parts voted one way, two the other. London and the majority of people in the big cities were on one side, rural and provincial England on the other. We are a country starkly divided between doing-well Britain and left-behind Britain, between the Britain that is essentially comfortable with globalisation and diversity and the Britain that feels its anxieties and anger about identity loss have not been listened to. (Rawnsley, 2016)

By later snapshots, this hybrid analysis was being widely echoed across the political spectrum – though the precise balance between the multiple, overlapping fault-lines the vote exposed was invariably skewed differently, depending on the particular (often partisan) discursive use to which it was put at any one time. In a thoughtful contribution to a multi-authored March 2017 *Guardian* opinion piece published as then Prime Minister Theresa May invoked Article 50 of the Lisbon Treaty, triggering the EU withdrawal process, Anglican priest and commentator Giles Fraser crystallized the nature of Britain's 'new political division' as one of 'old alliances being shattered and new ones coalescing' (Fraser, 2017). Arguing that 'the broad left' had 'been pushed to choose between an instinctive solidarity with those who have been left behind' and 'an allegiance to liberal internationalism', he said that, by 'often choosing the latter', they risked accusations of 'betrayal'. Echoing repeated analyses of Labour's middle-class drift since at least the Blair era, he added that people who had 'long thought of themselves as standing alongside the poor' had ended up siding with 'the global instincts of the City of London' *against* 'decaying outer-city housing estates of the north and the Midlands' – thus 'abandoning traditional Labour voters to the racist clutches of UKIP'.

Two-and-a-half years later, during the metaphorical heat of an icy winter 2019 election campaign, former Tory leadership rivals Johnson and Gove each drew from this hybrid left-behind playbook in quotes reproduced in the Brexit-supporting *Express*. Recalling the referendum, Johnson said Leave's victory had been delivered by 'many in our country' who 'felt powerless and left behind and wanted more control over their lives', while Gove spoke of 'overlooked families and undervalued communities' who believed 'the system' had 'not worked in their best interests' (quoted in Hall, 2019). In a diagnosis similar to those of Curtice, Rawnsley and other post-referendum pundits, he added that the vote 'didn't create divisions in society', but 'revealed them' – in the form of familiar oppositions 'between north and south, rich and poor, young and old' that 'politicians of all parties had failed to address'.

As with straight economistic framings of the left behind, hybrid readings were also widely voiced in Parliament. In a December 2016 Lords debate entitled 'National life: Shared values and public policy priorities', Lib Dem peer Lord Newby proposed a suite of policies to address the smorgasbord of 'concerns' he ascribed, normatively, to a 'frustrated and angry left behind'. These included growing public services 'in line with changes in population'; education gave people 'the skills they need' to meet labour shortages, and 'much more' was done to tackle a 'chronic' lack of affordable housing. But he also alluded to cultural divisions exposed by the vote, suggesting 'national institutions that bind us together' – from the BBC to the NHS – be harnessed to reunite the country. Two months later, in a Commons debate on the EU (Notification of Withdrawal) Bill, Labour MP Vernon Coaker proffered a similar view – summing up

Brexit as 'an emphatic shout of "Enough!"' from those 'left behind by globalisation' who felt 'economically, politically and socially excluded' (Hansard, 2017c).

LEFT BEHIND BY WHOM – OR WHAT?

Allied to the question of who or what the left behind *are* is the inextricably linked issue of who (or what) is *responsible* for leaving them behind. Notwithstanding more partisan perspectives, which invariably blamed specific parties/governments, the most widely shared diagnoses tended to revolve around three main culprits: the Westminster and/or EU establishment (often conceptualized, together or individually, as the dominant political 'elite'); the prevailing international capitalist system, or 'globalization', and the 'metropolitan' classes and major economic centres they inhabited (principally London), which were consistently framed as disproportionate beneficiaries of all of the above.

In addition to the aforementioned examples of articles and parliamentary interventions emphasizing the democratic deficit, a classic illustration of how elitist politicians were constructed as responsible for leaving swathes of Britain behind was given by Paul Sewell, chairman of the Humber Local Enterprise Partnership Business Board, in feisty comments reported in the *Hull Daily Mail* business section three months after the referendum. Deriding then Chancellor Osborne's 'Northern Powerhouse' as the 'Northern Poorhouse', he argued that 'our political system and its politicians' needed to 'review' how they related to 'the people they represent' – especially the 'disenfranchised and left behind' of 'the North of England' (quoted in *Hull Daily Mail*, 2016). This, he stressed, would take 'more than platitudinous initiatives', a 'couple of major cities getting some goodies' and 'the void in power and leadership that now exists'. A more nebulous iteration of this anti-establishment characterization had been aired ten days earlier by GP and writer Youssef El-Gingihy in a hyperbolic guest column for the *Independent*. Published online beneath a landscape-shaped photo of France's right-wing populist politician Marine Le Pen, her hand raised defiantly as she gave a speech before a large Tricolor flag, the piece described the Brexit vote as 'a howl of rage' from 'working-class communities devastated and left behind by decades of neoliberal policies including deindustrialisation' and 'a roar' of anti-elite anger 'framed in the discourse of immigration' (El-Gingihy, 2016).

Three years later, in a lengthy think-piece in the *Sunday Times* News Review section headlined 'The Strange death of Labour Britain' and topped by an evocative black-and-white photo depicting a line of cloth cap-wearing factory workers, Matthew Goodwin offered a detailed anatomization of the distinct forms of elitist disconnect associated with both Labour and Tory parties today – including the charges of wokeness threatening to undermine the former's 'historic bond with the working class' (Goodwin, 2019). 'With London Labour MPs seemingly more interested in defining everybody as a victim and by their group membership than making the case for economic redistribution', and 'centre-right parties' still 'dominated by high-income and economically liberal "merchant elites"' with 'scant interest in reforming a broken economic settlement', he argued, in prose straddling the fine line between the rhetorics of Corbynism and right-wing culture warriors, the 'left behind and left-out', people 'who want more economic security but also more cultural security', faced 'a new choice': whether to 'stick reluctantly with the main parties, defect to the populists or stay at home'. By contrast, a more questioning examination of similar tropes by the *Independent*'s Sean O'Grady outlined the battle-lines widely ascribed to the 2019 election in an op-ed that October defining 'the new culture war' as a conflict between two popular imaginaries: the 'Islingtonian metropolitan prejudices personified in Jeremy Corbyn' and 'Workington man', a 'typical Leave voter, unimpressed by the "Westminster elite"' and based in northern 'rugby league towns', whom he framed as 'socially conservative' and (echoing attitudes observed as far back as *The Affluent Worker*) 'Old Labour' purely out of 'tribal loyalty' (O'Grady, 2019).

Even more commonplace were references to wider forces perceived to have disempowered left-behind communities: principally, globalized capitalism. The day after the referendum, Trades Union Congress (TUC) General Secretary Frances O'Grady took this line in a *Guardian* comment piece arguing that, 'in too many parts of the UK, voters feel left behind by the pace of globalisation'

(O'Grady, 2016). On the same day, a hybrid take on the result was crystallized by political columnist Andrew Grice, who itemized the multiple fractures the referendum had 'exposed starkly' in 'a divided nation', including

> the gulf between a liberal metropolitan class and working-class people worried about immigration; between those doing well from globalisation and those 'left behind' and not seeing the benefits in jobs or wages; between Scotland and England; between London and the rest of England; between young and older voters and between the well and less well educated. (Grice, 2016)

Two weeks later, touching on similar themes, the billionaire founder of MoneySuperMarket, Simon Nixon, offered a wry take on the success with which Britain's most demonstrably elite politicians had activated the anger of under-privileged left-behind voters. Writing in *The Times*, he suggested everyone was 'eager to know' how 'the paradox' of a Brexit campaign 'led by radical ultra-liberal free marketeers but won by tapping into the anger of voters "left behind" by globalisation' would be resolved (Nixon, 2016). By the time the World Economic Forum convened for its 2019 deliberations over the major global economic, political and environmental challenges, even arch-globalizer and WEF founder Klaus Schwab was conceding that globalization was to blame: 'globalisation produces winners and losers', he admitted, adding that, though it had produced 'many more winners', the time had come 'to look after the losers' who had been 'left behind' (Wearden, 2019).

Globalized markets and neoliberalism were also a favoured target of parliamentarians. In his contribution to the December 2016 Lords debate about Britain's 'national life' and 'values', Lib Dem Lord Wallace offered an unusually internationalist diagnosis of how 'globalisation' had 'swept over' both disadvantaged regions of the UK – including his own West Yorkshire, which had witnessed 'the disappearance of mills and factories' – and 'the poor of Africa, the Middle East and South Asia' (Hansard, 2016e). Alluding to the concept of the precariat, he suggested 'millions of people' had been 'left behind by the transformation of work' – a theme echoed in a

July 2017 pledge by then International Trade Secretary Liam Fox, who committed to addressing 'negative aspects of globalisation' to ensure 'no one is left behind by the pace of change' (Hansard, 2017h). And, during a January 2019 Commons debate on the May government's ill-fated EU (Withdrawal) Act, Remain-supporting Lib Dem MP Christine Jardine reflected on the rationale underpinning many working-class voters' decision to back Brexit, emphasizing the economic drivers that had left 'an entire generation' worried that 'their children and grandchildren would not be as well off as they were', having been 'left behind and failed by globalisation' (Hansard, 2019b).

Just under a year later, outgoing Labour leader Corbyn framed the left-behind predicament in more overtly Marxist terms during the later passages of Johnson's European Union (Withdrawal) Bill, by criticizing aspects of the deal he feared would betray 'essential principles that we believe in' – primarily building 'a country that looks after everybody' and 'protects' communities 'left behind by the excesses of the free market' (Hansard, 2019k). Similar sentiments had been expressed during a September 2017 Commons 'Ways and means' debate by then Labour backbencher (and vocal Corbyn critic) Wes Streeting, who spoke of people 'completely left behind by the economic order', who had expressed 'their frustration through the ballot box' – by voting to leave the EU, which they saw as 'central' to this unequal system, and by electing Trump (Hansard, 2017i).

As noted earlier, one aspect of narratives focusing on the differential distribution of globalization's economic rewards and penalties was the recurrence of oppositions between its perceived winners and losers. These tended to be drawn in primary colours, often couched again as North versus South or (small post-industrial/coastal) town versus (large metropolitan) city. While some parliamentarians highlighted the existence of these oppositions as problematic real-world phenomena – magnifying societal divisions that needed addressing in the interests of national unity – others used them as politically convenient rhetorical tropes, often aligning themselves with 'sides' that had historically lost out. In this vein, future Chancellor Rishi Sunak, Tory MP for Richmond in North Yorkshire, used a November

2017 intervention in a debate on 'Transport in the North' to reel off a list of major infrastructural projects from which other regions, particularly London, had benefited – arguing that, to avoid 'the rural north' being 'left behind', 'we in the north' needed Ministers 'to back Northern Powerhouse Rail' (Hansard, 2017k).

By contrast, in a December 2018 Lords debate entitled 'Constitutional convention' (Hansard, 2018d), Labour's Lord Hain – himself a staunch Remainer – spoke regretfully about the 'bitter Brexit divisions' that had left 'our society' so 'hugely polarised', with 'towns left behind as metropolitan cities forge ahead', buffeted by 'never-ending austerity and widening inequality'. Similarly, in a March 2017 intervention during a Commons debate following then Chancellor Philip Hammond's Budget statement, Labour's Dame Angela Eagle argued against spending pledges disproportionately biased towards affluent areas, particularly marginal constituencies targeted by the Conservatives and seats they already held. Describing this as 'a Budget that continues to hit the poorest the hardest', she accused the Chancellor of ensuring that 'some people' were 'being left behind' while 'a chosen few, in certain chosen areas', reaped 'all the advantages' (Hansard, 2017f). Two years on, her Labour colleague Tracy Brabin, then MP for Batley and Spen, juxtaposed her seat with others benefiting from the new Stronger Towns Fund, by aligning it with the 'many' northern towns that were 'sick to death of being bypassed and left behind', with their 'banks closing, theatres closing, cinemas closing, Sure Start centres closing' (Hansard, 2019e).

LEFT BEHIND BY *OMISSION*: WHITHER THE NON-WHITE WORKING-CLASS?

One of the most problematic aspects of all the major left-behind imaginaries was their overwhelming emphasis on the normative concept of a 'traditional' and/or 'post-industrial' working class invariably constructed as white. To journalist after journalist, and one MP and peer after another, left-behind areas and communities were conceived of as weary bastions of a neglected and threatened minority, caught out of time and battered by the winds of unforgiving economic, cultural and/or political change. Articles and speeches referred to immigration as often as they mentioned globalization, neoliberalism, loss of sovereignty, or more 'abstract' macroeconomic contributors to the decline and disempowerment of left-behind groups. And through this divisive discursive prism, the left-behind debate was implicitly racialized, with pointed oppositions constructed between the under-siege in-group symbolized by 'indigenous' or 'native' workers and multifarious marauding 'foreign' out-groups: a montage of distant, uncaring EU elites; asset-stripping overseas investors; rapacious money markets, and invasive incomers, from Polish plumbers to alien faiths and cultures unfamiliar from the (supposedly) mono-ethnic histories of coalfields, potteries and ports.

Alongside the various other associated labels used in newspapers and parliamentary debates, between them the terms 'white working class' and 'white working-class' (hyphenated) were used as direct synonyms or corollaries for the left behind 33 times in the press in total, appearing in 29 separate articles. The same terms occurred at least half a dozen times in parliamentary exchanges – often during highly sensitive debates relating to divisions caused and exposed by Brexit. In his morning-after comment piece in Glasgow's *Herald* newspaper, Iain Macwhirter drew an explicit opposition between the 'white middle classes' of the 'comfortable suburbs', who 'do not experience immigration in the same way' as those 'at the bottom': the 'white working class' of 'post-industrial cities', who 'feel betrayed, left behind, ignored' and 'are sore at the rapid changes in their community and culture that they were never consulted about' (Macwhirter, 2016). Almost exactly a year later, Matthew Flinders, professor of politics at Sheffield University, would also conflate the left behind with white working-class people, in an article analysing the unexpected (and temporary) electoral resurgence of Labour in its post-industrial former heartlands, by eliding 'the white working classes, the "left behind"', with those who had previously 'rejected mainstream politics and led "the revolt on the right" seen in the popularity of UKIP in 2015' – an intertextual allusion to Ford and Goodwin's book of the same name (Flinders, 2017).

By contrast, only in a handful of pointedly counter-discursive articles and speeches was there any acknowledgement of the existence of a Black or multi-ethnic working class – let alone of the complex, multi-sectional disadvantages often experienced by such groups. Moreover, even on the numerous occasions when colour, race and/or ethnicity were not directly mentioned, implicit racialization was often at play. Although immigrants and economic migrants whose recent arrival in the UK may have impacted on already struggling communities were statistically more likely to be from white ethnic groups, the repeated emphasis placed by commentators on pressures caused by incoming population movements and culture clashes between 'incompatible' customs, values and beliefs had the effect (if not intention) of displacing blame from structural economic and/or political forces into tensions around nationality, ethnicity, culture and, ultimately, race. To demonstrate the pervasiveness of discussion of (im)migrants in newspapers alone, a keyword skim of the corpus found more than 400 references to 'immigration' and 66 to 'immigrants'. In placing so much emphasis on problems supposedly caused by mass (im) migration, such contributions revived timeworn tropes associated with discourses of 'Orientalism' (Said, 1978) and racialized 'moral panics' (Hall et al., 1978). They also echoed recent findings identifying the prevalence of 'invader' frames in press articles focusing on intra-EU free movement in the immediate run-up to, and medium-term aftermath of, the referendum (Morrison, 2019b).

The discursive effect of privileging disadvantages experienced by white working-class communities is doubly problematic. Firstly, it downplays (or omits) the – sometimes more severe and certainly more multidimensional – inequities experienced by low-income minority-ethnic people (especially migrants). Secondly, and more invidiously, it frames non-native and/or non-white settlers from overseas, at least partly, as the *cause* of economic and social hardships endured by 'traditional', 'post-industrial' working-class groups – thereby fuelling and legitimizing both inter- and intra-community divisions and prejudices. As we will see shortly, politicians and pundits' obsessive association of the term 'left behind' with the white working class – often in denial of economic and other disadvantages experienced by people of *all* racial, ethnic and (increasingly) social backgrounds – has not been without critics. Neither has the commentariat's presumptive tendency to speak *for* communities identified and/or identifying as left behind.

The next chapter uses a more in-depth analytical approach to move beyond examining the surface *framing* of the left-behind phenomenon: its construction as an economistic, culturalist and/or political imaginary. Drawing on critical discourse analysis (CDA), it unpacks how media and political actors have *problematized* both the left-behind narrative(s) – specifically, the manner and motives of its/their use – and the left behind themselves. Towards its end, the chapter begins to interrogate the absence (so far) of *solutions* to 'the left-behind problem': in essence, how to remedy the feelings and/or conditions of being left behind. This debate is further addressed in Chapter 4, through analysis of social media deliberation, before the final chapters develop and diversify the left-behind concept. They do so by widening its definition to encompass more multicultural and multidimensional demographics, while recognizing how latter-day transformations in the nature and quality of work have brought us to a point where young, urban and/or ostensibly 'middle-class' adults are now as likely to be found in the ranks of the precariat, 'new' working class and/or 'left behind' as those from the erstwhile industrial proletariat.

3

How to solve a problem like the left behind: Condescension or contempt?

The question of whether the left behind primarily constitute an economic, cultural or political phenomenon only addresses the first level of meaning enshrined in this discursive imaginary. Many lengthier speeches and more opinionated press contributions went beyond presenting them simply as areas and communities defined by this or that condition or characteristic. Instead, they attempted to consider more deeply the nature of the 'problem' the existence of the left behind presented for 'the body politic of the nation' (Rawnsley, 2016). In the context of Brexit (and subsequent democratic events), should they be considered victims or victors? Was the rebellious rage widely ascribed to them in the referendum and ensuing elections that of righteous revolutionaries – smarting from decades of abandonment and/or exploitation? Or was it an incoherent, misdirected outburst by an angry mob who only had themselves to blame for their failure to keep up with economic and cultural advancements of the modern age? Who was *responsible* for the fact that so many people felt left behind: capitalism, the state, the EU or the left behind themselves? And how did the existence of people experiencing such marginalization both manifest and deepen fault-lines in society – generating fuel for divisive forms of political populism?

After analysing how politicians and journalists addressed these issues, this chapter closes by considering some of the tentative 'answers' proposed for the left-behind 'question'. As we shall see, the endless deliberations fell short of proposing any magic formulae:

perhaps predictably, while full of performative concern, they were worryingly bereft of solutions.

In debating the multiple conundrums posed by the left-behind problem, commentators fell into multiple camps – but the two broadest standpoints, as might be expected, were defenders and critics. Each of these groupings, in turn, contained a spectrum of sub-positions which could sometimes (though not always) be aligned with wider ideological affinities. For example, many of those expressing sympathy for areas and communities considered left behind broadly came from the liberal Left. Where this was the case, they tended to emphasize the *economic* disadvantages experienced by left-behind groups and structural inequalities they blamed for fostering these. But sympathetic pundits and politicians could also be found on the Right. Often (though not always), these favoured culturalist and/or political interpretations of the left-behind condition – for example, focusing on the perceived erosion of cherished values and traditions, resulting from mass migration and the changing ethnic compositions of economically pressurized communities, and/or the sense that distant, unaccountable (EU and Westminster) politicians and bureaucrats were wilfully blind to their needs and concerns. In doing so, such pundits drew on well-worn tropes from the referendum campaign, ranging from nativist criticisms of the supposedly negative impact of immigrant pressures on housing, public services and local economies, to arguments that had historically played as well among well-heeled shire voters as the working class about the diminution of Britain's national sovereignty during its decades-long membership of the European Union.

Likewise, the opposing side – that which discussed the left behind more critically – was subject to intriguing variations. While some commentators (generally more right-leaning) resurrected tried-and-tested archetypes associating the left behind with earlier iterations of socially abject, pathologically impoverished imaginaries, such as the 'underclass', Left-inclined critics tended to adopt discursive positions that were more condescending than stigmatizing. These ranged from articles and speeches acknowledging the understandable grievances of left-behind areas while gently warning that leaving the EU was not the answer, to despairing assessments chastising working-class voters for backing Brexit in the mistaken belief it would solve their problems. The most dismissive critics metaphorically washed their hands of the left behind, with an elevated air of 'they've brought it on themselves.'

Significantly, the two broad competing camps – defenders and critics – often engaged dialogically with one another. Commentators who championed the left behind frequently did so in (explicit or implicit) opposition to those *problematizing* them. For example, a number of defenders condemned arch-Remainers for dismissing or patronizing the left behind as misguided, deluded, or ignorant for voting against their own best interests. In this vein, TUC General Secretary Frances O'Grady (a Remainer herself) used a *Guardian* opinion piece on the morning after the referendum to pointedly distance herself from 'the urbane sneering and social media memes about supposedly backward leave voters' (O'Grady, 2016).

Conversely, commentators who questioned or condemned the *views* ascribed to left-behind groups often did so by proxy: contesting the prescriptions and prejudices promoted by 'anti-elite' populists, rather than the left behind themselves. In a 29 June 2016 opinion piece in the *Times* business section, London-based fund manager Alberto Gallo conceded the 'city of London, the wealthy and the old' had 'benefited from' an 'asset-rich, wage-poor recovery' from the 2007–08 crash, while the 'rest of the country, the young and the have-nots' had 'been left behind' (Gallo, 2016). But he did so only to revert to a familiar refrain among elite pundits (and, as we shall see, social media users): that, while inequalities had grown unacceptably stark in recent decades, the EU was not a block to remedying them, but the solution. 'The English patient has been sick for a long time but Brexit was never the right medicine', he insisted, in an apparent intertextual allusion to Michael Ondaatje's eponymous novel. In directing responsibility for the vote squarely at England (where most Leave votes had been cast), Gallo argued that 'solving the UK's economic and social imbalances' required 'a lot more than building a border or kicking out an unpopular prime minister'; it was 'time to stop believing in promises' and build 'a more balanced growth model' (Gallo, 2016).

The following sections explore these competing discursive positions by drawing on the medium of critical discourse analysis (CDA). Put simply, CDA is the process of analysing the use of 'language as social practice' (Fairclough & Wodak, 1997). The mode of CDA applied here is based on Ruth Wodak's 'discourse-historical approach', which elicits meaning from texts by integrating 'available knowledge about the historical sources and the background of the social and political fields in which discursive "events" are embedded' (2001: 65). More details on the precise methodology are given in the Appendix.

DEFENDING OR DENIGRATING THE LEFT BEHIND? COMPETING IMAGINARIES OF 'REVOLTING SUBJECT'

As we have seen, the dominant characterization of the left behind to emerge from popular debate in the post-referendum period framed them as victims or casualties – whether of economic decline, cultural disconnection, political marginalization, or a confluence of two or more factors. Indeed, many shorter parliamentary records and simpler news articles adopting such frames were somewhat superficial, in that they portrayed the left-behind condition in highly descriptive, even normative, ways. However, at times when journalists and politicians took more opinionated/critical positions on left-behind voters – whether to understand, endorse, or query their grievances – they often penetrated beyond their surface framing to construct them (in relation to Brexit at least) as what sociologist Imogen Tyler has conceptualized as 'revolting subjects' (2013). Where attempts to critically engage with left-behind groups adopted positions *defending* them, the subjects were presented as having a legitimate case for 'revolting' – that is, rebelling against the status quo. By contrast, in cases where they were *criticized*, treated dismissively, or with contempt, they were painted as 'revolting' in a very different sense: at best, patronized as misguided or ill-informed and, at worst, derided as economically and/or culturally deviant and, as such, largely responsible for their own predicaments. In the next two sections, we explore how these two contrasting imaginaries of the left behind as opposing forms of revolting subject – righteous rebels versus abject anti-citizens – played out in the discursive arenas of press and Parliament.

The left behind as righteous rebels

In the days and weeks immediately after the referendum, the comment and opinion pages of Britain's national and regional press were characterized by a collective sense of dazed incomprehension. As the enormity of the electorate's decision to leave the EU slowly sank in, commentators on both sides of the great Leave–Remain divide directed their attention to the question of why so many working-class and/or low-income voters – often (though not always) located around post-industrial areas of northern England, Wales and the Midlands – had voted for Brexit. Never mind the fact that the biggest proportion of Leave voters was located not in down-at-heel ex-mining towns or faded coastal resorts, but the affluent South (Dorling, 2016); throughout the great post-referendum post-mortem (as in the months and years succeeding it), the spotlight was squarely trained on the left behind.

Though it would often be accused in later months of publishing condescending metropolitan-elitist commentaries about left-behind voters, the *Guardian* offered a notably reflective early attempt to understand the rationale underpinning the working-class rebellion in its Editorial on the morning after the referendum. 'The self-styled proponents of progressive politics must reflect', it warned, 'on why they have found it so tricky … to understand' the 'worry' of left-behind communities – let alone 'do anything useful to assuage it' (theguardian.com, 2016). 'One prompt for soul-searching', the paper suggested, should be the inability of liberal-Left politicians 'to change the tone of the conversation about immigration', which had been 'going wrong for a decade or more'. Another was 'a failure to reckon sufficiently early with all the towns and estates left behind by an international economic order' which had 'not treated them well' – places 'abandoned for decades', that had finally been 'given the chance to vent their rage at somebody'.

In a more bullish defence of the righteous rage of left-behind groups published in the same paper the following week,

Leave-voting priest Giles Fraser spotlighted the groundswell of working-class resentment exposed by the referendum, while (like others) downplaying the role of better-off voters; it was, he said, a 'battle over globalisation and its discontents', between 'the beneficiaries of a boundary-busting neoliberal economy' and those 'left behind by it' (Fraser, 2016b). Fraser illustrated this by recalling how he had visited Stoke-on-Trent several years earlier to investigate then growing support for the British National Party (BNP). There, one BNP recruit had told him how 'one day some Chinese guys in suits' arrived at the pottery factory where he worked, 'shaking everybody's hand' – before buying the company, bundling its kilns onto 'flatbed lorries', closing the factory and leaving him 'out of a job'. In a striking passage addressing the tension between his empathy for the redundant workers and his aversion to the racism and bigotry of the BNP, Fraser wrote:

> Some people will only hear the racism in this story. And yes, I think it is there. And yes, it absolutely must be challenged, ripped out and destroyed. But there is something else that needs to be carefully attended to – a cry of rage at the alien forces of a vampire capitalism that sucked his community dry. This was the rage that Brexit tapped into. And the far right were able to turn this against poor immigrants precisely because those who should have been listening were too busy worrying about their children's next trip to Paris or what their friends at Glastonbury would think if they challenged the liberal consensus. Precisely the same people who are now saying, incredulously, 'but I have never met a leave person', as if that were a good thing. (Fraser, 2016b)

Fraser's richly interdiscursive anecdote mobilized multiple tropes for rhetorical effect – not least a subversion of populist in-group/out-group discourse which condemned 'the far right' for pitting poor potters against 'poor immigrants', while simultaneously constructing *its own* (legitimate) us-and-them opposition between post-industrial Brexit voters and well-heeled Remainers who had 'never met a leave person'. In his vivid evocation of blood-sucking 'alien forces', he also appeared to implicitly allude to the book *Vampire Capitalism*, then recently published (to widespread acclaim) by late sociologist Paul Kennedy. Fraser's recollections would be echoed in sentiments expressed by Stoke-based voters interviewed by pollster Deborah Mattinson three years later for *Beyond the Red Wall*, as they rationalized their decisions to back Brexit and switch allegiance from Labour to the Conservatives. Emphasizing the fact that employment in pottery factories had shrunk from 50,000-plus in the 1950s to just 6,000 in 2020, Mattinson observed that, while 'many of the great names still exist', they had now 'shifted production abroad' – with both Wedgwood and its equally famous subsidiary, Royal Doulton, now relocated to Indonesia (Mattinson, 2020: 61).

The picture painted by both these accounts of globalization-driven asset-stripping and clinical overseas takeovers of treasured local industries was echoed in interviews with people living on Stoke's most disadvantaged estate for Chapter 5 of this book. It was also a refrain repeatedly returned to by MPs for the city in Parliament at various stages of the post-referendum aftermath. In a January 2017 contribution to a Commons debate entitled 'Leaving the EU: Security, law enforcement and criminal justice', Remain-backing then Labour Member for Stoke-on-Trent Central Tristram Hunt said his voters

> wanted to leave the European Union for three reasons: sovereignty and a return of national powers to this Parliament; a reaction against globalisation and a political economy that they thought had shut down the mines and steel industry and eliminated 80% of jobs in the potteries; and immigration. (Hansard, 2017a)

By describing the city's voters as having 'thought' the EU was responsible for these changes – and further distancing *himself* from this view, by stressing how he 'often put the case that the EU was a bulwark against the ripcords of globalisation' – this private school-educated Cambridge graduate and former television historian adopted a discursively hedged (or noncommittal) position which risked appearing to dismiss voters' perceptions, much like other politicians who expressed sympathy for voters' *feelings*, rather than empirical *experiences*, of being left behind. Nonetheless, Hunt carefully triangulated his position, by forcefully defending Stoke residents against accusations of xenophobia – asserting that concerns about immigration were 'not racism', but 'about the effects of large-scale migration' on wages and services in an 'already low-wage city'. In so doing, he used a discursive practice semioticians term 'judgement-based epistemic modality': statements of fact based on a speaker's degree of confidence in their truth (Cornillie, 2009: 44). Despite implicitly questioning the epistemic *basis* for Stoke voters' Euroscepticism, Hunt then went on to express considerable epistemic confidence in the legitimacy of their *concerns* about migrants (even if, in using the term 'concerns', he was continuing to hedge *his own* position on the subject). Moreover, by rhetorically weaponizing his working-class constituents' grievances in this way, this elite-educated scion of an upper-middle-class Labour dynasty acted as an exemplar of how the floating signification of the left-behind concept rendered it just as prone to exploitation by liberal-Left Remainers as right-wing Brexiteer culture warriors.

The discursive strand represented by others on the Left (like Fraser) who defended the left behind from broadly socialist perspectives can best be understood as manifestations of so-called 'Lexitism': a form of Euroscepticism rooted in one point or other on the political Left which became increasingly widely debated following a failed post-referendum coup against then Labour leader Jeremy Corbyn. The Lexiter label became attached to Corbyn himself, both during and after this contest, as he was consistently framed – by media, political opponents and rival factions in his own party – as, at worst, a closet Brexiteer and, at best, a reluctant Remainer whose lacklustre efforts to convert wavering voters had undermined the pro-EU cause. A key aspect of the mainstream 'Lexiter' case is a broadly economic-protectionist position drawing, in part, on a long tradition of statist thinking that can be traced back to the anti-Common Market rhetoric of (among others) Corbyn's mentor, the late Tony Benn, during the years of industrial unrest characterizing the proto-globalized 1960s and 1970s. A classic Lexiter intervention drawing on similar tropes to Fraser came during a January 2019 debate on the EU (Withdrawal) Act, when vocal Brexit-backing Labour backbencher John Mann (otherwise a staunch Corbyn critic) illustrated his opposition towards unfettered free movement of labour by recalling 'a demonstration I went on outside the power stations', in which 5,000 workers protested that their 'jobs were going to Portuguese workers' and they 'could do nothing … because of EU laws' (Hansard, 2019b).

Six months earlier, in a debate on 'strengthening the union', a similarly Lexit-tinged intervention had been made by Jo Platt, one of several Labour MPs representing strongly Leave-supporting constituencies, who would later break her party's whip to support a Conservative withdrawal agreement (though this failed to stop her losing her seat during the 2019 'red-wall' collapse). In a strident speech strongly framed around the *economic* impoverishment affecting many northern communities, she condemned the 'brutality' of 'austerity cuts', before segueing into a wider consideration of how these had contributed to embedding political marginalization – as the Government displaced 'responsibility and obligations' onto local authorities, city regions and regional mayors, 'while at the same time cutting their budgets and limiting their powers' (Hansard, 2018c). Over time this would prove a prescient intervention, given Boris Johnson's increasing success in redirecting blame for inter-regional economic inequalities onto *local* administrations and capitalizing on voter disillusionment with their provincial political establishments – often damaging Labour at the polls (see Mattinson, 2020). 'Power, resources and funding are tightly held by Whitehall, and communities across the country have little say in, influence over or even knowledge of the decisions affecting their daily lives', Platt emphasized, using a form of rhetoric known as 'over-lexicalization': an 'excess of quasi-synonymous terms for entities and ideas that are a particular preoccupation or problem in the culture's discourse' (Fowler, 1991: 85). Pointedly distancing *herself* from the left-behind label, she argued that, while 'some say' such areas had 'been "left behind"' – and 'too slow to respond to a rapidly changing country' – they were *not* 'behind' but, rather, 'held back' and left with 'no voice and no choice'.

Over the course of the three-plus years of this post-referendum/pre-Brexit timeline – the period between the vote itself and the UK's eventual departure from the bloc – there would also be strongly worded defences of left-behind Leave voters from Left-leaning journalists, politicians and other actors who stopped short of declaring their own Lexiter leanings. In a highly critical *Guardian* opinion piece published five days after the referendum, under the provocative headline 'The privilege of the elite fuelled the anger of the leave voters', writer Tim Lott voiced what soon became a well-worn piece of received wisdom, by arguing that Brexit had 'at least partially' been 'fuelled by a resentment about elites' (Lott, 2016a). 'The private and London metropolitan school elite' had, he wrote, 'reaped disproportionately the benefits of globalisation through their entry into key jobs at the higher end of society' – partly thanks to 'cheap global labour at the other end of the social spectrum', which 'subsidised' their 'lifestyles'. Lott's most contemplative passage (a foretaste of increasingly toxic debates to come) reflected on the growing media-political focus on intersections between Leave voters and an abandoned post-war working class. Alluding to a then mainstream political mindset its critics would later dub 'wokeness', Lott criticized 'the Labour party and Conservative party alike' for choosing to 'put class to one side in politics and concentrate instead on matters of identity', just as long as those identities were not that 'of Englishness'. As a result, 'the discourse' had 'not been about lifting working-class people into the elites', but 'lifting people from other disadvantaged groups', based on 'ethnicity, gender and sexuality'. Here again, as in other commentaries throughout the post-referendum period – from banker Gallo's handwringing lament about 'the English patient' to the increasingly nationalistic pronouncements of Brexiteers in the run-up to and aftermath of the 2019 election – both Brexit and the resentments that spawned it were implicitly framed as crises of English (not British) identity.

Returning to the theme of class three weeks later, Lott wrestled more explicitly with the latter-day complexities of this concept – arguing that, while hardwired, industrial-age distinctions between the working and middle classes had progressively dissolved in an age of mass consumerism and the post-industrial service economy, many people still strongly *identified* with working classness and felt left behind 'not only financially, but in terms of their status' (Lott,

2016b). Despite describing Brexit as a 'great white working-class howl of outrage', Lott addressed the increasing muddying of historical class distinctions revolving around income, wealth and education, by reflecting, 'I don't know what class is', other than that it 'has something to do with money, obviously'. But, in an implicit intertextual allusion to popular imaginaries of feckless low-income households familiar from tabloid mythology, Channel 4 docusoap *Benefits Street* and shows like *The Royle Family* and *Shameless*, he added that working-class people 'don't simply sit around drinking, fighting, gambling, signing on and watching TV' – contrary to myths reframing 'the salt of the earth' as 'the scum of the earth'.

Three years on, another working-class writer would address similar themes as Theresa May's government teetered on the brink of collapse amid ongoing Conservative infighting about whether to ratify her version of the EU withdrawal agreement. Also writing in the *Guardian*, Frances Ryan, whose 'Hardworking Britain' column had chronicled the hardships faced by low-waged workers and benefit recipients throughout the austerity years, sympathetically cited a Leave voter, 'Martin', whom she portrayed as typical of people 'characterised as "the left behind"' – a term she hedged, by arguing that it suggested some people simply 'could not keep up' (Ryan, 2019). Citing working-class academic Lisa McKenzie, and echoing the sentiments of Platt, she over-lexically argued that people like Martin were, instead, those who knew they had been '"left out" – of jobs, of wealth, of opportunities'.

Meanwhile, writing in the *Guardian* that December, shortly after the 'Brexit election' delivered a resounding victory to Johnson's avowedly pro-Leave Tories, Geoffrey Kabaservice, director of political studies at the Washington-based Niskanen Center, a libertarian social and environmental think-tank, reflected on the hubris of 'Corbyn's middle-class supporters', who (he argued) were content to blame their losses on 'the alleged racism, sexism and xenophobia of the working class' – an attitude he dismissed as the 'latest manifestation of longstanding middle-class condescension' toward 'the white working class'. Drawing on historical parallels, he reminded readers of the decades-old words of sociologist Richard Hoggart, author of *The Uses of Literacy*, who had grown up 'an orphan in the grim poverty of the back-to-backs in south Leeds', and once noted that 'many middle-class people angrily deny the persistence of class feeling' simply because 'the class-styles they themselves practise' are 'so embedded in their backgrounds and training that they quite fail to recognise them' (Kabaservice, 2019). In essence, then, Kabaservice framed such unconscious, taken-for-granted perspectives as a blinkered middle-class *self*-image, equivalent (and implicitly related) to discourses around the supposed failings and deviances of the *working* class: the unquestioning 'doxa' of 'welfare common-sense' problematized by sociologist Tracey Jensen (2014).

Evoking similar themes in the same paper a month earlier, Daniel Trilling, ex-editor of *New Humanist* magazine, criticized not just the condescension shown to economically disadvantaged groups, but the simplistic conflation of the left-behind imaginary with the 'white working class' – a term he dismissed as 'patronising and divisive'. The 'real problem', he argued, was the sense of 'abandonment, fear for the future' and 'lack of control' shared by (righteously rebelling) people from 'a far wider range of backgrounds than fit the stereotype' (Trilling, 2019). In doing so, he crystallized a discursive paradox implicit in popular preoccupations with such a narrow *view* of the left behind: the fact that a singular focus on the plight of a particular population segment (the white working class) effectively both stigmatizes *and* privileges it. Downplaying or omitting from the left-behind narrative multifarious other groups who have *actually* been left out and/or marginalized – economically, culturally and/or politically – is one of this book's central concerns. We return to it presently, in interrogating the discursive side-lining of everyone from minority-ethnic working-class people to precarious workers generally (*irrespective* of their objective 'class').

Away from the conflicted liberal-Left analyses of the left-behind problem, more vociferous defences of Leave-backing working-class voters were often mounted (perhaps unsurprisingly) in right-wing, Brexit-backing papers and/or by (small and large-c) conservative pundits and politicians. In a July 2016 comment piece in *The Times*, focusing on the contribution of democratic deficits to the left-behind condition, economics editor Philip Aldrick queried the accepted liberal-Left wisdom that the decision of many low earners to vote for Brexit was not 'economically rational' (Aldrick, 2016). Echoing McKenzie, Ryan and others, he argued there *was* clear 'sense' in this decision – notwithstanding 'the wilful deception of the Leave campaign', which he over-lexicalized as including 'its dismissal of recession warnings, the empty promise of more money for all' and opportunistic 'inflammatory anti-migrant UKIP sentiment' from 'a group led by pro-migrant liberals' (an apparent interdiscursive reference to historical speeches and articles by Johnson himself – who had vocally championed open labour markets while serving as mayor of London). 'For poorer households', he asserted, with epistemic confidence, Brexit was 'a rejection of a status quo' that had 'failed them' because they had 'been left behind'.

But perhaps the most powerful defence of left-behind voters appeared in the *Telegraph*, nearly three years after the referendum, in a richly intertextual comment by Leave-voting Cambridge University historian Robert Tombs foreshadowing the can-do, sunny optimism that would become a hallmark of Johnson's repeated COVID-era pledges to 'level up' and 'build back better' following Britain's EU departure. Training his sights on the 'misguided pessimism' of 'extreme Remainers', Professor Tombs, an expert on working-class political culture and author of two monographs on the 1871 Paris Commune, decried those who believed in the 'illusion' of 'Europe', before parading an acute understanding of the fusion of two superficially contradictory working-class mindsets Johnson would skilfully mine for electoral gain: a peculiar marriage of post-austerity righteous rebellion and vestigial Thatcherite aspirationalism. Condemning 'the bourgeois nature' of a liberal-Remainer 'mentality' that was 'indifferent if not hostile to the plebs', and often bereft of the 'practical experience' of 'trying to find a job, earn a living wage, or run a small business', he illustrated his argument by invoking a suite of disparate examples. These ranged from a London conference at which 'a middle-class lady literally quivered with indignation when she spoke of "that thing, England"' – intertextually framed as an attitude George Orwell had 'brilliantly mocked' in the 1940s – to *Times* columnist (and ex-Tory MP) Matthew Parris's 'cheerful boasting of his contempt for democracy' and Labour frontbencher Emily Thornberry's supposed 'disdain for working-class patriots' (Tombs, 2019). This was an interdiscursive reference to an infamous 2014 tweet in which, on the date of a parliamentary by-election in which the Conservatives had lost a seat to UKIP, Thornberry had posted an 'image from #Rochester' beneath a photo of two St George's Cross flags draped over a terraced house, with a white van in its driveway. The van image itself interdiscursively alluded to a symbol associated with a tabloid imaginary of patriotic, hard-working, *Sun*-reading, (white) working-class tradesmen – popularly termed, since the 1980s, 'white van man' (Conboy & Steel, 2010).

Similarly stout defences of patronized working-class voters could be heard in Parliament. A notable intervention came during a Lords debate on the June 2017 Queen's Speech, when Tory peer Baroness Stowell suggested much of the language directed towards Brexit-voting working-class people implicitly framed them as ignorant. 'Often, when we talk about those who are uneducated' about 'big political events', we use 'phrases such as "left behind"', implying that 'people who are not educated to degree standard are all failures', she argued (Hansard, 2017g). Echoing left-wing observers such as Ryan and McKenzie, she suggested that a 'better way of thinking about' such voters was 'cut off and left out', adding (with epistemic certainty) that they were 'not left behind' but 'right here, right now'. Accusing 'the educated side of the divide' of believing 'everything is so complicated that only the educated people can come up with the answers', the peer went on to draw on a similarly interdiscursive allusion to Prof. Tombs – reminding colleagues of 'the incident between Gordon Brown and Mrs [Gillian] Duffy'. This was a reference to a lifelong working-class Labour voter the ex-Labour prime minister had encountered on the 2010 election campaign trail – and to whom he was later recorded referring as a 'bigoted woman' (quoted in Curtis, 2010). Mrs Duffy had described herself as 'very upset', she reminded colleagues, because she viewed Mr Brown as 'an educated person'.

As time passed after the referendum, and a growing Brexit-shaped gulf emerged between working-class Leave voters and many of those on the political Left, conservative defences of the left behind were increasingly couched less as heartfelt expressions of camaraderie with their newfound bedfellows than gloating condemnations of the failure of (Remain-backing) liberal papers and politicians to keep on side their one-time core constituents. In this respect, such commentaries could be characterized as *appropriations* of the left behind: opportunistic expressions of an unlikely alliance between social groupings with shared Brexit ideologies but wildly differing material interests, rather than genuine efforts to empathize with disadvantaged groups with which they otherwise had little in common. In a forthright *Sunday Telegraph* opinion piece published three days after the 2019 election that took full advantage of the floating signification of the left-behind concept to frame it in unabashed 'culture-war' terms, US-born conservative philosopher and journalist Janet Daley explicitly likened the disdain some liberal-Left commentators were by then directing towards working-class Leavers to former presidential candidate Hillary Clinton's notorious 2016 dismissal of blue-collar Trump voters as a 'basket of deplorables' (Reilly, 2016). Raising the spectre of wokeness to sum up the reasons for the erosion of Labour's red wall, Daley wrote that, 'by concentrating on the denizens of this social media world, Labour ended up ignoring the real one with its urgent needs and fears' – a miscalculation she compared to Clinton's preoccupation with 'privileged women worrying about glass ceilings' over 'women in the rust-belt states' who 'worried about putting food on the table' (Daley, 2019). Interdiscursively alluding to now widely discredited scientific ideas about superior and inferior human characteristics, she suggested that Labour Remainers' 'snobbery' towards their erstwhile working-class base had 'mutated into what sounded like eugenics', until 'something' had 'snapped in the electorate' – and they 'humiliated their tormentors'.

A similar verdict was reached two days later by the *Daily Mail*, which improbably leapt to the defence of 'neglected millions' in 'former coal-mining communities and hollowed-out manufacturing towns' who had rallied behind the Tories' newly built 'blue wall', while alluding to longer-term trends that had seen working-class voters gradually drift away from Labour (*Daily Mail*, 2019). Red-wall voters, it argued, had 'dished up sweet revenge' after years of being 'betrayed over Brexit', 'left behind by globalisation' and 'ignored by the London-fixated political elite (even when New

Labour's shining stars represented those constituencies)'. Given the strongly Tory-supporting traditions of both *Telegraph* and *Mail*, it was hardly surprising that such commentaries should be framed more as attacks on Labour than the wider governing elite. Nonetheless, it was beyond audacious that such stout defences of the disenfranchised masses should be mounted by elite commentators in papers which had long been passionate cheerleaders of the very neoliberal free-market policies that had so immiserated the erstwhile industrial towns they now championed.

Some right-wing, Brexit-backing papers went even further in expressing performative sympathy for marginalized left-behind Leave voters – notably tabloids with historically substantial readerships in the C2DE 'unskilled' or semi-skilled socioeconomic grouping, like the *Sun* and *Express*. One device used to explore the predicaments of such communities in a more (superficially) layered and persuasive way was to unpack them through lengthier, reportage-style colour features, incorporating direct quotes from left-behind voters, rather than straightforward news stories or overt opinion pieces. Another was to outsource authorship to civil society experts whose work the papers otherwise rarely covered. For instance, a week before the 2019 election, the red-top *Sun* devoted a lengthy feature to a hagiographic profile of then Chancellor Sajid Javid: a rags-to-riches MP from an Asian background its public school-educated political editor framed as having grown up 'on Rochdale's mean streets in the early 1970s' (Newton Dunn, 2019). Using over-lexicalization to construct the image of a working-class boy-made-good who had risen from humble beginnings in 'a modest terraced house' in a 'South Pennines mill town' (a background visualized through a sprinkling of photos of Javid posing outside such dwellings), the feature framed him as poster-boy for others, 'full of talent', who felt they had 'been left behind'.

An example of an outsourced expert think-piece was a January 2019 article in the *Express*, written by Graham Duxbury, chief executive of Groundwork UK, 'a federation of charities mobilising practical community action on poverty and the environment across the UK' (groundwork.org.uk, 2021). In it, Duxbury drew on tropes that might have been lifted from one of Mattinson's focus-groups or the writings of Blue Labour thinker Maurice Glasman to stress how, for many Brexit voters, the referendum had been as much about reasserting a patriotic 'pride in the place where we live and a passion to make it better' as 'taking a swipe' at 'remote and uncaring' elites (Duxbury, 2019). In a passage echoing the can-do post-Brexit spirit of Prof. Tombs and Johnson, he said this patriotic spirit could be harnessed as 'a springboard' for projects to make communities 'more vibrant and welcoming' – creating 'a stronger social fabric that benefits us all'.

As the years and months passed, moreover, increasingly nuanced and reflective accounts of the position of left-behind communities and their frustrations at being economically and politically side-lined were also voiced by Left-leaning politicians and journalists – particularly during the later stages of the prolonged parliamentary wrangles over how (or whether) to implement Brexit. In a self-questioning intervention in the strongly pro-EU *Guardian*, deputy opinion editor Joseph Harker reflected how, while initially 'horrified' by the Leave vote, he had become 'more and more sympathetic to the people who voted leave' – arguing that they had been arrogantly ignored by a 'Westminster village' that had spent the ensuing years debating whether there should be a second referendum, or a 'meaningful vote', when they wanted 'meaningful lives' (Harker, 2019). 'Remember that brief moment after the referendum, when commentators started acknowledging the "left behind", admitting that they'd been ignored for far too long?' he asked rhetorically, recalling the post-referendum focus on 'swaths of the country beyond the M25 where industries had been lost, where communities had been torn apart, and where the idea of prosperity was a long-forgotten dream'. Drawing on binary 'North–South divide' imaginaries, Harker argued that all pretences of empathy with working-class Leavers had since dissolved, as 'the panic to stop Brexit' among Remainers had led to 'their stories' being 'forgotten' and the message from liberal elites being 'boiled down to two words: "Stupid northerners"'.

Similar sentiments were aired during a January 2019 Lords debate on the Brexit withdrawal agreement and political declaration by cross-bench peer and Keynesian economic historian Lord Skidelsky – who condemned as 'wrong and misleading' the tendency to 'label the leave vote' as that of 'the left-behinds or the ill-educated' (Hansard, 2019c). While conceding such phrases had 'a certain descriptive accuracy', in that they identified 'the damaging legacy of austerity and insecurity', he said it was 'wrong' to suggest 17.4 million people voted for Brexit 'because of these things'. 'That is not only condescending but to deprive voters of agency', he argued, adding that 'no one will tell you, "I voted to leave because I was left behind or badly educated", but they will give a reason', and 'unless these reasons are taken seriously' we 'risk drawing wrong conclusions on policy'.

Meanwhile, writing in the *Guardian* in the early stages of the 2019 snap election campaign, Lisa Nandy, Labour MP for Wigan, described how 'voters outside London' were 'wearily resigned to suddenly being subjects of much interest during election time, after years of events that loom large in our villages, towns and cities – extreme weather, transport chaos, drug problems and broken government promises – going largely unreported' (Nandy, 2019). Alluding to a term coined by working-class journalist Caitlin Moran, she added, 'we've also got used to journalists channelling their inner David Attenborough to travel to our towns to interview "leave voters" – that strange species that must apparently be observed in its natural habitat – before hopping on the train back to London.' She went on to condemn journalists' predilection for 'homogenous stereotypes' and 'dismal language about our towns as "left-behind" places and "wastelands"' where people had 'nothing left to lose' and 'entire communities' had 'apparently been "slung on the slagheap"'. Nandy's sentiments echoed the nearly three-year-old words of her fellow Labour MP, Remain-backing Member for Sheffield South-East Clive Betts, who had used a February 2017 parliamentary intervention to debunk the blanket characterization of people who had been 'left behind by economic progress over a number of years' as xenophobic because of their immigration concerns. Warning of the dangers of driving people 'into the arms of the racists' on the populist Right if mainstream politicians failed to heed their 'genuinely held concerns' about the impact of 'unrestricted immigration' on public services, pay and conditions, he emphasized how such fears had been expressed to him not only by 'white British residents' but 'people from different ethnic backgrounds' – including 'the Pakistani, Kashmiri, Bangladeshi and Somali communities' (Hansard, 2017c). Two months earlier, Ivan Lewis, then MP for Leave-voting Bury South, had delivered a speech containing an intertextual allusion to language popularized by politicians and military leaders during the Iraq War – defining Brexit as a 'shock-and-awe wake-up call' from righteous rebels who felt 'mainstream politics' was 'broken' and did not 'work for them' (Hansard, 2016f). Despite having served in a Blair government often criticized for taking working-class voters for granted and adopting open-door policies towards mass migration, Lewis displaced blame for the left-behind's anger on his party's leftward drift under Corbyn. 'Some senior Labour frontbenchers', he claimed, displayed 'contempt for those who have legitimate concerns about the pace and impact of immigration'.

The left behind as social abjects

The post-referendum positioning of left-behind groups and communities as righteous rebels – 'positive' variants of Tyler's revolting subjects – was only half the story. An intersecting but conflictual construction of disadvantaged working-class Leave-voters, and wider social grouping(s) with which they were aligned, cast them as, at best, misguided dupes or, at worst, a socially inferior rabble. Yet within this broad discourse of social abjection there were, as always, multiple gradations. Some commentators (often self-identifying Remainers) referred to the left behind with ambivalence: while ostensibly acknowledging their hardships and right to protest, they nonetheless patronized them by suggesting they had been *manipulated* into voting for a fantasy Brexit-shaped solution to their problems, invariably by nefarious populist forces. For others, the left-behind debate appeared to present an irresistible opportunity to reboot historical imaginaries that had often been used to legitimize more or less ideological forms of 'welfare reform' – most recently during the years following the 2007–08 financial crash, when the Coalition government had displaced blame for Britain's burgeoning budget deficit onto working-age benefit recipients and built a popular consensus in support of brutal cuts. While articles portraying the left behind as social abjects may have contained few explicit mentions of 'scroungers' or 'shirkers' – go-to tropes of the Coalition and its tabloid cheerleaders – a discursive DNA trail could be traced back to subtler aspects of 'underclass' framing in more sweeping caricatures of denizens of left-behind communities as unskilled and/or jobless, dependent on benefits and lacking agency.

Aside from its often subtle and insidious modes of expression, this latter discourse was distinguished from scroungerphobia of the past in that, unlike previously, it was as likely to be invoked by actors (nominally) on the political Left or Centre as right-wingers. In essence, there was no clear-cut correspondence between commentators that disparaged left-behind voters and their broader ideological or party-political affiliations. Instead, at a time when the rush to publicly champion the working class was beginning to be led by actors on the Leave-backing populist Right (Lexiters aside), stigmatizing imagery often occurred in the ruminations of Remainers – and were as likely to be voiced by Labourites or Lib Dems as Tories. In this respect, one curious – and highly significant – takeaway from the public negotiation of the floating signifier 'left behind' in the months after the referendum appears to be its early articulation and mirroring (underappreciated at the time) of the creeping realignment of many working-class voters with parties and movements on the populist Right, rather than those on the Left – a repositioning which would manifest itself most starkly in the waves of losses Labour suffered to the Tories in the 2019 general election and 2021 English local elections. It also provides succour for the argument – rehearsed by Matthew Goodwin, Maurice Glasman, Jon Cruddas and others – that the much-discussed 'falling out of love' with Labour among the working class had been both reciprocated *and* precipitated by that party's ever greater preoccupation, over time, with courting a middle-class, metropolitan electorate.

Another intriguing pattern to emerge was the close correspondence between relatively *more* stigmatizing commentaries and the *culturalist* frames outlined in Chapter 2. Overall, comments that merely patronized working-class Leavers for assuming Brexit would solve their problems were generally voiced in articles and speeches framing the left behind as an *economic* phenomenon

– the Left's initial default diagnosis. By contrast, those that were more sharply critical of left-behind voters largely framed them in cultural or values-based terms, insinuating that immigration concerns, for example, could be put down to bigotry or racism. Of these two frames, culturalist characterizations of the left behind proved especially mutable. In other words, the floating signification of the left-behind concept – and the ideas around values, worldviews, patriotism, identity and status loss attached to it in culturalist readings – could either be operationalized in *defence* of an under-siege, justifiably aggrieved 'traditional' working-class (often, though not exclusively, by those on the political Right) or in *condemnation* of one that was retrograde and burdensome (the underlying default position of many liberal-Left commentators). Here then – peeping through in plain sight – were the embryonic fault-lines of the since widely debated 'culture war' (Sobolewska & Ford, 2020).

An early (if atypical) example of the gently admonishing positions some broadly liberal-Left newspapers adopted towards left-behind voters appeared in the *Scotsman* two days after the referendum, in a verbatim transcript of an address by Scottish First Minister Nicola Sturgeon to left-leaning think-tank the Institute for Public Policy Research (IPPR). In her speech, Sturgeon acknowledged that many people had voted Leave because of 'a feeling' that 'they were being left behind' – a condition she normatively characterized as relating to 'the effects of austerity and an economic system that doesn't work for them'. However, in itemizing the factors she argued had contributed to their decision – from the UK government's 'decision to make ordinary people pay the price of a financial crash they didn't cause', to 'its cynical collusion in the myth that cuts and public service pressures' were 'the fault of migrants', rather than 'a direct result of deliberate economic policy' – she aligned herself with the view of her economic adviser, Marianne Mazucatto, that 'blaming the EU was a category error' (quoted in scotsman.com, 2016). 'If the leave campaigners were right about how many felt about life and work in Britain today', she ventured, quoting Mazucatto, they were 'wrong' about both 'the causes' and 'solutions'. While careful to direct *responsibility* for this 'category error' towards elite actors leading the Leave campaign, then, Sturgeon steered uncomfortably close to extending her definition of those who were 'wrong' to blame the EU for inequality to voters *themselves.*

Similarly, in a comment piece published on 2 August 2016, as both Conservative and Labour parties were commencing their protracted post-referendum leadership battles, *Independent* economics editor Ben Chu lamented the 'irony' of Cornwall voting to leave, given that it was 'a very good example of the direct economic benefits of EU membership', thanks to investments in the Eden Project, 'built on the site of an old China clay pit' (Chu, 2016). Indeed, over the months and years following the referendum, there would be much talk of 'irony' to counterpoint the (presumed) *intentionality* of left-behind Brexit voters with the (predicted) *consequences* of their decision. Thus, in his *mea culpa*-like intervention in *The Times* a week after the vote, multimillionaire fund manager Alberto Gallo had argued that, while 'pointing the finger at the EU' had been 'an easy political strategy to capitalise on these issues', the 'irony' was that many Leave voters would be among those 'most hurt by a weaker currency, rising inflation and job losses from divestments' (Gallo, 2016).

Meanwhile, by January 2019, as then Prime Minister May mounted yet another heave to force her ill-fated Brexit withdrawal Bill through the Commons, Labour's London Mayor Sadiq Khan was stressing 'the irony' that staying in the EU would have given voters 'the best chance of finding the solutions' to their grievances' 'root causes' – framed (in classic economistic terms) as the sense of being 'left behind' by a 'new world', in which 'benefits of economic growth increasingly flow to only a few at the top' (Khan, 2019). This point would be echoed by *Independent* columnist Patrick Cockburn at the end of the year, as the dust settled on the Tories' snap election victory. Cockburn mulled over 'one of the most extraordinary and contradictory developments in modern English political history': the fact that '"left behind" and "left out" places' had 'decided to retaliate against a British establishment that had long ignored them' by 'scapegoating the EU', despite the fact it had often been 'the only governmental institution that did anything to help them' (Cockburn, 2019).

While clearly empathetic towards the parlous economic position of left-behind voters, then, these commentaries were united by a common condescending refrain: that, in voting against their own best interests (as they undoubtedly had), they had done something 'ironic', 'contradictory', or (in the words of Sturgeon's adviser) plain 'wrong'. Again, these sentiments were repeatedly echoed by Remainer politicians in Parliament. In an uncompromising rejection of the impulses perceived to have driven so many left-behind voters to back Brexit during a January 2019 debate on the then EU (Withdrawal) Act, outspoken Remainer MP David Lammy referred to 'friends on this side of the House' who had urged him 'to appease Labour voters in industrial towns' – the 'former miners' and 'factory workers' who 'feel that they have been left behind' (Hansard, 2019b). Instead, he argued with epistemic certainty, 'we must not patronise them with cowardice' but 'tell them the truth': that they had been 'sold a lie' by 'parts of the media' who used their 'fears' to 'sell papers and boost viewing figures' and by 'Nigel Farage and the right hon. Member for Uxbridge and South Ruislip [Boris Johnson]'. Directly addressing left-behind Leave voters in terms that came close to justifying Baroness Stowell's characterization of Remainers as those who believed 'only the educated people can come up with the answers', Lammy accused Brexit populists of exploiting the tabloids' anti-foreigner 'prejudice' to blame 'immigrants' for their economic misfortunes – when, in truth, it was 'our schools and colleges' that had 'failed to give you skills'.

Lammy's words contained strong echoes of an earlier speech by outspoken Lib Dem peer Lord Wallace, who, while stressing it was vital for 'voices of the poorer regions of England' to be 'represented' in the process of leaving the EU, over-lexically patronized 'ignored, underpaid and undertrained' Leave voters by suggesting they had been lured by the prospect of 'lots of goodies' following Brexit (Hansard, 2018b). Similarly, during the following month's Lords debate on a prospective UK-EU Trade Bill, Lib Dem peer Lord Fox suggested hard-pressed communities had been duped into scapegoating European economic migrants by Ministers keen to 'vilify' them to displace blame for issues caused by 'government mistakes and mismanagement', such as their 'woeful performance in housebuilding'. 'The evidence points to the need not to stop the beneficial flow of economic migrants' but for 'targeted government investment' in communities that 'have generally been termed to have been left behind', he argued – adding that such communities would 'not be benefited by making Britain poorer' (Hansard, 2019d). Fox's comments were notable for their use of multiple discursive modes. In confidently asserting that 'evidence' showed economic migrants had been 'beneficial' to Britain and ending free movement would make the country 'poorer', he employed a form of epistemic modality drawing on unspecified evidentiality which was rhetorically reminiscent of the similarly certain economic warnings issued prior to the referendum by the official Remain campaign. By stressing the 'need' for 'targeted government investment' in left-behind areas as Britain looked to its post-Brexit future, meanwhile, he employed a form of 'deontic' modality: a discursive practice emphasizing the speaker's *desire* for something to happen (Kreidler, 1998: 241). In a more pessimistic address just weeks earlier, Tory Remainer Baroness Altmann had condemned Brexit in similarly over-lexicalized terms to Fox – intertextually ridiculing the ongoing delusion that it could 'solve lack of infrastructure investment, the housing crisis, education standards, the need to improve productivity or the social care crisis' as 'Alice-in-Wonderland thinking'.

One of the earliest examples of a more overtly condescending, even stigmatizing, representation of left-behind groups appeared in a news story in London's *Evening Standard* in July 2016. Headlined 'UK "paid price for lack of investment in schools"', it focused on a speech to a French business conference by 'top investment banker' Tidjane Thiam, then chief executive of Credit Suisse, which returned to the framing of left-behind Leave voters as uneducated (or under-educated) as an explanation for their Brexit voting (Tobin, 2016). Thiam was quoted striving to balance his recognition of 'desperate levels of inequality' he had 'witnessed' during '15 years living in Britain' with a diagnosis that a key cause of the result – framed as 'bad for the country' – was 'a chronic lack of investment in education'. In other words, working-class Leavers were as likely to have backed Brexit because they were uneducated and ignorant as out of any (justifiable) desire to protest at what Thiam himself acknowledged as governments' inaction to 'even out the impact of globalisation'.

A more common refrain, however, was for the left behind to be framed as vulnerable to the predations of manipulative, unscrupulous populists – in essence, too weak, undiscerning and/or nativist to avoid being duped into supporting divisive, dangerous policies. In a rueful May 2019 meditation in the *Scotsman* on the 'contempt' in which the 'entire political class' was now held, the SNP's Kenny MacAskill pointedly distinguished between 'younger voters' who had 'switched off' and now preferred 'more radical or environmental politics or parties' – a reference to unfolding debates about so-called 'woke' causes – and 'the poor', who had been 'left behind' and were increasingly 'disengaged, contemptuous of failed promises' and 'open to manipulation by populist parties' (MacAskill, 2019).

Even think-pieces striving to paint more graded portraits of the left behind were often only a nuance away from conflating the traditional values, pride in place, insular cultures and social conservatism ascribed to them empathetically by Glasman and Mattinson with bigotry and racism – in so doing, tainting their analyses with remarks verging on the contemptuous. In a lengthy reflection on the resurgence of political demagoguery published days before the referendum but preoccupied with the impending prospect of Trump's election (as signposted by the headline: 'Welcome to the age of Trump'), *Guardian* deputy comment editor Jonathan Freedland had spotlighted the popular imaginary of the 'angry white male' – whom, he reflected, was 'now more politely referred to as the white working class' (Freedland, 2016a). During a lengthy passage introducing an early focus on the *cultural* dimensions of the left-behind condition, he observed how the US had 'grown steadily more liberal over the last two decades, with a loosening of attitudes to diversity, gender equality and sexuality', especially 'among the young and well-educated'. 'Symbols' of this revolution – including 'a black man in the White House' and 'the law that allows same-sex couples an equal right to be married' – had been 'deeply unsettling' for 'angry white males', as a 'society that gives a prominent and equal place to, say, black men or gay women can seem to contradict the values in which these traditionalists (some would want to call them reactionaries) were raised'.

Though aspects of Freedland's argument recalled Chapter 1's exploration of the gradual erosion of status experienced by industrial working-class men – as manufacturing jobs had been jettisoned, outsourced abroad and subordinated to service and financial sectors – his use of a hedged rhetorical device in the bracketed phrase 'some would want to call them reactionaries' hinted at his own unease at the resultant ('anti-woke') backlash. While acknowledging the *material* causes of working-class resentment, such as the increasing elusiveness of a 'job' and 'affordable home', he placed less emphasis on these negative changes than on the (positive) *cultural* aspects of how the traditional 'social hierarchy' had been disrupted: through the levelling of a structure in which working-class men (repeatedly racialized as 'white', in terms recalling critiques by Haylett, Skeggs and others) had once been 'validated' above 'the gay, the non-white and the female'. Tellingly, Freedland directly referenced the book *There Goes my Everything: White Southerners in the Age of Civil Rights, 1945–1975* – Jason Sokol's 2007 exploration of the decline of white supremacy in the US.

This tacit equation of left-behind voters with uneducated, uncivilized, nativist values also emerged from parliamentary exchanges. During a bad-tempered February 2017 Commons debate on the then proposed state visit of newly elected Donald Trump, Labour MP for Cambridge Daniel Zeichner pointedly elided Britain's readiness to welcome the divisive US president with the emerging 'culture-war' debate between (supposedly) disadvantaged post-industrial working-class communities and those with more internationalist worldviews determined to stand up against 'intolerance, ignorance and hatred'. 'We have heard about the people who have been left behind', he said, in hedged terms tinged with distaste, before juxtaposing them with the favoured in-group of his own constituency: framed as 'another place that values tolerance, education, understanding and learning'. This was 'the kind of city Cambridge is', he declared, with epistemic certainty, adding that standing up to Trump was 'about who we are and about our values' (Hansard, 2017d).

Perhaps the most openly stigmatizing comments, however, were those that began appearing towards the end of the sample period, as three-and-a-half years of interminable post-referendum divisions culminated in a decisive general election that would finally deliver Brexit. By this time, much of the commentariat had exploded into a bitter, polarized blame-game tinged with aspects of moral panic – often with working-class Leavers cast as folk-devils (Cohen, 1972). Amid the rawness of the post-election period, depictions of the (real or imagined) Leave-voting masses – invariably framed as the white working class – were often couched in contemptuous terms. In a television review in the *Independent* which read like a parody of bourgeois condescension, critic Ed Cumming awarded a Christmas 2019 edition of the ratings-winning sitcom *Mrs Brown's Boys* with a single star, deriding it as 'Brexit TV' and a 'programme that puts two fingers up at the snooty metropolitan elite', while ventriloquizing the assumed opinions of viewers who 'feel left behind' by 'fayncy high-falutin comedy out of that London' (Cumming, 2019). Bearing the headline 'This panto is pure Brexit telly', the review ended with a lament that the show's star, Brendan O'Carroll, did not capitalize on his 'rare command of his audience' by being 'more rigorous with his material' or (swiping at its millions of viewers) finding 'a more discerning audience'. This could easily be interpreted as both a dig at the Brexit-voting masses and an allusion to populist politicians, like Farage and Johnson, whose crowd-pleasing tactics O'Carroll had (it was implied) imported into the domain of popular entertainment.

More typically, though, disparaging portrayals of left-behind voters appeared in newspaper comment sections – often emerging from wider-ranging reflections on the election's outcome. In a 15 December *Scotsman* column condemning Labour left-wingers for the party's seismic defeat, Euan McColm accused them of having 'no idea about the reality of working-class existence', and instead holding a 'distorted' and 'deeply condescending' view of 'the working class as perpetual victims', like 'characters from a Ken Loach movie' – an intertextual reference to the work of the Corbyn-supporting, multi-award-winning, working-class director whose most recent films, *I, Daniel Blake* and *Sorry We Missed You*, had been widely praised for their authentic insights into the precarity of the present-day benefits system and gig economy (McColm, 2019). McColm's most useful contribution was the nuanced definition *he* gave of the working class, which he characterized as both 'often more socially conservative than Corbynista cultists would find comfortable' *and* 'aspirational': a rare acknowledgement of the complex interplay between traditionalist worldviews ascribed to many post-industrial red-wallers and the upwardly mobile mindsets held by embourgeoised post-Thatcher voters that (in combination) formed the nexus of Johnson's support base.

However, while McColm made a powerful case for the limitations of Corbynistas' 'romantic notions of the noble poor' – which framed 'politics as a war against a brutal elite', rather than 'a process by which the worker might advance' – he reverted to problematic characterizations of the *most* impoverished groups, in a passage normatively identifying 'an underclass of people', who were 'left behind and struggling to survive'. By implicitly associating the term 'left behind' less with its customary corollary (socially conservative workers and pensioners) than those at the very bottom of the economic pile, such as the long-term unemployed, McColm juxtaposed these twin imaginaries in terms that might easily have been lifted from a 1980s Conservative Party Conference speech – with its stout defence of aspiration and implied distinction between a deserving and undeserving working class (if not poor). While recognizing that 'victims' of government policies 'need defenders', he argued politicians must balance 'the needs' of 'the family struggling on benefits' with 'those whose, perfectly reasonable, wish is to have a second car in the driveway of their new-build semi'.

Three days earlier, a similarly casual association between the left behind and underclass stereotypes blighted by welfare dependency had been made by Allister Heath, Brexiteer editor of the *Sunday Telegraph*, in an election-day rallying cry evoking populist tropes pitting 'the people' against 'the elite' – a timeworn binary to which we return in Chapter 4 (Mudde, 2004). Under the hysterically over-lexicalized headline, 'Today is our final chance to save Brexit – and even democracy itself; Capitalism vs Marxism. The people vs officialdom', he framed the poll as 'the most important' of 'our lifetime', and Johnson's 'Levelling Up' agenda as a way of tackling 'the plight of the UK's left-behind areas' that did not 'simply chuck welfare cash at them' (Heath, 2019). Heath's comments recalled a similarly framed intervention two years earlier in a Lords debate on 'Intergenerational fairness in government policy'. In a speech condemning Britain's reliance on 'cheap jobs' and lack of spending on 'new generations', cross-bench peer Lord Bird, founder of the *Big Issue*, had said he wanted 'social security' to be turned into 'social opportunity', so 'those people' who were 'left behind' stopped 'costing us an arm and a leg as they tread water' (Hansard, 2016d).

Among more left-wing commentators, meanwhile, disbelief and disapproval over the left-behind's Brexit folly had, by the time of the 2019 election, given way to despair at their ongoing political masochism: unconcealed incomprehension that, three years on from a referendum in which they had committed the 'category error' of blaming their woes on the EU rather than UK governments, they had now voted *en masse* for the same party that had historically inflicted on them such social and economic misery. In a *Guardian* comment published the morning after the Conservatives' landslide win, Labour-supporting columnist Zoe Williams warned balefully that 'whoever feels "left behind" today' – a term pointedly placed in speech marks – 'should see how they feel tomorrow, or next month, or a year from now' (Williams, 2019). A week later, Ian McConnell, business editor for Glasgow's *Herald*, predicted that 'former Labour voters' in 'the likes of the north of England' who backed 'Boris Johnson and his "Get Brexit Done" mantra' were 'likely to be among those hardest hit' by Brexit: 'those who believe they have been left behind' were 'likely to experience a huge intensification of this feeling after even just a little while of being disadvantaged by the policies of Mr Johnson and his Government' (McConnell, 2019). In an epistemically certain passage asserting the 'plain and simple fact ' that Tory 'economic policies' had 'hammered' communities once 'dependent on heavy industry', he added, with barely concealed irritation, that this 'seems to have escaped' voters who 'switched allegiance because of a new-found passion for Brexit' – especially 'those old enough to remember', who were willing to let their 'zeal' for Brexit overshadow 'memories of the Margaret Thatcher era'.

COUNTERING WHITE WORKING-CLASS PRIVILEGE: SPEAKING UP FOR A MULTI-ETHNIC LEFT BEHIND

If it is possible to speak of a coherent *counter-discourse* about the left behind, beyond comments problematizing the values and attitudes ascribed to them, this could be found in the small but significant number of interventions challenging the quality with which it was most persistently associated: its whiteness. Racialization of left-behind areas and communities as a primarily white working-class grouping, or cluster of related groupings, was a recurring discursive trope throughout the three-and-a-half years of debate and reflection over the outcome of the referendum. Alternately privileged (as a group whose suffering was recognized over that of all others) or stigmatized – as a culturally backward and socially inferior 'ugly contradiction', both 'abject and white' (Haylett, 2001: 352) – the dominant left-behind imaginary was cast as a stubbornly monocultural, mono-ethnic construct.

As the post-referendum debate unfolded, however, a steady strain of counter-hegemonic argument slowly emerged, both in Parliament and sections of the national and regional press. A primary strand of counter-discourse was that the racial and cultural composition of many post-industrial communities, both in the present and (to a lesser extent) past, was significantly more multi-ethnic and multicultural than commonly supposed. A secondary argument was that, while many traditional working-class areas might indeed have been historically white, most economic challenges they faced today – from low-paid, precarious work, to benefit cuts, to depleted public services, to a lack of good-quality, affordable housing – were precisely the same as those endured by the more racially diverse urban 'precariat' (Standing, 2011), 'emerging service workers' (Savage, 2015) and/or umbrella 'new working class' (Ainsley, 2018) latterly identified by social scientists. Meanwhile, a third strand sought to subvert the dominant discourse more substantially – by emphasizing demographic data showing that, far from merely experiencing *comparable* levels of economic disadvantage to the white working class, Black and minority-ethnic households and communities were *disproportionately* affected by poverty and associated inequalities, with lower life expectancies and poorer health and/or education outcomes than white ones.

An early flavour of the argument that economic disadvantage was no respecter of colour or ethnicity played out in a May 2017 news story in the *Bristol Post* – published a few weeks ahead of that year's snap general election. Focusing on the recommendations of a Bristol University-hosted community workshop exploring ways of uniting Remainers and Leavers following a divisive referendum, the story's opening lines reheated the popular narrative that Leave voters, 'fed up of being left behind' by the city's creeping gentrification, were 'sticking two fingers up' to 'politicians and politics generally' (Cork, 2017). In reported remarks, the PhD student leading the project acknowledged that many Leave voters were 'older, white, working-class men' who had been '"left behind" by rapid social and economic processes' and backed Brexit 'out of frustration with the EU and mass immigration'. However, she added, 'the stereotype of ethnic minorities as (passive) victims of hate crime rather than active participants in the referendum' was 'no more helpful' than 'stigmatising the white, working-class Brexiteer as making the "irrational" choice to Leave based on racial prejudice'. Importantly, she went on to directly quote a workshop participant who had asked, "we always hear about the white working class as left-behind. What about the black working class?"'

Writing in *The Times* around the same time, columnist David Aaronovitch framed his particular countervailing point along generational, rather than explicitly racial, lines – arguing that, contrary to popular belief, the 'old, white working class' were actually 'super-served' by politicians determined to chase the grey vote through triple-lock pension protections, while Britain's 'truly left behind' were 'the young', who were priced out of education and housing, and forced into menial, insecure, temporary and/or underpaid work. He also implicitly acknowledged the debate's racialized dimensions by arguing that the country's latter-day discursive preoccupation with the plight of white working-class people could be dated back to the 'fateful encounter' between Gordon Brown and Gillian Duffy seven years earlier – an incident that had given 'eagle's wings to' a then 'emerging narrative of the Great Ignored' (Aaronovitch, 2017). Aaronovitch's argument was rather muddled at times, misleadingly conflating the 'old, white working class' on whom it initially focused with 'white working-class people' in *general* when it later proved discursively convenient to do so. However, he rightly observed that, 'in the guise of not being allowed to talk about immigration', Britain's leaders had spent much of the period following the notorious Brown-Duffy exchange discussing 'almost nothing else' – to which he added that 'the intention of making amends for not noticing the plight of the white working class' had led to it noticing 'no one else'.

Three years later, the lead-up to another election saw an articulate, detailed expression of a more overtly race-critical case voiced by Alana Lentin, associate professor of cultural and social analysis at Western Sydney University. Writing in the *Guardian*, Dr Lentin criticized the 'elite obsession with the "left behind" white working class' as having 'badly damaged' any 'hopes of solidarity between communities' commonly 'ravaged by cuts' (Lentin, 2019). While white and other ethnic groups might have shared, or analogous, experiences of economic disadvantage; however, 'white people' were not subject to 'state-sanctioned harm' in 'the same way' as people of colour. In a passage stressing the multiple measures by which many minority-ethnic people arguably had a *stronger* case for feeling left behind than the white working class, she itemized a litany of inequalities disproportionately favouring the latter – including their higher life expectancy, better job prospects, and the fact they were 'less likely to be arrested or incarcerated' or suffer from mental illness.

FROM DIAGNOSIS TO TREATMENT: ADVANCING THE LEFT BEHIND

Whether framing the left behind as righteous revolutionaries or social abjects, what *remedies* (if any) did the incessant post-referendum commentaries selectively sampled above propose for their condition? A remarkable feature of these often erudite, lengthily reflective and interdiscursive interventions was that they seemed to have so little idea how to quell the anger or assuage the suffering of Britain's disadvantaged communities. In some cases, not only did they fail to suggest solutions: they showed little interest in finding them. This was especially true of pundits and politicians approaching the problem from a Remainer and/or liberal-Left inclination. Aside from occasional *mea culpas* at the failure of elite actors (implicitly including themselves) to address the grievances driving so many to lash out against the EU and wider establishment, they focused less on actions that might *resolve* this situation than those that (in their view) would make it worse. In other words, many commentators offered little more than a re-tread of their approach to the referendum campaign itself: principally, dire warnings of impending economic doom that played into the hands of those keen to dismiss the Remain cause (however unfairly) as 'Project Fear'.

In one sense, this may have been unsurprising – given that post-referendum debates played out against the backdrop of an interminable three-and-a-half-year fight between those determined to implement, re-run, or reverse the outcome of the vote. However, when the *Guardian*'s Freedland predicted 'the Regrexit sentiment' would 'grow' when 'some of those leave voters' realized that Brexit had 'not brought back the good jobs of old, that housing is still in desperately short supply and that a migrant family still lives round the corner', it was hard to read into his words much more than an inflated degree of epistemic certainty that low-income Brexiteers would reap the whirlwind caused by their misguided actions – and an early foretaste of arch-Remainers' gathering determination to overturn the result (Freedland, 2016a). Similarly, when London Mayor Sadiq Khan wrote in January 2019 that 'only through being a proper part of Europe' could Britain exercise 'power and influence on the world stage' and ensure 'all citizens share in the fruits of globalisation', an obvious retort from left-behind groups was to ask why this had not happened before – and where had the EU been during a previous decade of swingeing cuts to local authorities, services and social security?

Moreover, such protestations risked displaying all the attributes of the unkindest 'Remoaner' clichés: symbolizing a collective failure to reflect on the mistakes of a sterile, technocratic campaign that had over-relied on zigzagging line-graphs predicting economic doom as a means of swaying people for whom such fears seemed meaningless, given the daily dilemmas they already faced about whether to put food before fuel after years of grinding austerity. In place of a persuasive championing of the existing settlement, or a sufficiently progressive prescription for change (based on a recognition that many communities' pre-Brexit position was grim), came stale re-runs of earlier campaign warnings about what might be (further) lost if this mistake were to go ahead. Far from offering visionary plans for rebalancing the economy, investing in communities, enhancing local democracy, or improving integration in areas facing serious population pressures (whether or not directly related to EU migration), Remain-backing commentators reverted to warning that the left behind's position would only worsen with the coming apocalypse: a denialist rejection of the inevitable need to reimagine Britain's social settlement in the *absence* of the Union.

But if liberal and/or Remainer commentaries were notable for their collective lack of vision and failures of imagination, both Lexiter and more conservative Eurosceptic opinion-formers also reverted to type – either by recalling the inequities of the neoliberal economic system they associated with Britain's EU membership, or exhibiting exactly the kind of airy optimism about the prospect of post-Brexit Utopia that had typified the heady, un-costed promises and flag-waving 'Britain is best' rhetoric of both official and unofficial Leave campaigns. Many such interventions were characterized by an air of 'good riddance' to the old order, combined with an idealistic certainty that the simple act of fulfilling the people's choice would offer a recipe for a bounteous new era for Britain's left behind. In so doing, they took full advantage of the floating signification not only of the left behind but Brexit itself – promising that the latter would magically unlock the nation's pent-up potential by liberating it from the perils of rigid red-tape with which the EU was associated. It was in this spirit that the intro of a January 2019 editorial in the strongly Leave-backing *Telegraph* pronounced Brexit a milestone offering 'fresh opportunities for a more outward-looking Britain' (telegraph.co.uk, 2019). Five months later, Prof. Tombs would use the same paper to frame the 'Remainer mindset' as 'an irrational one based on cultural pessimism', contrasting this with a 'Leaver mindset' characterized as 'optimistic about our future as a successful, self-governing' and 'happy country' – provided, that is, 'Brexit happens' (Tombs, 2019).

This, then, is where we leave the discourse of the left behind at the end of this chapter: in a curious conceptual space stuck somewhere between a dubious consensus on the primarily white working-class composition of this disputed grouping and a more complex understanding of those who might legitimately claim to have been left behind (whether or not they had voted for Brexit). It is on a similarly open-ended note that we leave the debate around *what to do about* the left behind: principally, how to balance competing concerns about economic, cultural and/or political factors that had contributed to their feelings and experiences of neglect and marginalization, and how to heal the divisions that these had fuelled. In the next chapter, we pick up both these strands again as we turn to considering how the position of the left behind has been negotiated, understood and (especially) responded to in that extension of the 'political public sphere' (Habermas et al., 1974: 114) that exists beyond the arenas of the mainstream press and Parliament: social media.

4

Fear and loathing on social media: Trolling and championing the left behind

The story of how the debate about the – or *a* – left behind unfolded on social media after the 2016 referendum and into the longer term is a tale of two competing, but interlinked, imaginaries. One account of the vote in favour of leaving the European Union framed it in terms all too familiar from Chapter 2 and 3's analysis: as a righteous rebellion against the socioeconomic and/or political status quo, powered (or led) by a disenchanted social grouping broadly identified as the post-industrial working class. In the alternate version, many posters self-identifying as Leavers collectively constructed *themselves* as something altogether more intriguing: newly empowered agents of a far wider coalition of anti-establishment voters more akin to a large-scale popular uprising than a backlash by one or more disgruntled segments. One of these imaginaries therefore cast the dissenters in Orientalizing terms, as an *outgroup* – an economically, culturally and/or politically impoverished *minority* (if a suddenly vocal and audible one). The other conceptualized them as a wider-scale, socially diverse *ingroup* – one with which many enthusiastically associated *themselves*. In asserting their membership of a groundswell of hitherto unheard or unheeded voters drawn together from *across* society – as a largely *political*, if also partly *cultural*, iteration of the left behind – such posters collectively crystallized themselves as 'the people' or a hitherto 'silent majority'.

The idea that there exists a great ignored 'silent majority' – a *politically* left behind – and the association of this concept with a mass of 'people' who have (supposedly) been locked out of democratic decision making takes us squarely onto the rhetorical and ideological terrain of populism. In an important 2004 theoretical paper, political scientist Cas Mudde described as 'essential to the discourse of the populist' a 'normative distinction between "the elite" and "the people"': a purist 'Manichean outlook, in which there are only friends and foes' (Mudde, 2004: 544). In other words, 'opponents' of 'the people' – deviant out-groups intrinsically antithetical to the virtuous or pure in-group – are regarded as 'not just people with different priorities and values', but 'evil'; rendering any attempt to 'compromise' with them 'impossible', because 'it "corrupts" the purity' (ibid.). This populist conception of 'the pure people' versus 'the corrupt elite' has since been applied to the context of Brexit specifically by international relations scholar Alexander Spencer and political scientist Kai Oppermann, who have described how Leave won this binary battle by constructing a 'largely consistent romantic narrative', in stark contrast to the muddled story presented by Remain's 'mixed narrative genres' (2019: 666). This romantic narrative took the form of an 'exciting and entertaining story involving conflict and adventure', alongside doses of 'sentimentality and exciting emotions': one which activated long-standing populist tropes that 'rely on a romantic emplotment' involving 'the moral people' resisting 'an unjust order' by standing up 'to fight for a better world against powerful adversaries' (ibid.: 671, 679–80). Even more apt, perhaps, is the work of political sociologists Carlo Ruzza and Milica Pejovic, who are among the few scholars to have examined the negotiation of popular discourses around Brexit on social media (2019: 442). In so doing, they identified a strong strand of populist criticism of EU institutions on Facebook, stressing 'the cleavage between the people and elites' – one they explicitly related to Robert Ford and Matthew Goodwin's distillation of the left-behind mindset in *Revolt on the Right* (2014).

Returning to this book's purview, what was – or were – the dominant characteristics and identities ascribed to economically and/or politically left-behind 'peoples' through the sites of online deliberation considered here: Twitter and newspaper comment threads? How were the two competing imaginaries of the economically and/or politically ignored masses discursively configured, both individually and in relation to one another? What distinctions, if any, emerged through the ways in which marginalized, excluded and/or disenfranchised populations were imagined in these two discursive arenas? And, finally, how did social media actors *respond* to the (supposedly) decisive influence of left-behind voters on the referendum and subsequent election results – and the groundswell of disaffection and rebellion these were seen to symbolize? To address these questions, this chapter begins by examining the broad picture, through a high-level analytical breakdown of the multiple ways in which these popular 'backlashes' were articulated and accounted for across a broadly representative cross-section of national newspaper comment threads – an approach repeated later for Twitter conversations. The methodology used for this purpose was a form of qualitative content analysis drawing on manual sentiment analysis techniques, as employed in other recent social media studies, including those focusing on marginalized groups (e.g., Lopez et al., 2012; Serna et al., 2017; Morrison, 2017 and 2019b). The chapter then unpacks the nature of the discourses that emerged from these (often febrile) debates by drawing on the discourse-historical approach to critical discourse analysis (CDA) applied to press articles and parliamentary texts in Chapter 3.

ANALYSING COMMENT THREADS: A BRIEF WORD ABOUT METHODS

The sheer scale of online debate and deliberation around the question of who voted for Brexit (and why) during the three-and-a-half-year study period meant it was necessary to drastically narrow down both the range of newspaper comment threads examined and the timeframe(s) around which analysis focused. An initial sample of all UK-wide national newspapers' coverage of the five discursive events that formed the basis of Chapter 2's framing analysis identified only a handful of titles that published comment threads beneath their articles. Moreover, several threads that *were* published accompanied news stories focusing on parliamentary manoeuvrings over various EU withdrawal agreements, rather than the outcomes of democratic events involving public participants. In such cases, user comments tended to focus on criticisms of Parliament and politicians and/or speculation about the future of then incumbent governments – rather than the nature and characteristics of social groupings contributing to the referendum outcome and/or subsequent UK election results. For these reasons, combined with the need to rationalize the overall sample size, analysis was confined to comment threads published in response to the two key democratic events in the lifetime of Brexit to date: the 2016 referendum itself and the 2019 general election.

To ensure consistency in the threads sampled across the two snapshots, enabling meaningful comparisons to be drawn, a decision was taken to extract them from the same newspapers in each case. This helped narrow the range of eligible titles, as several papers only ran threads responding to one or other of the two events. In making a final selection, care also had to be taken to ensure that sampled papers broadly reflected the overall ideological balance of the UK national press. In the end, neither of Britain's two mid-market nationals, the *Daily Express* or the *Daily Mail*, were considered eligible: the former because it did not run a thread to accompany news of the referendum outcome; the latter because its 23–24 June 2016 article and attendant thread focused not on the vote's result or those who delivered it, but the dramatic resignation of then Prime Minister David Cameron. The final news-sites chosen were those of www.theguardian.com, website of centre-left quality paper the *Guardian*; www.thetimes.co.uk, online version of centre-right quality paper *The Times*, and www.thesun.co.uk, the web platform of right-wing red-top the *Sun*. Appendix 3 gives a detailed explanation of the approach to sampling and analysis.

Initial datasets assembled for the two discursive events were manually cleaned to remove numerous comments irrelevant to the primary focus of this analysis: the framing and conceptualization of rebelling/left-behind voters. These included various posts that simply reacted to or commented in general terms on the referendum or election results and/or their likely consequences for Britain as a state or union of nations – rather than specific communities, areas, or social groupings. In the end, comments retained for analysis were all those that made an explicit reference to specific segments of the electorate, voters in general and/or more abstract collectives – or floating signifiers – such as 'the left behind', the 'working class', 'the people', or 'the silent majority'. Given that some articles generated hundreds of comments, it was necessary to rationalize the datasets prior to analysis, by confining final samples to only the first few pages of posts and prioritizing those ranked as 'most liked' or 'most rated'. For example, the *Guardian*'s thread from the night of 23–24 June 2016 ran to 942 comments, of which only the first five pages (250 most 'recommended') were sampled, together with their replies. The final sample of snapshot 1 comment posts across all three titles – the night of the 2016 referendum – numbered 353, while the total for snapshot 2 (the date of the 2019 election) numbered 282. Posts were coded into a total of seven categories identified in initial immersion in the material. Significantly, these not only included comments defending and criticizing groups/communities associated with the left-behind concept, but also defensive/critical posts focusing on the more expansive imaginaries of 'the people' or 'the silent majority', and a further category of posts mentioning the electorate more generally. Examples of such comments included a number responding to the 2019 election result that argued for electoral reform to ensure future outcomes genuinely reflected the people's will. These included one singled out by editors as a '*Guardian* Pick', which argued that only by introducing proportional representation would we ever 'know' what people really thought about 'socio-economic problems & climate change'. Breakdowns of the balance of sentiments towards the two intersecting imaginaries are given in Tables 4.1 and 4.2. A detailed methodological explanation is given in Appendix 3.

POWER TO 'THE PEOPLE': ANTI-ELITE POPULISM IN POST-REFERENDUM ONLINE DISCOURSE

An abiding pattern to emerge from the divergent ways in which Britain's left behind were collectively imagined by reader-commentariats of the three sampled news-sites was that the dominant discourse on each site's thread was strongly conditioned by the way its journalists framed the specific voter-types or population segments seen to have determined the outcomes of these two momentous events. Significantly, nearly every article inviting comments adopted at least some element of *culturalist*

Table 4.1 Comment thread snapshot 1: Left-behind discourse at Brexit referendum

Newspaper	*Defending left behind*	*Defending 'will of the people'*	*Neutral comment on left behind*	*Left behind duped*	*Left behind backward or bigoted*	*Posts critical of 'the people'*	*Other posts about voters*	*Total*
Guardian	189 (73.8%)	2 (0.8%)	36 (14.1%)	8 (3.1%)	18 (7%)	1 (0.4%)	2 (0.8%)	256
The Times	9 (12.3%)	39 (53.4%)	0	2 (2.7%)	2 (2.7%)	11 (15.1%)	10 (13.7%)	73
Sun	0	11 (44%)	0	1 (4%)	1 (4%)	7 (28%)	5 (20%)	25
Total	198 (55.9%)	52 (14.7%)	36 (10.2%)	11 (3.1%)	21 (5.9%)	19 (5.4%)	17 (4.8%)	354

Table 4.2 Comment thread snapshot 2: Left-behind discourse at 2019 general election

Newspaper	*Defending left behind*	*Defending 'will of the people'*	*Neutral comment on left behind*	*Left behind duped or misguided*	*Left behind backward or bigoted*	*Posts critical of 'the people'*	*Other posts about voters*	*Total*
Guardian	15 (16.9%)	14 (15.7%)	16 (18%)	5 (5.6%)	8 (9%)	11 (12.4%)	20 (22.5%)	89
The Times	12 (10.6%)	61 (54%)	2 (1.8%)	3 (2.7%)	0	11 (9.7%)	24 (21.2%)	113
Sun	11 (13.3%)	41 (49.4%)	6 (7.2%)	0	0	5 (6%)	20 (24.1%)	83
Total	38 (13.3%)	116 (40.7%)	24 (8.4%)	8 (2.8%)	8 (2.8%)	27 (9.5%)	64 (22.5%)	285

framing – in contrast to the overwhelming dominance of *economistic* portrayals of the left behind in overall press coverage. The editorial strategy of specifically inviting readers to participate in discussions responding to articles incorporating aspects of the emerging us-versus-them 'culture-war' thesis strongly reflected wider approaches to hyper-commercial online news practices designed to engage and enrage readers by involving them in polarizing debates (Morrison, 2019a: 234). Given this priming, it is perhaps unsurprising that culturalist discourse was far more prominent in the comment-thread (and related Twitter) datasets assembled for this chapter than in the wider newspaper sample. However, this disparity between a dominant overall press thesis favouring *economistic* factors and a disproportionate focus on *culturalist* ones in our much smaller comment thread/Twitter sample also suggests that, for all the indignation expressed by self-styled champions of the 'ridiculed' masses – from *Spiked Online* to the *Telegraph* – the cliché that discussion of the left behind primarily acts as a locus for the channelling of disdain towards the lower orders by a privileged, Remainer, liberal elite is misplaced. It also raises questions about the plausibility, perhaps even the existence, of a 'culture war'.

An example of the partially culturalist ways in which Britain's ignored, marginalized and/or disaffected publics were *framed* could be clearly seen on the night of the referendum itself. The main 'morning-after' article under which comments were solicited on www.theguardian.com centred around the (hitherto anticipated, but now apparently accomplished) mass revolt against the EU status quo among 'working-class' voters in Labour's erstwhile industrial heartlands. Written by Matthew Goodwin, co-author of *Revolt on the Right*, this lengthy think-piece carried the provocative headline 'Labour's traditional voters no longer share its progressive values; Today's working class care more about community, solidarity and belonging' (Goodwin, 2016). Hardly surprising, then, that more than 97 per cent of sampled posts this article generated (251 out of 256) were preoccupied with debating the nature, condition and worldview(s) of today's post-industrial working class: a social grouping Goodwin himself normatively conflated (in terms he had previously helped patent) with 'the left behind'. Of these, more than three-quarters (189 out of 251) defended the communities concerned, often by condemning their perceived neglect and marginalization by Westminster politicians over preceding decades, while just one in 10 (26) adopted positions critical of such voters – the remaining 14 per cent (36) posting comments that could best be described as neutral or balanced. A typical example was 'angryboy's' post minutes before polls closed, which strongly echoed the substance of Goodwin's thesis without indicating their own bias. In it, they summarized many of his underlying points, observing that 'Labour's traditional voters' were 'largely patriotic, don't want large scale immigration and despise welfare dependency'. Echoing McKenzie and Silver's observations half a century earlier in *Angels in Marble*, they added that working-class people tended to vote Labour (if in ever-dwindling numbers) out of 'tradition' – not because they were enthused by 'so called "progressive" values'.

In contrast to the *Guardian's* framing, the immediate post-referendum article inviting comments on www.thetimes.co.uk was a news story headlined simply 'Britain votes for Brexit' (Elliott & Coates, 2016). Opening with an introduction announcing that the UK was 'heading out of the European Union today' after a referendum that 'remakes the country's political landscape', the story reported how 'swathes of England and Wales' had backed Brexit to 'express their anger over immigration and inequality' in 'a popular revolt' that had 'left the country deeply divided'. Given this framing, it was perhaps unsurprising that 48 of the 73 comments coded (more than 66 per cent) focused not on debating the plight or protestations of a disadvantaged left-behind grouping, but the role played by a much wider imaginary of 'the people' or 'the silent majority' – with 39 posts (53 per cent) celebrating this popular rebellion and/or proudly declaring themselves to be part of it.

A similar frame characterized the 24 June referendum report leading reader discussion on www.thesun.co.uk (like www.thetimes.co.uk, a Conservative-leaning news site owned by News UK, whose majority shareholder is Rupert Murdoch). Beneath its triumphantly capitalized, pun-ridden headline 'SEE EU LATER!' the story emphasized its 'popular revolt' framing through a standfirst trumpeting, 'Britain votes to LEAVE the EU on a dramatic night as [then UKIP leader] Nigel Farage declares "victory for ordinary people'" (Tolhurst et al., 2016). Again, this forcefully framed portrayal of the night's dramatic events appeared to prime a similarly populist sentiment in most sampled posts: 11 out of 25 (44 per cent) focused on the role played in delivering the Brexit vote by an at times abstract conception of 'the people' or 'the public', rather than specific communities or types of voter. Moreover, while seven out of the 20 posts commenting on people who voted Leave adopted counter-discursive positions, by criticizing them and/or warning about Brexit's consequences, several posters self-identified as participants in the uprising – as might be expected among readers of a long-standing Eurosceptic paper (Anderson, 2004).

The agenda-setting influence of individual newspaper frames on the nature and emphasis of their comment threads was also apparent during snapshot 2. The article beneath which the *Guardian's* main comment thread ran was a soberly titled editorial piece headlined, 'The Guardian view on the 2019 election result: a new political landscape' (theguardian.com, 2019b). For anyone still in any doubt about the paper's reading of the election's significance, the accompanying standfirst left little room for interpretation, with its stark prognosis that Boris Johnson had 'redrawn the map'; both Labour and the Liberal Democrats were 'in disarray', and not only would Brexit now 'pass', but the union itself stood threatened, as 'Scottish independence' would likely 'move to the centre of the stage'. With the article itself framing the election as 'a Brexit-dominated contest' in which Labour had mustered its 'lowest total' of seats 'since 1935', while the Conservatives had 'swept through constituencies in the Midlands and the north of England' that Labour had 'rarely lost in its history', the scene was set for a lively thread focusing squarely on the collapse of the only recently conceptualized (but already widely recognized) 'red wall'.

Sure enough, more than six out of ten comments (44 out of 69) focusing on the voter groups/communities responsible for the 80-seat Tory majority concerned themselves with the role played by disaffected working-class defectors in once solid Labour-voting seats – returning to the three-and-a-half-year-old narrative thread sown by Goodwin's article on the eve of the referendum. Intriguingly, though, there was also space on this occasion for a wider-ranging debate about the nature of the improbable winning coalition the Tories had assembled between their customary support-base in the shires and newly annexed post-industrial territories. As a result, four out of ten posts focusing on the nature of the new Tory electorate (25 in total) were concerned with wider definitions of righteous rebels as 'the people' or 'the majority', with a particular focus on the idea that the election had played out as a proxy for a second Brexit referendum – and, ultimately, a repeat of the Leave vote. Given the paper's positioning on the broad liberal-Left, and its (qualified) pre-election endorsement of Labour (theguardian.com, 2019a), in the raw aftermath of the vote it was perhaps unsurprising that many posts expressing opinions about working-class defectors to the Tories openly criticized them: disregarding neutral comments, 45 per cent (24 out of 53) of those expressing a viewpoint condemned or questioned their decisions, compared to 55 per cent (29) who empathized with their position (often, as previously, while despairing at Labour's failure to earn and/or retain their loyalty). This 45–55 split was the same whether discussion focused on working-class/left-behind groupings or 'the people' more generally.

In clear contrast with the *Guardian*'s continuing preoccupation with *conventional* conceptualizations of left-behind/marginalized voters, the overwhelming focus of comments on the *Times* and *Sun* threads was the roar of defiance expressed by the electorate *overall* – the clear implication being that Tory victory symbolized a popular backlash against Parliament's then ongoing obfuscation over Brexit. Some 72 out of 86 *Times* posts commenting on the nature of voters responsible for the result and/or their motivations (eight out of ten) focused on 'the people' or a (hitherto) 'silent majority', with 85 per cent of these (61) defending their rebellion and/or associating themselves with it. On the *Sun*'s website, 46 out of 63 posts about the nature of the Tory coalition (73 per cent) emphasized the imaginary of a cross-class pro-Conservative/Brexit mass movement – nearly nine out of ten expressing their own support for it. However, given that the socioeconomic profile of the *Sun*'s core readership traditionally lies among C2DE manual and/or 'unskilled' workers, it was intriguing to note posters' recognition of the role played by working-class voters – with 17 out of

63 (one in four) remarking on this, compared to 17 out of 86 (one in five) on the *Times* thread.

As in both papers' coverage of the original referendum result, these silent majority-focused threads had been primed by articles bearing headlines stressing the need to finally end Brexit-tinged societal divisions reopened by the election – by finally delivering on the referendum result. In tune with the consistent framing of the poll as a 'Brexit election', both by the Tories themselves and Murdoch-owned media outlets, notably *Sky News* (Wring & Ward, 2020), the headline on www.thetimes.co.uk focused on the Leave/Remain fault-line – not the role played by (or likely impact on) particular groups. Declaring 'UK election results: Boris Johnson offers an olive branch after Tory win', it presaged a standfirst describing his appeal to 'Remainers' (rather than ex-Labour voters) to 'let the healing begin' (Elliott et al., 2019). A similar message was carried by that day's headline wordplay on www.thesun.co.uk: 'MERRY BREXMAS!' It was accompanied by a standfirst stressing Johnson's quest for '"closure" over Brexit', so Britain could 'heal', and his vow to 'make the NHS top priority' (intertextually echoing his 2016 Leave battle-bus slogan).

In summary, then, the *version* of left-behind – or left-*out* – voters around which online deliberation cohered on each site depended to significant degrees on how the will of voters was framed in the articles to which it responded. The two right-wing papers adopted frames focusing on the drama of the UK's decision to leave the EU, underpinned by a celebration that the will of 'the people' *overall* – or a substantial 'silent majority' of righteous rebels whose views had previously been ignored – was finally being heard, first in the referendum itself, then the decisive 'Brexit election' that sealed the deal. By contrast, the framing adopted by the liberal-Left *Guardian* conceptualized the outcomes of both referendum and election as consequences of decades of neglect of a particular *type* of left-behind voter/electoral segment, defined through a complex intermeshing of identity components, embracing economic position, socio-cultural values, geographical location and/or social class. Here, then, the left-behind concept was framed much more narrowly, as a forgotten or overlooked socio-cultural minority: the post-industrial, or 'traditional', working class.

CONCEPTUALIZING A NEW CLASS CONFLICT: FROM RISE OF THE LEFT BEHIND TO FALL OF THE RED WALL

A central question underpinning debate around the role 'traditional' working-class voters played in the referendum outcome was that of whether/to what extent it was 'liberals' (particularly *Labour* politicians) that had left these people behind – by switching their focus to courting a predominantly urban, university-educated middle class. A strong current underpinning this thesis, articulated in Goodwin's referendum-night article framing the *Guardian* thread, was that Labour's slow-burn abandonment of its erstwhile voter-base had both worsened the *economic* malaise affecting their communities and deepened an *ideological* rift with them over its increasingly divergent social and cultural values – particularly during periods when it had been in 'government', whether at national and/or local levels. In other words, as Labour nationally had evolved into a more metropolitan, bourgeois political movement, by embracing a more diverse coalition of members and activists, it had drifted away from moorings that had once attached it to the more rooted forms of 'community, solidarity and belonging' prized by communities whose identities intrinsically sprang from their collective industrial working-class heritage (Goodwin, 2016).

Primed by this framing, most comments posted on the *Guardian*'s referendum-night thread squarely focused on the contribution made to the result by this specific voting segment: the 'post-industrial' or 'traditional' working class, particularly those located in long-time Labour heartlands in the North and Midlands. Not only this: the majority of these comments accepted the broad thesis that an apparently unbreachable chasm had opened, over time, between the party and historically loyal supporters. By contrast, on both www.thetimes.co.uk and www.thesun.co.uk, posts preoccupied with this conventional conceptualization of the left behind were in a minority – reflecting the fact that the papers had framed their threads as responses to the overall referendum result, rather than the agency of any particular group of voters. Though the *Guardian*'s single-minded preoccupation with working-class voters was far less marked in its election coverage, its readers continued to give this aspect of the result considerable attention, as the fabled 'red wall' crumbled. Significantly, there was also a notable upswing in interest in this segment among *Sun* readers.

But turning to a more deep-dive sentiment-based analysis, what did 'positive', 'negative' and 'neutral' characterizations of left-behind voters actually *look like* – whether imagined as the 'traditional' or 'post-industrial working class' or any of various (interchangeable) floating signifiers? How did audiences posting in the online echo-chambers of the three sampled news-sites collaboratively construct the concerns and conditions of this discursive imaginary in the immediate aftershocks of these seismic democratic events? Specifically, how did this spectrum of characterizations map onto the taxonomy of left-behind frames identified in our analysis of *media and political* discourse(s), and which of the three dominant archetypes emerged most strongly: the disgruntled economic casualty, 'anti-woke' cultural throwback (or custodian), or political reject/pawn?

Moreover, what (if any) ancestral DNA did these late-modern, post-crash uprisings against the inequities of neoliberalism, globalization and/or deficient democracy share with earlier incarnations of class-based conflict with which Labour was historically associated? The following sections unpack this nexus of dimensions as it unfolded over our two key snapshots: the referendum and the 2019 election. From there we turn to analysing the emergence and discussion of the rival left-behind imaginary that emerged through online deliberation primarily on the two conservative news sites: 'the silent majority' or 'the people'. The final section examines how both concepts were deliberated on Twitter.

DEFENDING THE DISILLUSIONED: CHAMPIONS OF THE WORKING-CLASS LEFT BEHIND

Of the 344 comments about working-class/left-behind voters sampled from the two snapshot periods, seven out of ten (236) characterized them as a grouping that had been mistreated, misrepresented and/or misunderstood. The discursive position such posters adopted was therefore one that championed the cause of the left behind, invariably by condemning one or more external forces (economic/cultural/political) seen to have adversely affected them. Primed by the frames to which they were responding, such posts also tended to (implicitly or explicitly) contest the ways in which left-behind voters were perceived and portrayed by other people – including, at times, on the platforms where they were posting.

As by far the biggest share of all comments about this conventional iteration of the 'left behind' (295 out of 344, or 85.8 per cent) appeared on the *Guardian*'s thread, it is perhaps unsurprising that this was where their most fervent defenders could also be found. Altogether, 204 of 236 posts defending lower-income voters across the three sites (86.4 per cent) were published on www.theguardian.com – vastly outnumbering negative posts. In fact, of 243 *Guardian* comments adopting any form of obvious *viewpoint* on the left behind, only 39 openly criticized them – meaning that 'positive' posts (those championing them) outstripped 'negative' ones more than six to one. Given that 251 out of the 344 comments about such voters – nearly three-quarters of the total published across all three sites – were posted beneath the paper's 2016 article spotlighting the growing chasm between Labour's 'progressive values' and working-class voters' social conservatism, by far the most prominent frame among posters was that focusing on *cultural* aspects of the left-behind condition. As a result, a striking disjunction was visible from the outset between the *economistic* reading of the left behind that dominated overall press coverage (and political discourse) and the *culturalist* one prevailing on sampled threads.

For many posters, Goodwin's framing was the perfect trigger to unleash feelings of frustration (or anger) over the suggestion that the values of voters and their communities were somehow at fault, let alone 'behind'. Often this irritation was articulated through counter-attacks on a middle-class liberal establishment (in this case, Labour), which stood accused of neglecting or jettisoning them. Political elites were therefore framed as responsible for the schism: if the left-behind concept meant anything, it described a process by which Labour had *wilfully* shed, or left behind, those in which it was no longer interested, rather than any suggestion that voters themselves were backward or behind. 'Those voters were not "left behind"', but 'abandoned' by Labour 'to pursue what you [Goodwin] call a "progressive" agenda', retorted one poster

– explicitly contesting the author's use of this term to describe working-class voters who no longer had faith in the party. In a similar vein, for 'FFC800' it was 'not the working classes' that had changed, but Labour – especially under the 'internationalist, EU-supporting, big business supporting New Labour'. 'Working class people' had 'always been about local solidarity and workers' rights against big business', but Labour's increasing embrace of globalization 'just isn't in line with that'.

An openly mocking tone was adopted by 'tomo123456', who channelled the spirit of David Goodhart's 'Somewheres' in asking rhetorically, 'who knew the working class like living among their own families and communities' and prefer 'stability' to 'the more atomised values shared by many middle class liberals'? But a more intriguing question was posed by 'Vaudevillian', who contested the entire framing of this supposed Labour–working-class culture war as a conflict between 'progressive' and 'traditional' (or 'socially conservative') values. Directly querying the line from the article's standfirst characterizing contemporary working-class values as those of 'community, solidarity and belonging', they asked, 'when did these cease to be progressive values?' Picking up this line of argument, several posters suggested that, in pontificating over (but distancing themselves from) traditional working-class values, metropolitan Labourites were guilty of the same mix of hypocrisy and Orientalism that had characterized the writings of Victorian social explorers. 'The new middle class "Labour" idealists' seemed to believe such qualities should be 'admired and protected within exotic and faraway cultures' but 'denigrated' when displayed by their 'own fellow countrymen', remarked 'RussWYD'. His post drew a direct response from 'WasterofTime', who confessed to being 'fascinated by the extraordinary Anglophobia of the middle-class English', which 'projected their own racism onto the "working-class", the working class of other nations and ethnicities they continue to condescend' to as 'forever in need of their patrician intervention' – recalling comments by Deborah Mattinson's red-wallers who accused Labour of seeking to keep 'the poor poor' (2020: 131). Similarly, another poster argued that the 'intellectual and bourgeois Left used to treat the working class as *the-other-that-needs-saving*' (original emphasis). The arrival of 'more attractive identity groups' had left working-class people 'abandoned by the intellectuals', in favour of 'new victims-that-need-saving': principally, 'ethnic minorities, gender, sexuality, post-colonial amends-making'.

Others were even blunter in condemning sweeping statements about working-class people. The 'middle class left despise the working class every bit as much as the right wing do', asserted 'fairshares', accusing liberals of 'wilfully choosing to ignore' them – and dismissing them as 'racist, xenophobic "little Englanders"'. Indeed, the suggestion that *Guardian* debates about the diverging 'values' of middle-class liberals and Britain's vestigial 'traditional' working class were smokescreens for snobbery, often couched in subtly stigmatizing language, was widespread on its threads. 'Labour left the Working man, not the other way around', argued referendum-night poster 'AnotherGlassDarkly', adding that 'the sneers, scorn and vulgar comments of the Labour commentary' left them thinking, 'no wonder I voted Leave'. 'You think the electorate are stupid', one poster remarked as constituency results flooded in early on 13 December 2019, adding that 'people on here keep making this mistake of losing an election and blaming the voters.' Such criticisms were often made by 'evidence-based' posters: contributors whose comments included assertions of first-hand knowledge based on personal experience (Morrison, 2017). 'I am from a working-class community in the north of the country, and I know for a fact that people there (who are disproportionately voting to leave) still remember well "bigotgate"', declared 'allom8', with epistemic certainty – alluding to the notorious 2010 encounter between Gordon Brown and Gillian Duffy. It was 'hard for a party to give the impression' it cared about working-class people when it kept 'letting the mask slip' and showing its 'contempt'. Another poster said Labour had 'arrived at a place' that would have been unrecognizable to their 'staunchly Methodist, working class grandparents' – overtaken by 'a pampered, London-centric, upper middle-class cabal' who 'sneer' at working-class values, as if they are from 'another planet'.

More nuanced defences of post-industrial left-behind communities often addressed specific tropes associated with dominant elite discourses. These included the widespread framing of today's working class as monocultural and/or predominantly white and the perceived preoccupation of middle-class liberals with concerns about identity rather than (economic) inequality. Posts in the latter category often rehearsed emerging 'culture-war' arguments, by problematizing not working-class social *conservatism* but bourgeois social *liberalism*. 'Progressive politics seems to be about identity only rather than income inequality', remarked one repeat poster, who added that even 'this article' was 'about identity', rather than 'the real problem faced by those left behind': a 'lack of money, not helped by immigration', which would 'be less of an issue' if communities 'weren't living under conditions of a permanent recession'.

Meanwhile, in an implied intertextual reference to the row provoked by an infamous Gordon Brown speech vowing to preserve 'British jobs for British workers', another poster pointed out the disjunction between Labour's latter-day reluctance to discuss pressures around immigration and the fact that its first leader, Keir Hardie, had 'started his career leading demonstrations' against Polish and Lithuanian miners employed in Scottish coalfields. 'The alliance of the middle class "progressive" left with the working class protectionist left was always an uneasy one', they observed, adding that 'early trade unionism was driven by skilled workers protecting their jobs and income levels from unskilled workers.' Such struggles were 'every bit as much a part' of Labour's roots as 'the Fabian Society and the Webbs' (a reference to Sidney and Beatrice Webb, authors of the party's constitution).

Similarly, 'Trefelsg' asserted that it was *Labour* (not working-class voters) that had 'moved away from' values the two once shared: 'best summed up as conservative with a small c, royalist, traditionally patriotic but prepared to agree with and vote for socialist ideals with a small s'. Drawing on similar arguments to those voiced elsewhere by Lisa McKenzie and *Guardian* writer Frances Ryan, they added that, if middle-class Labour elites were to 'visit a school in a working class area', they would find it often contained 'more mixed race children and disabled children, just as many gay/trans families as anywhere else', while the imagined traditional working class lived on 'the same estates and in the same inner city areas' as recent immigrants – meaning they were 'living the multicultural modern life' middle-class people *talked* about but were 'less exposed to'.

Compared to the cultural dimensions of the working-class left-behind condition, comment thread discussion of the *economic* and *political* aspects of what it meant to be/feel left out or marginalized were generally treated as secondary and tertiary concerns – an intriguing fact, given the overwhelmingly economistic framing favoured by newspapers and politicians themselves. Nonetheless, when posters applied an economic frame, their criticisms of politicians, parties and other actors who had ignored (or exacerbated) the working class's plight were sometimes scathing. In a merciless 13 December 2019 post on www.thetimes.co.uk, one poster condemned 'self satisfied, virtue signalling, wealthy champagne socialists' who 'no longer support the less well off' and had 'nothing in common' with 'hard working voters who once proudly voted Labour'.

Three-and-a-half years earlier, similar sentiments could be found in a *Guardian* post tinged with old-style class nostalgia, in which 'Justanotherwageslave' defined the referendum as 'about class' and a Labour Party that had increasingly 'abused it's natural supporters in the pursuit of power' and 'become a slightly nicer wing of the establishment', instead of delivering for 'the people' who need 'futures other than wage slavery and shrinking public services'. And, in a romantic evocation of the variously tough-but-dignified industrial jobs valorised by Goodhart and others, another referendum poster accused 'the average labour mp or minister' of having 'no understanding of working class ties to their land, the country that their toil has helped build or the blood that has been spilled to protect it'. A more philosophical take on Labour's latter-day struggle to hold together its complex electoral coalition was offered by 'Sudders', who described it as merely the latest in a succession of ideological tightropes the party had navigated – balancing an internationalist outlook on worker solidarity with more nativist economic protectionism which put British jobs first. This had been articulated by juggling a 'socialism-in-one-country, trade union wing', concerned with improving the lives 'of "their" people' with 'an idealistic, radical, liberal wing more concerned with remaking the world in general'. Meanwhile, a lengthy confessional post by someone implicitly identifying with Labour's metropolitan turn reflected on how 'we turned a deaf ear' to 'communities in the midlands and the north that had been decimated and cast adrift without hope by the effects of de-industrialisation', because 'we were too enamoured by' the 'chattering class of Hampstead' to care about 'what happened north of Watford Gap'.

While discussion of the left behind as a largely working-class imaginary was more dominant on the *Guardian* threads than those of either *The Times* or *The Sun* – where the focus was wider-scale anti-establishment revolts – some posting to these Conservative-leaning sites could not resist ridiculing Labour for losing its customary supporters. 'The political elite claimed Britain was financially better off in [the EU], ignoring the giant elephant in the room, immigration, while the people, particularly in less prosperous areas, said NO', declared one strident *Times* poster, as the referendum result emerged in the early hours of 24 June 2016. Responding to the news that the Tories had successfully annexed chunks of Labour's former red wall on the night of the 2019 election, another poster cast Johnson's appeal in the mould of earlier One Nation leaders who had forged successful election-winning alliances between working-class conservatives and the more moneyed middle and upper classes. 'Let's see working class conservative Christian values – authentic marriage, the family, the right to life – back at the heart of the party', they pleaded, describing the result as a 'boost for authentic conservatism', rather than post-Thatcher 'neoliberal corporate globalism'.

Perhaps unsurprisingly, though, many posts championing left-behind voters focused more on their rebellion against distant, disinterested politico-metropolitan elites than economic injustice. In a colourfully interdiscursive celebration of Brexit evoking images of the proletarian uprising of the French Revolution, one *Times* poster warned 'the perfumed princes of Brussels' to 'make some meaningful changes that do not include micromanaging our daily lives', if they wanted to avoid 'guillotines being set up in public squares' across 'the streets of Europe'. Meanwhile, one of several *Times* posts parroting the can-do post-Brexit optimism of Johnson's 2019 campaign spoke up for 'those forgotten areas' Labour had 'treated like dirt' which might now 'get decent and fair representation'. For others, Johnson was a symbol of the same elitist disconnect widely ascribed to Labour. According to election-night *Guardian* poster 'GoldBrickRoad', the 'main problem' was that no political parties 'listen to the people' – and 'Boris' was 'just another arrogant toff who thinks the working class is below him'.

'WE, THE PEOPLE' AND 'THE SILENT MAJORITY': WIDENING THE LEFT-BEHIND IMAGINARY

Although this book's main aim is to analyse how the term 'left behind' has been mobilized in relation to a newly vocal minority affected by economic disadvantage, cultural disconnection and other forms of inequality, it is worth briefly examining the much wider imaginary of a discontented, rebellious, *politically* 'left-behind' population that gained traction on comment threads around our two key discursive events. 'Oh no! The silly little people have voted the wrong way! Quick! Get them to vote again! And make sure they get it right next time!' mocked one *Times* poster, in a referendum-night post presaging condemnations soon to be aimed at the sneering attitudes of 'the new elites' towards the 'howling little people' by Brexiteer commentators, such as *Spiked Online's* Brendan O'Neill (2016). In a more direct statement of similar sentiments, another poster castigated the 'left leaning metropolitan elite', before proclaiming 'victory for the small otherwise ignored man' previously 'trampled on by the EU juggernaut' – and declaring, 'the mouse has bloody well roared!!', in an apparent intertextual allusion to the eponymous 1959 Peter Sellers comedy movie.

Another distinguishing feature of this more expansive imaginary of 'the people' of 'left-behind Britain' was the eagerness with which some posters associated it with *themselves*. A textbook illustration was *Times* poster 'Deep Joy's' condemnation of a 'political establishment' that had 'long since ceased to represent the people of this country', in favour of 'their chosen few, the Eurocrats, bankers, city traders, TUC etc.' that 'we' were 'expected to meekly follow': an elite this imagined 'we' had told 'where to go and how to get there'. And, in one of many election-night invocations of the will of 'the silent majority', a *Sun* poster described how it had 'marched to the polling stations to deliver Brexit' and 'stop a Marxist Labour trashing the country'. In an apparent swipe against popular rebellions over more *liberal* causes, another used near-identical imagery to disdainfully contrast 'protest marches' with the righteous rebellion of 'the silent majority' who had 'finally had their say'. Such sentiments were also visible among *Times* posters – one of whom used a lengthy broadside against the 'hysteria, distortions and outright lies' of 'fanatical remainers' to praise 'British people' for forcing Parliament 'to live up to its responsibilities'. In an interdiscursive reference to the notorious descriptor Hillary Clinton had used to dismiss blue-collar Trump supporters before the 2016 US election, they stoutly defended Leavers against any charges that they were 'a basket of deplorables', let alone 'knuckle-dragging racists'.

BASHING THE BIGOTS AND BACKWARD PEOPLE: CRITICS OF THE LEFT BEHIND

The vast majority of comments focusing on one or other left-behind imaginary – eight out of ten of those adopting non-neutral positions (404 out of 498) – came out in clear *support* of them. Many, as we have seen, directly identified with their own preferred iteration of the righteous rebels. Nonetheless, a small minority were unafraid to out themselves (in open conflict with most of their fellow posters) as outspoken *critics* of the left behind.

Given that the *Guardian* threads focused more on the mass desertion from Labour of traditional working-class voters than the scale or composition of the Brexit/Tory-voting alliance generally, the most direct and vocal attacks on conventionally defined left-behind communities were unsurprisingly to be found on that site. Among various comments positioning such voters as ignorant, bigoted and/or xenophobic on referendum night were a succession of dismissive posts by 'TwoScoopz' focusing on the susceptibility of disgruntled left-behind voters to populism. This predicted that UKIP would 'claim the dregs of the working class', like 'every far-right party' across Europe. In an earlier comment, the same poster had asked who such 'beef-wits' would blame for their 'shit wages and poor working conditions', soaring rents, 'inability to get their child a place in a school within their catchment area' and 'oversubscribed doctor's surgeries and hospitals', once Britain had left the EU. This *schadenfreude*-tinged sentiment was echoed by an election-night poster who gloated that they could not wait for 'the yellowbellies' (a colloquialism for people from Lincolnshire) in Grimsby and 'Scunny [Scunthorpe]' to 'discover they've been had'.

For both 'oldcornishlefty' and 'TalkingBollox', meanwhile, the Leave vote marked the point when the Left should part company with working-class voters unwilling to sign up to its liberal agenda – the latter explicitly suggesting 'progressive labour and regressive labour' should 'go their separate ways'. 'If the people are moving to the ignorant racist right then labour cannot follow them', added the former. And, in a nuanced comment addressing the complexities of what it meant to *be* 'working class' in socially atomized times when precarious workers were as likely to live alone in run-down urban flats as with their families in traditional post-industrial settings, 'ID2016C' mocked the characterization of working-class values as those of 'community, solidarity and belonging' with the following tirade: 'Come on! I am in a bedsit in Dartford and that is just horseshit. Utterly surreal. And I fear tomorrow all around me will be vile and smug about their vileness too, having had their squalid beliefs validated by political process.'

Another exasperated poster querying the disputed assertion of what *constituted* latter-day working-class values – and why these were judged so incompatible with Corbyn Labour's focus on tackling disadvantage and inequality – simply asked, 'why does nobody ever list these mysterious values which [are], according to you, being ignored'? Equally disparaging was 'MrTitan', who derided the 'vaunted working class' for failing to 'engage their brains and see what was happening under the Tories from 2010', before warning that Labour could no longer 'survive on the fickle working class who will pander to neo-cons and racists'. In a similar vein, a foodbank volunteer using the nom-de-plume 'Ifyoudotoday' despaired of encountering 'more and more of the people' at work who 'don't blame the Tories for their condition', but instead 'blamed immigrants, the EU and voted for Brexit and were going to vote Tory' – leaving him 'conflicted' about 'why I volunteer' or 'should care'. And in a lengthier autobiographical comment on the website's election-night thread – singled out by editors as a '*Guardian* Pick' – a poster from the (now former) red-wall seat of

Mansfield wrestled with how currents of small-c conservatism he had witnessed growing up in the East Midlands one-time industrial town appeared to have morphed into the big-C variety. Recalling an insular 1980s town of 'pits and working men's clubs', from which 'many people' had only travelled the 15 miles to Nottingham 'once or twice in their lives', he dismissed it as 'a place trapped in the past', where 'social attitudes of people young and old were extremely conservative'; 'hostile to outsiders, let alone foreigners'; and 'barely tolerant of gays'. 'People say it's a big political journey from Labour to Conservative', but 'on certain measures it's not at all', he reflected. Picking up on this 'young-and-old' focus, an intriguing post on the paper's election-night thread framed working-class Leavers in terms starkly at odds with the 'angry old white men' imaginary – echoing an argument put forward the previous year in Eatwell and Goodwin's 2018 book *National Populism*. Instead, the widely debated concept of intergenerational conflict among the electorate was upended to position both Brexit and Tory victory as consequences of a betrayal of the voting traditions of working-class post-industrial communities by *younger* voters: older people in the North and Midlands who had 'fought to keep their industries and communities' had 'been shat on by their sons and daughters'.

Of posts critical of the Brexit/Tory-voting public *generally*, meanwhile, the most vocally disparaging were also to be found on www.theguardian.com. A flavour of these included an election-night comment playing up all the caricatures of defensive Leavers, unashamedly branding them 'racist little Englanders', and an intertextual post quoting an observation attributed to nineteenth-century economist and Liberal MP John Stuart Mill that, while it might not be true that 'all conservatives' were 'stupid people', it *was* the case that 'most stupid people are conservative.' Yet another post remarked that there had been 'no mention of the real reason' the Tories won, which was the fact that Britain was now 'a nation of small minded, immigration obsessed nationalists'. But not all such sentiments were confined to this site. Reacting to the election, one *Times* poster dubbed Brexit voters 'moronic' and another 'ignorant and easily led'. A third expressed themselves 'stunned' at 'the nation's capacity for stupidity'. Meanwhile, a poster likening Brexiteers to 'non-thinking types' in her mother's care home trained her fire on the generational split between Leavers and Remainers – despairing that some 'old people' were 'so stupid', 'so ignorant', 'so racist', 'so prejudiced'.

Although most posts castigating both working- and inter-class left-behind voters appeared on the Remain-supporting *Guardian*'s threads, perhaps the most openly stigmatizing criticisms of the former appeared (as one might expect) on those of the two right-wing sites. In a classic example of 'scrounger discourse' (Morrison, 2019a), a *Times* poster using the alias 'Newminster' dismissed another's suggestion that EU migrants had cost British workers their jobs, by arguing that 'the jobs were there for the taking', but 'Brits' were 'too idle or too conceited to work for the minimum wage and would rather sit on their obese backsides gawping at [daytime TV show] "Cash in the Attic"' – leaving them for those 'prepared to travel halfway across Europe to work'. And, in a curious exchange between two posters conflating Labour voters with unemployed benefit recipients, one raised the prospect of them waking up to a shock 'around 11 am', when they 'get up' to 'get their giro'. Another playfully suggested it was now Tory and Brexit Party supporters who would be 'happy when they get up to collect their giro', in an implicit association between red-wall Labour *defectors* and welfare dependency. In a similar conflation, tinged with a vicious strain of 'scroungerphobia' (Deacon, 1978), an election-night *Sun* poster ridiculed the failure of Labour's 'youth vote' to withstand the Tory assault – arguing that 'morning teenagers, layabouts and junkies were overwhelmed by actual taxpayers who voted later in the day, after work ends.' An even more abusive poster, 'Scorpio', used the familiar scrounger trope of the 'scrote' to distinguish between deserving and undeserving left-behind groups, by lumping together various supposed un-worthies in a comment also tainted by racism. 'This is a vote for working class', it declared, 'and not for the scroats and breeding pakistanis!' Normative scrounger discourse also surfaced in posts defending 'deserving' left-behind voters: one referendum-night *Times* poster suggested that, now 'the people' had 'spoken', 'a fairer society' could be built for 'the poorest (and they're not all workshy benefit-addicted layabouts)'.

CHAMPIONING AND CHASTISING THE MASSES: COMPETING PERSPECTIVES IN THE TWITTERSPHERE

The story of how the two rival imaginaries of (previously) left-behind voters played out over our two Twitter snapshots is that of a punchy, snappy, sometimes vicious debate – which, like that unfolding on comment threads, contained a strong culturalist dimension. Although tweets adopting clear discursive positions on working-class voters and/or 'the people' only amounted to half of those included in the referendum-night dataset (52 per cent, or 50 out of 96), this proportion rose to three-quarters of the election-night total (59 out of 79). This is significant because, in the years between the two events, Twitter doubled the number of characters allowed in a single tweet – from 140 to 280 in 2017 – enabling lengthier comments to be posted. This appeared to facilitate publication of argumentative posts that articulated clear viewpoints, in place of shorter tweets describing or retweeting (for example) electoral statistics, factoids, or quotes from articles. Also reflecting this was the noticeable drop in the number of neutral posts between snapshots: while one-thirds of all referendum-night tweets were 'neutral', this applied to fewer than one in five (15 out of 79) in 2019. Conversely, the percentage of tweets *critical* of 'the people' rose markedly over time. Only 15 of 96 in the 2016 sample overtly criticized left-behind voters and/or the 'silent majority': three in ten (15 out of 50) of those expressing views either way. By 2019, the number of people criticizing Brexit/Tory voters had risen to four in ten (24 out of 59) of those that took a position.

Before considering the nature of Twitter discourse in detail, it is important to briefly explain the sampling method. As observed elsewhere, constructing Twitter samples is more problematic than for comment threads, in that '*automatic* data-sets' do not exist in the same way as they do on newspaper websites, where they can simply be scraped (in whole or in part) from beneath the articles they accompany (Morrison, 2019a: 205). The retrospective nature of the snapshots analysed also necessitated the use of Twitter's 'advanced search' function for data-gathering, rather than a tool with more functionality, like Twitonomy, which is designed for contemporaneous searches and real-time analysis. As with threads, details of precise search terms used to construct the samples are given in Appendix 3. The final breakdown of tweets by category is given in Table 4.3 overleaf.

FROM PULLED PUNCHES TO SLIPPED MASKS: SHADES OF TOXICITY ON TWITTER

If one standout feature distinguished tweets about left-behind/left-out voters on referendum night from those posted around the December 2019 election, it was the shift towards an angrier, more polarized tone over time. When tweeters expressed opinions about either imaginary in their immediate online reactions to the referendum, these were generally couched in measured, unconfrontational terms – barring occasional abusive outliers. But by the point that Brexit was finally on the cusp of being realized, at the tail-end of 2019, much of this surface civility had broken down, and tweeters critical of voters on the other side of the Leave–Remain (or Tory–Labour) divide were no longer so content to pull their metaphorical punches. Instead, claims and counter-claims became more strident and aggressive, with many anti-Brexit/Tory tweeters unleashing bitter, stigmatizing invective – especially towards voters from culturally and/or economically left-behind communities.

More specifically, on referendum night, posts critical of such voters tended to adopt tones that were regretful or (at most) gently admonishing towards them – sentiments familiar from early commentaries by liberal newspaper pundits examined in Chapters 2 and 3, such as the *Guardian*'s Jonathan Freedland, who had warned they were likely to be adversely impacted by Brexit. By the time of the 2019 election, however, this sense of underlying sympathy for left-behind voters (however partial or condescending) seemed to have largely evaporated among critics unhappy with the result, who lined up to label them as (among other things) 'gobshites', 'cretins', 'inbred', 'xenophobic' and 'racist twats'. Given the relatively small scale of the two main Twitter snapshots, it is perhaps worth pausing briefly to offer one or two glimpses of how this gradual processing of attitudinal hardening towards the left behind began emerging at earlier stages in this evolutionary process.

Table 4.3 Twitter snapshots: Left-behind discourse at referendum and 2019 election

Discursive event	*Defending left behind*	*Defending 'will of the people'*	*Neutral comment on left behind*	*Left behind duped or misguided*	*Left behind backward or bigoted*	*Posts critical of 'the people'*	*Other posts about voters*	*Total*
2016 referendum	31 (32.3%)	4 (4.2%)	32 (33.3%)	8 (8.3%)	4 (4.2%)	3 (3.1%)	14 (14.6%)	96
2019 election	30 (38%)	5 (6.3%)	15 (19%)	14 (17.7%)	5 (6.3%)	5 (6.3%)	5 (6.3%)	79
Total	61 (34.9%)	9 (5.1%)	47 (26.9%)	22 (12.6%)	9 (5.1%)	8 (4.6%)	19 (10.9%)	175

As tweeters started to debate the unfolding 2017 election outcome, a provocative early post in which 'Flying Rodent' speculated that the 10 p.m. exit poll would signal that 'it's time to at least pretend to be racist' prompted a relatively reasoned retort describing the result as 'a wake-up call to the entire political class' who had consistently 'ignored' the concerns of 'left-behind Somewheres' – a clear allusion to the concept of rooted, parochial but proudly patriotic communities then recently popularized by Goodhart (2017). But by December 2018, a discursive pinch-point at which then Prime Minister May faced the latest of several knife-edge Commons votes on her ill-fated Brexit 'withdrawal agreement', posts had become more binary and brutal. One tweeter subverted the tropes of scrounger discourse to discriminate between 'the *real* left behind' (original emphasis) who 'get treated with contempt in brexshit Britain' – including those 'sleeping rough', who 'deserve help' – and 'the real underclass, loud mouths in Britain' they implicitly associated with normative left-behind *archetypes*. And, amid an otherwise nuanced discussion about the precise breakdown of the Brexit vote, which saw one poster point out that 'the romanticised myth about the "left behind"' ignored the fact that 'the very poorest were less likely to vote leave', a tweeter targeting stereotypical working-class Leavers suggested that 'troops' would be needed when 'those who voted for Brexit because they felt left behind' realised 'the EU wasn't to blame.'

To illustrate how the tenor of critical tweets intensified between the referendum and 2019 election, posts gently admonishing left-behind voters immediately after the initial Brexit vote were typically couched as warnings that they had voted against their own best (economic) interests, were likely to regret their decision, and/or would only have themselves to blame when Brexit backfired. In a colourful response to a normative tweet describing the referendum result as 'a "protest vote" & "wake-up call" by citizens who feel left behind & who want to work but can't', another poster derided this as 'a protest vote where they burnt down their own home' and 'sunk their own ship!' Three-and-a-half years later, similar sentiments would be voiced by a tweeter suggesting that 'if people in the north who voted for Brexit/Tories felt left behind before', then 'OOH BOY here we fucking go'. A more exasperated criticism in a similar vein had been posted on the night of the referendum by 'Gothiron', who juxtaposed a line from an article posted by another tweeter – a normative statement about 'towns that have been left behind' – with the (ironic) fact that such areas were 'usually recipients of EU funding when no fucking government' could 'give a stuff'. Another warned that Brexit was 'likely to decimate what's left of British manufacturing' but lamented, 'left-behind voters were&are no longer listening.' And, echoing the impatient *Guardian* poster who had implored left-behind voters to enlighten them on the nature of their 'values' that were 'being ignored', a further critic asked whether, given that '"grievances" seem to revolve solely around foreigners', these were 'what we now have to "understand"?'

This latter tweet was significant in being one of very few from referendum night signalling an overt unwillingness to engage with what it implicitly framed as the prejudice of left-behind Brexiteers. By dismissing such voters' demands for 'understanding' about their immigration concerns with the withering aside 'well, I don't want to', it prefigured a much angrier refrain that would circulate in the small hours of 13 December 2019, as the scale of the Tory election victory unfolded. Among the most vicious was this expletive-ridden rant: 'By the way if you're working class and you voted for Boris because you wanted to get Brexit done, fuck you, you utter fucking moron. I don't want to hear any more about the "left behind". You deserve to be left behind. Cretins.'

Other notable election-night critics included an evidence-based tweeter who recalled their time living in Carlisle, whose residents they dismissed as 'racist twats' who were 'terrified of anyone different'. The suggestion that some voters had seen Brexit as a magic bullet to transform their fortunes was ridiculed in a tweet confidently predicting that not 'a single constituency in the UK that feels "left behind"' would be 'better off from Brexit'. Another mocked the assumed tabloid-reading habits of red-wall voters by describing them as a 'Sun loving, Daily Fail believing working class' who were naïve or stupid enough to 'think he [Johnson] is one of them'. Meanwhile, a US-based tweeter implicitly elided Brexit-backing working-class voters with blue-collar 'Trump people' with whom they worked. Drawing an interdiscursive analogy between Brexit and the then US president's pledge to build a wall to block illegal immigration through the US's porous Mexican border, they added, 'the wall ... is stupid and xenophobic but probably not as self destructive to our economy.'

Perhaps unsurprisingly, plenty of tweeters on both occasions *championed* left-behind/working-class voters – or, at least, repeated increasingly normative truisms about their economic and/or cultural marginalization over the years prior to the referendum. Given that such tweeters were generally on the winning side(s), their tones tended to be less angry than those of disgruntled Remainers/anti-Tories – though some could not resist adopting a triumphalist air. Election-night tweets defending under-represented working-class voters included one echoing remarks by various MPs, 'Lexiter' commentator Giles Fraser, Mattinson's red-wallers and several interviewees quoted in the next chapter by stressing the long-term neglect suffered by post-industrial Stoke under the previously dominant local Labour regime – asserting that they had talked to 'people' in the city who felt the party had 'left them before Corbyn.' Another interdiscursively referenced Clinton's notorious dismissal of blue-collar Trumpists, describing Brexit as 'a howl of rage from left behind "deplorables" [in] ex industrial heartlands' – and warning that (prospective Democratic Party presidential nominee) 'Bernie [Sanders]' would 'crash too' if he ignored it. Conversely, others grateful for the Tory win were keen to stress the importance of Johnson rediscovering 'his Liberal Conservative roots' (as one poster put it) by delivering on his promises to address regional economic inequalities. In an intertextual reference to a 1990s BBC socio-political drama of the same name, they added that 'we need to recognise and reward Our Friends in the North who have made this fantastic result possible.' And, in a succession of tweets that might have been lifted verbatim from the writings of Glasman, Goodhart, or Mattinson, a referendum-night tweeter commented that 'leave won partly by tapping into a labourist common sense' that had 'lain dormant since the 1970s' and was concerned 'not just about immigration' but also 'producerism, contributory welfare, masculinity, patriotism, and majoritarian populism.'

As for the hitherto ignored mass of 'the people', this wider conceptualization of politically and culturally (if not economically) left-behind voters was markedly less evident in Twitter datasets than on comment threads. While references to 'the people' and 'the population' surfaced at times, the term 'silent majority' (so prevalent on threads) was almost totally absent, even if the imagined in-group to which it pertained remained evident. This pattern seemed to point to the relatively greater salience among tweeters of the *working-class* left-behind imaginary than any more all-encompassing one – at least as a locus for debate about shifting patterns of voting in Brexit's shadow. Intriguingly, though, when tweeters criticized Brexit/Tory voters *as a whole*, they tended to be more condescending than condemnatory, let alone socially stigmatizing – in so doing, widening their canvass to critique the imagined silent majority (albeit not in so many terms). One suggested that the Tories had managed to 'fool the population', while another added, dismissively, that 'people will not join up the dots' or recognize 'the consequences of their (voting) action'.

But the most remarkable exploration of the motives ascribed to voters choosing to, in turn, 'take back control' and 'get Brexit done' through these two epochal events was played out in microcosm in a lengthy two-way exchange between an election-night tweeter and a BBC journalist. This lively discussion was initially sparked by a tweet from correspondent Nikki Fox about voting patterns in some working-class areas. It prompted a response lamenting the 'depressing' fact that 'people seem more concerned about Brexit' than 'what is going on in this country'. In a direct reply, Fox argued that Brexit *was* 'about what's going on in this country', as it was 'a protest that people are being left behind': a statement accepting normative characterizations of left-behind voters that arguably strained the bounds of journalistic impartiality. This opened up a remarkable strand of deliberation between two individuals, in which the very terms of the left-behind debate – and understandings of what it *meant* to be (or feel) left behind – became openly contested. 'The people who are being left behind are those living on the streets, those going to foodbanks' and 'Brexit will not make their lives better' argued the tweeter, to which Fox responded that she understood 'people voting' to be 'the working class, electricians, builders, people working their arse off and hoping for a better future for their children'.

Though careful to acknowledge she was 'heavily stereotyping', Fox's characterization played into the well-worn media-political imaginary of the virtuous 'hard-working family/household' (Morrison, 2019a: 121). Perhaps the most significant turn in this exchange, however, came when the tweeter responded by declaring *himself* to be 'working class' – prompting Fox to ask, 'what makes you working class?' In itemizing a list of tropes identified as markers of his working-class status – encapsulated in the over-lexicalized phrase, 'I work in a factory, don't own my house, school education, working class town' – the tweeter offered an intriguing insight into measures of working-classness that were almost entirely *material*, rather than relating to values or worldview. In so doing, he reopened questions around the validity of discourses that manipulate the floating signification of the left behind label to prioritize the *cultural* dimensions of contemporary working-classness over the *economic*.

Perhaps more significantly, this illuminating (if brief) two-way dialogue addressed issues about the nature and motivations of the left behind – or *multiple* left behinds – that moved well beyond the familiar 'culture-war' or economistic characterizations infusing much of the surrounding election-night discourse. In transcending these taken-for-granted tropes, it captured the essence of concerns that dominate the next chapter. These include questions around how we might *widen* normative definitions of the left behind to embrace a more socially, culturally and ethnically inclusive array of economically disadvantaged groups; how such disadvantages intersect with multiple other forms of inequality; how forms of financial and material hardship common to post-industrial communities relate to precarity experienced both *universally* and at the micro level of *individual* households and, crucially, whether current definitions of the term 'left behind' can be considered fit for purpose.

5

Speaking up for the left behind: The voices of disadvantaged Britain

Julie volunteers in a foodbank. Despite suffering from bipolar disorder, she has spent most of her working life juggling low-waged, precarious but demanding jobs while surviving years of domestic abuse. A former NHS mental health support worker, she was forced to quit her last post, as an overnight carer, after being laid off with stress caused by a punishing shift rota requiring her to work 100 hours a week. Although eligible for both Universal Credit and Personal Independence Payments (PIP), she is allowed to keep just £7 a month from this combined income after being cautioned for welfare fraud by the Department for Work and Pensions for using benefits to repay a loan shark. She still owes the DWP £13,000 and fears being indebted for life. Her teenaged daughter has lived since birth with Julie's mother in the next village along the Norfolk coast – an arrangement designed to spare her Julie's abusive former relationship with a 'lifer'. At 39, Julie has never had a foreign holiday.

Sixty-one-year-old Tom has spent most of his life in Bentilee, an area of Stoke-on-Trent classified among the 20 per cent most deprived in England. The son of a miner killed in an industrial accident, aged 22, he worked as a labourer in a textile factory before taking his A-levels at college, then studying for a degree in computing. On graduating into the early 1980s recession, Tom found himself stranded in a city once blessed with abundant employment in mines and pot-banks but now subjected to such rapid de-industrialization that 'it seemed like all the jobs had disappeared.' Alternately rebuffed for being over-qualified or bereft of the right skills to compete for the rapidly depleting industrial jobs on offer, Tom has since spent much of his life unemployed – punctuated by bouts of seasonal data-entry work for Royal Mail at

Christmas-time, deciphering addresses on parcels that computers are unable to read.

Anne-Marie is a 36-year-old married mother, from Rhondda, south Wales, who grew up wearing her big brother's hand-me-down clothes, as her working mother and stepfather struggled to survive on meagre earnings topped up by benefits. After training as a community development worker, she took a career-break to look after her first child, but her family's income plummeted when her husband had to accept a £10,000-a-year pay cut – sending her back into the job market just as the COVID-19 pandemic struck. Anne-Marie's £1,700-a-month take-home pay barely covers her three-year-old son's nursery costs and the couple only manage to avoid relying on foodbanks thanks to emergency loans from family members. As someone who works directly with communities once 'built around' the coalmines, she regularly visits households blighted by long-term illness, overcrowding and reliance on 'cash-in-hand work' or 'zero-hours contracts' for insecure, low-paid jobs.

Zaria is a 49-year-old mother-of-two, from Glasgow, who spent her early adulthood caring for her disabled mother and younger brother before entering into an unhappy Muslim arranged marriage with a man from Pakistan. A former supermarket checkout-worker, she was forced to give up her job after developing hereditary arthritis and degenerative disc disease in her lower back. Having spent years disentangling herself from her ex-husband, she now lives on £128 a week in Employment and Support Allowance, after losing much of her limited income when her youngest child left school – bringing to an end years of child benefit and tax credits. Despite using her local foodbank, in south Glasgow, Zaria often has to choose between heating and eating. She is used to having so little food in her stomach that she 'can't sleep at night', because the one meal a day on which she survives 'doesn't fill me up'.

Tales such as these – of precarious employment, interrupted earnings, punitive benefit sanctions and 'First World' hunger – are hardly peculiar to de-industrialized, left-behind places like Great Yarmouth, Stoke-on-Trent, Rhondda, or Glasgow. Across the UK, in January 2020 (two months before the coronavirus outbreak), 2.8 million people were living on such low incomes that they had to claim the main working-age benefit, Universal Credit (UC) – more than a third of them (36%) in employment (gov.uk, 2020). According to the government's own statisticians, the wealthiest fifth of the population earned twelve times as much as the poorest 20% that year (£107,800 to £8,500), with increasing inequality over the preceding decade directly related to the 'the diminishing effectiveness of cash benefits to redistribute income from the richest to the poorest' and a freeze to the annual uprating of benefits in line with inflation that had outlasted successive earlier periods of austerity and fiscal retrenchment between 1987 and 2016 (ONS, 2021: 2). This is to say nothing of the impact on household incomes of the pandemic itself, which saw some 8.7 million workers 'furloughed', on partial wages, under the UK government's emergency Coronavirus Job Retention Scheme (CJRS); 2.4 million self-employed people claiming help from the Self-Employed Income Support Scheme (SEISS) (Delestre et al., 2020); a near-doubling of UC claimants, which soared to 6 million adults (one in five of the workforce) between 12 March 2020 and 14 January 2021 (gov.uk, 2021a); and a record 200,000 households penalized by the benefit cap of £20,000 (£23,000 in London) – a rise of 13% between February 2021 and the previous quarter (gov.uk, 2021b).

But while Julie's, Tom's, Anne-Marie's and Zaria's stories reflect the experiences of economically precarious people *throughout* Britain, post-industrial places like Great Yarmouth, Stoke, Rhondda and Glasgow all have disproportionate numbers of households in such positions. Fewer than 66% of adults in Great Yarmouth were employed or self-employed during the calendar year January to December 2020, compared to more than 75% for the UK overall, according to labour market figures from the Office for National Statistics (Nomis, 2020a). Of the remainder, 6.5% were unemployed – a rate nearly 2% higher than the 'official' national average of 4.6%. A further 27.4% were classified as 'economically inactive', putting them in a hazy category encompassing everyone from full-time students to carers and those either temporarily or long-term sick/disabled. This compared to a rate of 20.9% for Britain as a whole. Earnings levels were also well below the national average, at just £473 per week for full-time workers, compared to £587 nationally, while only 37% of people had professional or managerial jobs, when the UK-wide level was 50.2%.

Data for the county borough area of Rhondda Cynon Taff was similarly stark, with only 67.3% of the labour force working or self-employed (although the official unemployment rate was the same as the UK's overall). A further 28.8% of adults were 'inactive', 35.5% of whom had long-term illnesses or disabilities – significantly higher than the 23.6% figure for Britain as a whole (Nomis, 2021b). Both gross weekly pay for full-time workers and the percentage of people in professional or managerial jobs were again below national averages, at just under £536 and 48.1% respectively. Although the employment figures for Stoke were fractionally *above* those for the UK – with 75.5% working, compared to 75.4% nationally – 5.3% were unemployed. Of the above-average 22.1% of people counted as 'inactive' in the metropolitan borough, 34.8% were long-term sick or disabled (Nomis, 2020c). As in Great Yarmouth, the proportion of professionals and managers severely lagged behind other areas, numbering just 37%, and weekly full-time earnings were substantially below average, at £512.30. Glasgow City's employment rate was well below the UK average, at 69.6%, with 27% of people inactive – 32.5% of them long-term sick or disabled (Nomis, 2020d).

Places like Great Yarmouth and Stoke also tend to be characterized by a confluence of factors beyond those purely relating to economic disadvantage, according to the Local Trust's 2019 England-focused report *Left Behind? Understanding Communities on the Edge*. These range from their specific demographics (stagnating population growth, disproportionately high white British compositions, above-average levels of lone-person households, and relatively low home-ownership rates) to the fact that they generally have worse health outcomes; lower skills levels, household incomes and 'job density' rates; and commensurately higher post-crash unemployment than other deprived areas (Local Trust, 2019: 12–13). Compounding these problems, the report highlighted that such areas lacked three crucial 'domains' that (when absent) could leave them 'feeling the most "left behind"' (ibid.: 9). These were 'proximity to key community, civic, educational and cultural assets', such as pubs, libraries, green spaces and leisure facilities; 'connectedness', in the form of transport and digital infrastructure, and ease of access to medical services; and 'an engaged community', defined in terms of measurable levels of neighbourliness and activism, and the presence of charities, third-sector organizations and civil society groups, such as community associations (ibid.).

While this book accepts the essence of many aspects of the above definition, it is important to add some important qualifications. Given that the trust was originally founded as a taskforce for operationalizing David Cameron's 'Big Society' agenda, its founding philosophy was underpinned by strong elements of neoliberal ideology, including an underlying belief in the virtues of self-help and entrepreneurship, rather than direct state intervention, as primary tools for promoting economic advancement. Even today, its trustees include Charlotte Pickles, director of centre-right think-tank Reform and a long-time adviser to Coalition Work and Pensions Secretary Iain Duncan Smith, the architect of its punitive 'welfare reform' programme – though it also counts among its board members more left-leaning policy specialists, such as Miatta Fahnbulleh, director of the New Economics Foundation.

Nonetheless, despite offering a far from definitive crystallization of what it means to be left behind, the trust's three 'domains' present a useful starting-point for this chapter, which explores the perspectives of people from places consistently bracketed as such about the nature and complexity of the challenges (and opportunities) they and their communities face. Alongside further testimony from people like Julie, Tom, Anne-Marie and Zaria, we hear from a range of other voices selected from more than fifty semi-structured individual interviews primarily focused on six local clusters representing regions across England and Wales. These interviews were concentrated in and around the former mining town of Edlington in Don Valley, South Yorkshire (North East); the one-time cotton and coal town of Leigh in the borough of Wigan, Greater Manchester (North West); the east coast holiday resort of Great Yarmouth, Norfolk, and its surrounding villages (East); England's erstwhile capital of the potteries, Stoke-on-Trent, and its surrounding hinterland (Midlands); the faded fishing and shipbuilding port of Bideford in Torridge, North Devon (South West), and the former Welsh valleys industrial hub of Rhondda (Wales). Of these, the biggest three clusters focused on Leigh, Great Yarmouth and Stoke – specifically the post-war housing estate of Bentilee and its neighbouring wards, which are among the most deprived in the city. Although this sample did not cover all English and Welsh regions (omitting, for example, England's far North East and the South East), it offered a series of snapshots that, taken together, gave a broadly representative regional spread of left-behind places. Moreover, while the initial interview sample focused on the English and Welsh clusters, these were supplemented at a late stage by twenty interviews with people from left-behind groups in Scotland, including several from two cities identified as facing the 'double whammy' of being historically 'left behind' and 'vulnerable to the immediate economic fallout from the pandemic' in a 2020 Institute for Fiscal Studies report: Glasgow and Dundee (Davenport & Zaranko, 2020: 316).

In selecting interviewees, every effort was made to identify as varied a mix as possible of individuals who could speak from personal experience about what one might crudely term the 'left-behind condition'. Alongside representatives of grassroots civil society organizations – community associations, parish councils, local chambers of commerce – and one past and one present MP, they include people directly affected by economic disadvantage. Crucially, they extend beyond wage-earners on low incomes to pensioners, unemployed benefit recipients and people with disabilities, and Black and minority-ethnic people, as well as those conforming more straightforwardly to classic 'white working-class' left-behind archetypes. We also hear from retired ex-miners, textile and pottery workers, and others with long memories of their areas' past glories – the riches their neighbourhoods and communities have lost over time – as well as representatives of disadvantaged groups sidelined in the national conversation around the left behind, including refugees and asylum-seekers. Full details of the interview methodology, including the sampling approach, are given in Appendix 4.

To help unpack these diverse testimonies, the chapter builds on the Local Trust's 'domains' to propose a tentative taxonomy of *dimensions of left-behindness*. These are common themes, issues and understandings of the challenges facing disadvantaged communities, places *and* individuals that (alone or in combination) might be seen to give meaning and definition to that elusive concept: the *experience of being* left behind. In identifying these dimensions, and recognizing the importance of 'place' to many people affected by economic disadvantage, the chapter strives to move beyond lazy, default diagnoses of the left-behind condition that frame it solely, or principally, as a *situated* phenomenon peculiar to particular (homogenous) groups, such as the post-industrial working class. Instead, the taxonomy aims to recognize aspects of the condition that are much more widespread – even universal – and, as such, experienced by more heterogenous populations.

In so doing, it is worth emphasizing how, with the notable exceptions of the final two, the dimensions identified by representatives of left-behind groups themselves overwhelmingly prioritized the *economic* aspects of what it means to be/feel left behind. This strengthens the argument that, while the left-behind condition undoubtedly encompasses certain important cultural (and political) dimensions, its underlying *drivers* are economic. Moreover, it adds considerable ammunition to the case that the fashionable thesis among politicians and pundits keen to stir the 'culture-war' pot by attributing the resentments of left-behind groups (particularly post-industrial communities) primarily to divergent worldviews may be seriously misplaced.

The proposed taxonomy acts as our guide for much of this chapter, before we briefly turn to considering a question overlooked in the more dispiriting, defeatist narratives about left-behind *localities*: what strengths and advantages do these communities possess, in terms of collective historical identities, legacy industrial infrastructure and present-day social capital, and what signs of progress, rejuvenation and hope are some already starting to see? The five 'dimensions' that form the central spine of the chapter are as follows:

- Degradation of work: precarity, falling wages and long-term economic decline
- Disconnection: weak transport links, poor communication and being cut off

- Erosion of place: industrial shrinkage, decaying infrastructure and heritage loss
- Contested identity: shifting demography, (im)migration and cultural change
- Democratic deficits: feeling unheard, invisible, ignored, forgotten

Degradation of work: Precarity, falling wages and long-term economic decline

One of the most striking themes to emerge from the interview clusters was a sense of communities being fractured, even threatened, by generations of industrial decline and economic stagnation. A common refrain was that mass employment in one or more major industries had offered job security, meaningful skills-based training and reliable (if largely unremarkable) wages, as well as a collective continuity of purpose and solidarity that transcended the workplace to infuse wider civic life. While workers and employers had often been in conflict, the historical strength of trade unions gave them a voice at the negotiating table with legal, moral and material force. Moreover, the work people did – in manufacturing, mining, or other 'heavy' industries – invariably produced physical artefacts that held what Karl Marx termed intrinsic 'use-value' (Marx, 1859 [1911]). By contrast, today's job market offered little more than pockets of precarious, part-time and/or sub-minimum wage employment, invariably in forms of work that seemed to have little purpose. In place of the old certainties of unified, unionized industrial endeavour – and guaranteed employment for anyone willing and able to take it – was a Wild West of zero-hours contracts, unintentional self-employment and periodic bouts of involuntary idleness, as work simply dried up.

'At five o'clock the pavement would be full of people walking back, [because] there was full employment', recalled 75-year-old Jean of her 1950s childhood in Stoke-on-Trent's sunnily named Goldenhill suburb. 'The potteries weren't well paid – it was a very *replaceable* workforce – [but] I don't remember strife and deprivation. I was out a lot and the kids I played with were all in the same road. In Goldenhill, you didn't have posh bits: it was all the same.'

Jean's memories were echoed by Andrea, also 75, who worked as a secretary for a manager of one of Stoke's leading pottery companies during the 1960s. Though scathing about the highly gendered, hierarchical structures and wage differentials that prevailed both within the pottery industry and between it and other sectors, she remembers a time of job security and abundant opportunities. 'The wages were absolutely awful, the jobs were just as awful', she said, describing how potteries were staffed by 'mainly women', working 40-hour weeks as 'a secondary income' that paid far less than their husbands earned in mines or steelworks. 'The snobbery end was the decorating end – Wedgewood and Dalton were the top end – [and] you were considered skilled if you were wheeling', whereas 'you would go down to what they called the "clay end", where you were working on the lumps of clay.' As for the upper echelons of the enterprise, 'the management were really stuck-up and snobbish' and 'had no idea about their own workforce', she said, adding that 'they were all rich, rich, rich – it came from their fathers and their grandfathers – and they had upstairs what they called "the club".' However, what the pottery industry consolidated, in terms of wider class inequalities, it partly made up for by providing thousands of people with stable, secure incomes, skilled apprenticeships and long-term, full-time jobs. Though intense competition between rival factories suppressed wages, at times so many vacancies were available that dissatisfied workers could hawk their wares from one to the other in search of a better deal. 'You could go to one factory in the morning and be at another one by the afternoon', Andrea reflected.

Such memories chimed with those of ex-miner Mike, from Leigh, who described the former pit town as 'a fantastic place to live' when he grew up in the 1960s – a period when 'nobody was claiming benefits, and if they were they were ill.' Though several decades Mike's junior, Great Yarmouth borough councillor Jade Martin also recalled rosier times – remembering how 'everybody used to love to come' to the east coast resort in the years before its appeal was challenged by the increasing availability of cheap overseas package holidays. Today, its other old industries (chiefly North Sea oil and fishing) are also declining and, while it has started to benefit from new investment in offshore wind farms, for now it remains characterized by low-waged seasonal work and a looming social care crisis she blames (in part) on ex-London Mayor Boris Johnson's policy of incentivizing the council to rehouse older people relocating from the capital in retirement. More than 350 miles away in North Devon, meanwhile, another councillor remembered a childhood 'watching salmon fishing on the [river] Torridge'. 'The crane is there, but you don't see ships coming in', observed Jude Gubb, wistfully, of the skyline of her deprived ward of East-the-Water, Bideford – stressing the contrast with a period when 'you used to get two or three ships a week' and she could 'watch the clay trains coming back from Torrington'. Bideford's neighbouring market town was a one-time centre for the extraction of ball-clay deposits exported as a raw material to Stoke's pot-banks, as part of an inter-regional industrial virtuous circle. Reflecting on this, Peter Jones, parish council chair for Forsbrook, a village just south of Stoke, recalled raw materials for pot-banks coming in from other counties, with imports of Cornish china clay ensuring that the potteries were 'not just an industry' in themselves: by 'buying in from other parts of the country', they had bolstered industries elsewhere that were now 'all closed'.

For all their fond recollections of this proud industrial past, many interviewees' memories were scarred by images of its sudden, brutal demise. Reflecting on his part in the 1984–85 miners' strike and the loss to Leigh of 30,000 coal jobs under John Major's 1992–97 government, Mike, 62, recalled the poverty he, his wife and four children endured after his years of secure paid work suddenly ceased. 'You don't know you're in poverty: other people tell you', he said. 'They say, "what's happened to you?"'

Andrea recalled a shameless, unsentimental sell-out of Stoke's pot-banks by the same managers who had lorded it in the good times. Echoing the images of rampant industrial asset-stripping evoked by Labour's John Mann and columnist Giles Fraser in their post-Brexit critiques of globalization, she recalled how, after 'Thatcher finished the mines', the potteries' management 'let us all down, by breaking the industry' – sending skilled potters to the Far East to train the local, low-waged workers who would ultimately replace them. 'My brother-in-law was what they called a mould-maker and he was asked in the early 90s to go to Indonesia to show them how to do this', she said. 'He did go, and then they closed the factory down.' Cllr Jones had similar recollections. 'Where there used to be 100 firms producing tiles, there's one', he said, adding that Stoke's iconic Wedgewood brand was 'now based abroad', as it had become 'cheaper to make it in Spain and Portugal than it was here'.

Such memories were not confined to those whose relatives worked directly in the old industries. Stephen Ruffley, a librarian and project officer for Leigh Neighbours Project, launched in 2012 to spearhead a ten-year programme of sustainable improvements to the town, said industrial jobs had been so plentiful in his youth that, for all the hierarchies of skills and wages, the landscape of entry-level opportunities was far more egalitarian than today's. A preponderance of mills and pits meant 'there was a job for *everyone*' – in other words, 'people of all abilities'. 'If you leave grammar school you're one of the managers or something', he recalled, adding, 'even if you've fluffed every exam you've taken', there was 'a job sweeping up'. Describing previous generations' 'intense pride' at 'being' a 'coal town', he recounted how things had begun to change in the 1970s and 1980s, when 'the pit closed' – with 'all the money that took out of the community'. Shaking his head, he added glumly:

> I knew a guy who was a miner at Parsonage [Colliery], and then he went to work at Golborne, and then Golborne closed, and all that money that goes out of the community … It's like a plant that you've not given enough water to. It's still there – all the kind of infrastructure's still there – but it's just … I'm kind of shrugging my shoulders now … It becomes *wizened* … .

In the eyes of Rhondda's Labour MP Chris Bryant, the slow-burn decay, and eventual collapse, of Britain's industrial base had also produced damaging long-term knock-on effects – undermining work-life balance and family cohesion. 'Within three, maybe four, generations you've got from 110,000 men working underground to none', he said of the coal industry that once dominated life in his constituency. While 'underground [work] was close to your home, using your hands and fists', work was no longer 'done in your area', but 'on a computer or on a phone 45 minutes or so away from your home'. And, far from commuting to well-paid city jobs, like many professionals travelling into London from counties in the prosperous South East, Rhondda's commuters were often 'on quite a low income', working 'in a coffee shop or as a cleaner in Cardiff' – their travel costs soaking up 'at least one or two of the hours you work'. Describing how the landscape of Rhondda was once 'black' with coal, but now had 'herons in rivers and things like that', Bryant likened its single-purpose pit-towns to Soviet Russia's 'monogorods': places purposely 'devoted to a single industry', as 'a deliberate function of communism'. 'Somewhere like Rhondda just did coal – not because someone decided that but because there was so much coal here', he recalled, 'so we became a monogorod, which meant we then had all our eggs in one basket and when that basket no longer provided, there weren't any [more] eggs.'

To some younger interviewees, a drastically depleted industrial base and de-skilled, precarious job market had combined with deepening inequalities around education, training and skills to beget an increasingly polarized local economy – with those brought up in neighbourhoods enduring long-standing disadvantages locked out of the already limited opportunities that still (notionally) existed for other people. Reflecting on the large numbers of children 'excluded from school' in her area, Keri Anderson, a town councillor in the former mining town of Edlington, near Doncaster, said there were 'very few opportunities for employment other than shop workers', meaning that 'young men', in particular, 'tend to find other ways of making money to support their families'. A single mother of three school-aged children, Keri claims Universal Credit herself – to top up her limited income as a sales consultant. But she has a degree in criminal justice; owns her own home on the town's salubriously named Royal Estate; benefited from supportive, relatively 'affluent' parents; and originally trained as a classical ballet dancer before an injury stopped her performing. Though proud of having taken 'every opportunity that was thrown at me', believing that 'it may be advantageous in the future', Keri recognized that 'not everybody has that' – and spoke with evident distaste of the stigma heaped on poorer parts of town by employers, estate agents and older residents nostalgic about the glory days of low crime and full employment. 'If I was looking to purchase a house in this area I would be told about high unemployment rates, particularly in males, young males, a lot of youths not being in schools, single-parent families [and] low-skilled workers', she said, adding, 'to a certain degree, even employers will look at the area that you live in and perhaps peg you with that.' It was 'normal' for people from the 'very large demographic of over-65s' to complain that 'in my day that would never have happened' – helping to 'perpetuate this idea that all youth are bad'.

Concern about younger generations missing out on employment and other opportunities enjoyed by their parents and grandparents was voiced by numerous other interviewees. Reflecting on the decline of his county's once 'thriving' paper factories, Jonathon Prasad, project officer for Lancashire BME Network, described how 'there isn't any industry' today – leaving young people of colour with whom he worked 'feeling hopeless'. In a similar vein, Mike lamented how today's 'kids' were missing out on the 'a job for life' or apprenticeship that, in his day, could 'support a wife and family' – driving many of them towards drugs and crime. For Annie Platts, membership and services manager for Greater Manchester Chamber of Commerce, the lack of clear pathways for young people from school to college or workplace-based training in areas with emerging skills gaps (especially post-Brexit) was spawning an 'invisible' or 'hidden generation' of people who were 'literally coming out of high school or university and … just disappearing' – because 'they're not signing on the jobcentre and they're not working.' The picture was similar in Bentilee, Stoke-on-Trent, one of Europe's biggest post-war housing estates, where a general malaise bequeathed by decades of decline and neglect meant poverty was 'worse', according to community association chair Janet Mason. 'So many people' had 'no expectations', she lamented, adding that young people 'don't have a chance'. Highlighting the plight of 'excluded children' barred from accessing the limited opportunities on offer locally, she said that even 'schools don't want them in because they're from families that have huge problems.'

Disconnection: weak transport links, poor communication and being cut off

Another subject guaranteed to unite interviewees in frustration was their communities' inadequate connectivity to the wider world. The litany of gripes ranged from erratic broadband and mobile signals to closed post offices to a lack of motorways, A-roads and rail links. But by far the most frequently voiced criticism was the state of local bus networks. 'They say the high street has gone downhill – which it has – but why? There's no buses!' exclaimed Cllr Jones, itemizing a range of ways in which this encumbered older people and those without their own transport in the Staffordshire village of Forsbrook. 'You go through [Forsbrook] and you can't get what you want. You want to go into town to get it but there's no bus to take you there', he complained, adding that 'if you want your hair done, there's 11 hairdressers, [but] if you want a post office we haven't got one.' Buses were similarly elusive in nearby Stoke, where, in contrast to the pre-1980s era of the National Bus Company, today 'only one bus goes up' Tom's road in Bentilee each day.

For disabled single mother Dorothy, from Gorleston-on-Sea, a small town to the south of Great Yarmouth, inadequate bus routes presented much more serious problems – at times stopping her accepting job offers or even attending interviews. Dorothy, who had alternated between spells of unemployment and periods working as a care-worker and foodbank volunteer, said 'a lot of the jobs' she 'wanted to go for' were inaccessible, simply because she could not afford her own car and had no other way of reaching them. She recalled once having to walk 'all the way down to the seafront' in Yarmouth for an interview, because there was no bus to take her to the other side of the River Yare (which bisects the town) – making it 'impossible' to reach the appointment 'unless I could get a boat across'. Dorothy's description of bus woes on the Norfolk coast was echoed by Margaret Greenacre, a parish councillor in the neighbouring village of Belton with Browston. She detailed how, despite having a substantial 4,000-strong population, many of them pensioners, Belton no longer had a single GP surgery, after its last one (based in the village hall) closed due to

NHS cuts. As a result, patients now had to travel three miles to nearby Bradwell – forcing many to rely on lifts from neighbours, because there was 'no bus link' between the villages. Both Dorothy and Margaret's accounts of a dysfunctional public transport system failing to meet the needs of those forced to rely on it echoed the experiences of several Yarmouth residents interviewed by novelist Kerry Hudson for *Lowborn*, her 2019 memoir about growing up in 'Britain's poorest towns'. In one encounter, a former schoolfriend explained to her that its town centre had become 'so much quieter' because 'the shops had moved outside' – so 'if you didn't have a car you couldn't get to them' (Hudson, 2019: 224).

As with their memories of better economic times, people's frustrations over deteriorating public transport were invariably tinged with nostalgia for a vibrant, connected past. Lamenting the loss of two out of three train stations that once served Great Yarmouth – the first under the notorious Beeching cuts – Belton parish councillor Ken Botwright recalled how the village had once been 'one big market garden', until the rail links vanished and 'the market garden disappeared.' Asked what magic bullet was needed to revive the area, Ken was unhesitant. 'Infrastructure', he replied. 'If you've got the infrastructure – the roads, the trains etc. – people can get to jobs, but also businesspeople will then be encouraged, if the infrastructure's there, to set up business in that location.' It was a similar tale in North Devon, where trains to the pretty port of Bideford stopped carrying passengers in 1965 and the station shut down completely in 1982 – 127 years after opening. Since then, the only rail link to North Devon – an area of 165,000 people – has been a 'cattle-truck' shuttle, with 'request stops', between its biggest town, Barnstaple, and Exeter in the south, leaving substantial population centres like Bideford and the faded resort of Ilfracombe (whose own station closed in 1970) accessible only by winding A-roads limited to single carriageways for much of their length. 'That was a knife going in', mused Jude, recalling how the closure of Bideford's rail-link soon after her family moved to the town in 1976 had been a catalyst for a 'downward spiral'. 'There were fewer closed shops [then] – you'd go through Mill Street and High Street … Mill Street would be bustling', she recalled, reeling off a list of failed attempts at gentrifying the town centre that have since been thwarted by high rents and business rates for retailers. These include recent efforts to revive the town's 140-year-old 'Pannier Market', which she described as 'empty'. 'The market is owned by the [district] council, but Bideford Town Council lease it [and] they decided they wanted to … refurbish it, so they got rid of everybody and … put in little lodges, like studios, but the rent was too high.'

Far from being a problem confined to coastal backwaters, however, poor train links were also a common complaint among politicians and business leaders across England's post-industrial North and Midlands. 'Stoke is brilliant to get to – it's such an easy place to get to by rail, by car, by train – but once you get here it's a nightmare', Stoke City Council leader Abi Brown said bluntly of the city's internal transport links, adding, 'we have a high percentage of people who don't own their own car and rely on public transport, but our public transport is rubbish.' While this means 'you can get here really easily on the train', a city already encumbered by its 'polycentric' topography was crucially devoid of 'good internal train connectivity'. Weak public transport links was also an issue for businesses across the similarly dispersed town centres of metropolitan Greater Manchester. 'Our tram system runs out into each of the boroughs, but when it gets to the boroughs there's no connection', complained Annie Platts of the dramatic drop-off in provision between well-served Bury and neighbouring market towns like Ramsbottom, while Susan Gredecki, chair of Leigh Neighbours Project, described hers as 'the biggest town in the country that hasn't got a railway station'. Dane Anderton, who represents the deprived ward of Leigh West on Wigan Borough Council, agreed that trains were 'a big issue', as 'only certain parts of the borough' were 'connected to the rail network' – though he added that Leigh had recently benefited from 'a guided busway to Manchester', which was returning on its investment.

Many interviewees emphasized how the sense of being *physically* cut off from other places – including both neighbouring and more distant areas with which they once enjoyed close trading relationships – was exacerbated by inadequate communication infrastructure. 'We have the worst TV signal, the worst mobile coverage [and] theoretically we are all sorted for broadband, but it doesn't feel like that', was Bryant's blunt assessment of the digital and telecommunications services endured by Rhondda residents. Recalling similar problems in North Devon, Rob Passmore, a freelance strategy consultant who recently moved home to Bideford with his family to develop a sustainable economic strategy for the area after a successful career in London, said he was only able to return because of improvements to its digital network, as 'the connectivity wouldn't have been there' previously. To others, poor mobile signals and weak broadband were symptoms of double standards they saw as privileging London (and the South East) over the rest of the country: another manifestation of the real/perceived 'North–South divide' reflected in media-political discourse. Recalling his disappointment on realizing that a flyer posted through his letterbox promising a £23-a-month deal for 'superfast broadband' was meant 'only for the London area', Tom sighed, 'it seems you can't get as fast a speed round here as you could down South.'

Erosion of place: Industrial shrinkage, decaying infrastructure and heritage loss

Closely related to the many impassioned laments about the degradation of contemporary working life; the blight of disused factories, mills and mines; and communities cut off by inadequate roads and closed or mothballed railway lines were interviewees' numerous reflections on how lack of attention paid to conserving, or reviving, Britain's decaying industrial infrastructure had contributed to a creeping loss of civic pride – and, ultimately, community identity. 'It's like a devastation of the past, in a sense', remarked Jean of the demolition of much of Stoke's industrial fabric, adding that the authorities had 'just knocked it down', leaving the city resembling 'a wasteland'. She had 'always had a sense in Stoke-on-Trent that certain areas that should have been treasured have not been treasured by the council or whatever', with only the Gladstone Pottery 'kept as a replica'. Now living in the market town of Leek, on the edge of the Peak District, Jean can survey the flipside of Stoke's abandoned industrial heritage: the slow-burn gentrification of its more picturesque eighteenth- and nineteenth-century buildings. 'I live on a street where there are three mills ... It's been preserved and it's become apartments', she sighed, reflecting how, back in Stoke, locals had 'fought hard' to keep 'in its place' the Spode factory that once revolutionized mass production of bone china – only for it to be converted into 'a "multi-use" thing'. Unsympathetic regeneration attempts had, she argued, undermined locals' 'pride' in their city and the 'sense of home' it had once symbolized. 'Work was hard and there was a lot of illness', she said, reflecting on the Stoke of her childhood, 'but there was "humour": people overcame all that with humour.'

For some, denuded levels of civic pride, and the resulting disconnection with a now widely erased industrial past, were responsible for many uglier trends of recent years, including rising crime. Explicitly reflecting on the disconnect between classroom lessons about the industrial Lancashire of cotton mill-owner Richard Arkwright, Jonathon said, 'we are all aware of that, but it doesn't speak to us – that tradition isn't part of my tradition', adding, 'if I'm being honest, our modern entrepreneurs are the drug-dealers.' Describing how her grandly titled 'Royal Estate' had gradually deteriorated from the 'very, very nice' area it had been when she first moved there to 'the rough end' portrayed by today's local press, Keri said a toxic mix of scarce opportunities, low expectations and lack of tangible connections to Edlington's industrial heritage had combined with the media's tendency to 'continually rake up' its negative reputation to reinforce criminal behaviours – a process Stanley Cohen conceptualized in *Folk Devils and Moral Panics* (1972) as 'deviancy amplification'. While condemning criminality, Keri mused, 'if you tell people what they *are* enough times', they 'start to believe that, and they decide to meet that kind of characteristic.' Wrestling with how a process of industrial decline, and successive failed attempts at renewal, had removed hope and aspiration from younger people, she reflected, 'Edlington itself was associated with the mining industry, but the mines shut down, so people didn't have that industry identification with the area.' While it was still 'a very warm and welcoming community', it had 'been economically deprived for so long' that this had 'become its identity'.

In her community development work in Rhondda, Anne-Marie encountered symptoms of dismantled industry and economic abandonment daily – in the form of gross health, education, employment and income inequalities. She described one of the areas on her patch, the erstwhile colliery district of Ely and Caerau, as 'the biggest council estate in Wales' and, until recently, 'the biggest council estate in Europe', with an average lifespan '20 years younger than in Cardiff' and 'three generations of unemployed'. Like others, Anne-Marie blamed successive governments for allowing whole industries to be erased and washing their hands of responsibility for replacing the jobs that vanished with them. 'They had, like, three factories there but they were all closed down' and 'nothing else was put in', she said. To 39-year-old single mother Jenny, who grew up in Bentilee, the dismantling of Stoke's industrial legacy not only effaced the *positive* civic identity of the past: it bequeathed *negative* 'new' identities which, she feared, were fast becoming antisocial badges of pride for many residents of poorer neighbourhoods. A learner support worker for young people with special educational needs, she recalled the lengths to which she had gone to move her son 'off Bentilee', because, though 'people aren't all bad', she did not 'want him to get involved in gangs'. Describing how 'if you're not from round there [Bentilee] it's not a place where you would want to go in the pub', she added, 'you're either, "oh, I'm from Bentilee" or you want to get away.' Her image of the estate was given a more positive spin by Andrea, who said that 'people love Bentilee', were 'proud to live there' and 'wouldn't want to be living anywhere else'. In describing the neighbourhood in this way, such accounts recalled ethnographer Lisa McKenzie's description of the pride in place displayed by residents of her own estate, St Ann's in Nottingham, where '"being St Ann's" meant a great deal' to locals – almost *because*, not *in spite*, of the fact they were othered by 'those outside of the estate' (2015: 71).

While younger interviewees (especially parents) were preoccupied with social problems caused by decades of decline and underinvestment, those from older generations largely focused on their lucid memories of once-treasured infrastructure and attendant aspects of civic life that had been lost with the collapse of industries recalled from their youth. 'I can remember so clearly starting at the central library in Leigh … one of those fantastic 1960s buildings – contemporary art gallery, meeting room, the vision of the local council in a small mining and cotton town in Lancashire', reminisced Stephen, adding that Leigh's Parsonage Colliery had recently been transformed into 'the Parsonage Retail Park'. 'Even now I can see the winding gear and – there's a kind of traffic light junction – and I can remember sitting there in my car and thinking, "blimey, there's a big sweep on this", and then this coal lorry came round at me', he recalled, reliving his realization: '*that's* why there's a big sweep on this', because it was one of 'these huge bloody coal lorries'. Today, beyond the former colliery-turned-retail park, with its Marks & Spencer, Sainsbury's and out-of-town parking, and one incipient cotton mill conversion into a community/cultural hub, there were only early signs of the plush warehouse conversions crowding the skyline in central Manchester. 'There are large buildings, including ex-cotton mills – if they were in Manchester they would be really swanky apartments and they're empty', he reflected, adding, 'it's just about *investment*: places like Leigh are left behind because they haven't been invested in.'

Among those nostalgic for the lost industrial heritage of these communities were politicians who had represented them, including past and present MPs. Caroline Flint, who lost the Don Valley parliamentary constituency she held for Labour for 22 years in the face of the Conservatives' 2019 'red-wall' insurgency, recalled how 'the dominance of one industry brought not only work but identity and a social glue enhanced by the clubs, culture and sports facilities in each pit community', at the same time creating 'local supply chains and a working community which supported local shops and businesses'. For Bryant, who retained his Rhondda seat with a reduced majority, the old industries fostered not just 'social cohesion' but a spirit of individual and collective self-improvement. He described these spatially isolated, insular communities in terms that sounded more intellectually and politically curious than the socially conservative cultures retrospectively ascribed to them today by the likes of Deborah Mattinson or Maurice Glasman. Using as a touchstone the village of Maerdy, located 'at the top end of the Rhondda valley', and 'very geographically isolated', he characterized it as 'entirely a coal town' – where, in its heyday, 'everyone' was 'working in the mines'. As in other such enclaves, 'the Miners' Welfare Hall would have a library and dances and bars and talks on improving subjects, and all sorts of things like that, as well as sort of a health service' – evidence of how 'the mines promoted a particular version of camaraderie.'

Contested identity: Shifting demography, (im)migration and cultural change

While crumbling collieries, closed railway stations, derelict brownfield sites and swanky mill conversions had all contributed to eroding communities' connections to their industrial legacy, if one other force was at work to undermine their traditional ideas about collective self-identity, it was shifting demographics. In several areas, this was seen to have manifested itself in generational terms, with growing levels of *outward* migration by younger people, lured away from the towns of their birth by the pull-factors of better educational and employment prospects elsewhere – and their more rooted parents and grandparents left behind. But demographic change was also evident in the forms of *inward* migration affecting these communities, as wealthy urbanites and retirees bought up picturesque, if dilapidated, old buildings to convert into plush second homes and Airbnb lets, while residents of run-down estates found themselves living next door to low-waged migrants or rehoused asylum-seekers. While population movements were on a relatively modest scale, in the overall scheme of things, some interviewees suggested their impact was magnified by the economically depressed, self-contained and/or monocultural character of neighbourhoods affected.

In more impoverished communities, such as former pit towns and Stoke's Bentilee estate, the comparatively 'sudden' arrival of visible numbers of additional people, often with complex material and other needs of their own, had caused tensions over the already parlous provision of local services that occasionally turned ugly. Andrea described Bentilee folk as 'quite bigoted' about recent migrants to the area from central and eastern Europe. 'They are saying, "see how they've got that house? It's not right ... My granddaughter can't have that house"', she said, qualifying her comments by suggesting, 'I don't think it's as much *racist*' and adding that 'younger people' were less likely to resent new arrivals and more prone to mix with them socially, because they had been 'brought up with these people'. While Janet dismissed the idea that there had been 'major problems' over immigration, she conceded, 'what people are saying at the school is that nobody speaks English!' Nevertheless, Jenny said she had witnessed at least one example of outright hostility, recalling 'this lovely Polish lady' and 'crimes against her because she was Polish' – though she attributed such incidents less to racism than the fact that 'there aren't enough jobs for people', so 'they've got nothing to do on the estate' other than 'cause trouble'. Reflecting on simmering resentments of a similar kind in Great Yarmouth, Jade dismissed anti-migrant sentiment as 'misdirected anger' over a lack of affordable housing and reasonably paid jobs. Some people, she said, had it 'glued into their heads that refugees come here and are instantly offered a home'.

Stephen recounted how the historical monoculturalism (bordering on mono-ethnicity) of post-industrial Leigh first hit him when he arrived there from central Manchester in the 1980s. 'I can remember coming to Leigh and thinking, "this is so *white*"', he recalled, reflecting on recent tensions he had observed between people from different ethnic groups. Measuring his words, he added, 'People like [Nigel] Farage have legitimized ... being *rude* to people, being rude *about* people' – attitudes he now noticed in the town's surrounding 'rugby league corridor'. Susan, whose grandfather was Polish, recalled how Leigh was once 'known as "white Wigan"'. However, while acknowledging that racism still existed – and had both been expressed and exacerbated by the Brexit vote – she said there was nothing new about resentments between white working-class people and those from other cultures and ethnicities, particularly at times when they were competing for access to the same pressurized public services. 'Through the ages, when people came over from the Caribbean they weren't welcome, the Irish weren't welcome', she said. 'Now it's the Europeans.'

A more uncompromising view of racially tinged resentments and abuse suffered by new arrivals to neglected post-industrial areas was offered by Stuart Crosthwaite, joint secretary of South Yorkshire Migration and Asylum Action Group, who works with refugees and asylum-seekers relocating to escape persecution and trauma in their home countries. He blamed a powder-keg of long-term underinvestment, deep-seated social deprivation, years of post-crash austerity and the lack of a meaningful attempt by central or local government to facilitate integration between native and incoming communities, for the hostile receptions many incomers endured. Pointedly distinguishing between the city of Sheffield and the rest of South Yorkshire, he described how the former's 'strong civil society' had been less 'battered by the 80s and Thatcher' than, say, neighbouring Barnsley, which '*was* mining': 'Sheffield is a university town, there's more money in Sheffield so there's a more diversified industrial base, the biggest employers are the health service, there are 40,000 students here [and] in the centre of Sheffield it's not unusual to see someone with a different colour', whereas 'go to Barnsley and it's a different story'. While not wanting 'to stereotype people in Barnsley', he said there was 'not that culture there' – and, in some pit villages, 'if you are from five miles away you are seen as an alien.' While not quite 'mono-cultural', Stuart described such areas as 'more so than Sheffield', adding, 'when we organize events in Rotherham or Barnsley we are thinking about security.' Condemning the folly of relocating traumatized asylum-seekers to 'already shit-poor' areas, he said he knew people who had 'been put in former mining houses in pit villages', often by private firms contracted to house them by the Home Office, and this had not 'worked out'. In one instance, a 'guy said to me it wasn't so bad as where he came from because at least he only had his windows smashed here!'

In his Lancashire BME Network role, Jonathon also works directly with people affected by racism – though many are British-born casualties of prejudice, rather than first-generation migrants or immigrants. Like Stuart, he attributed much of the *cause* of these racial tensions to systemic economic neglect and underinvestment, even if their outer *expressions* sometimes suggested they owed more to the simplistic narrative of an invidious, simmering 'culture war'. With Lancashire scarred by overcrowded, poor-quality housing, fuel and food poverty and some of the 'worst health outcomes' in the UK, often disproportionately affecting people from minority-ethnic backgrounds, he said politicians needed to make it 'an appealing area to invest in for businesses' – arguing that the region's people, especially those from BME groups, were 'excluded from conversations until the point that they [politicians] *have* to face the difficult realities of what austerity has done to our communities'.

Jonathon's own personal story speaks to the dynamics of the other big demographic changes seen to have affected left-behind post-industrial areas: a generational shift involving significant levels of outward migration by younger people looking for better jobs and opportunities elsewhere. 'Because there aren't jobs … people tend to move away', he explained. 'That's exactly my story – I got qualified and moved away [and] it's only this past year I've come back to the area, for my parents.' This picture of large-scale outflows of younger people was also familiar from Bideford, where retired teacher and veteran district councillor Peter Christie had witnessed 'a huge out-movement of young people' in his decades as a further education lecturer, with 'virtually all' his students migrating 'to large cities'. The only *inward* population movements of any scale had arisen from a combination of 'young families' with no historical connection to the area relocating, often 'for environmental reasons', and 'old people' moving in 'to retire' – thereby further ageing the population and bringing additional long-term NHS and social care pressures. Highlighting a similar inward trend among affluent retirees nestling in the scenic but impoverished Welsh valleys, Chris Bryant described how a 'significant number of people' had 'moved from wealthier parts of England' to buy retirement homes 'where they can see the mountains'.

Democratic deficits: Feeling unheard, invisible, ignored, forgotten

If there was any other recurring concern aired by interviewees across the piece – from people battling disadvantages themselves to those representing groups affected by inequalities – it was the sense that they, their communities and others like them had consistently been ignored, neglected and/or under-represented by national and regional politicians and policy-makers. Although numerous interviewees criticized the lack of private-sector investment in their areas, ultimate blame for this was generally directed at the political class – often conceptualized as a mangled montage of distant, unaccountable Ministers, absentee local MPs and unresponsive councils. It was mention of *these* inequities, above all others, that triggered the widest-ranging discussions, with reflections about being *politically* sidelined leading to (or reanimating) complaints about *economic* neglect and feelings of being left behind.

For Keri, herself an elected town councillor, Edlington felt like 'a left-behind community' because it was somewhere 'that both central government and local first-tier authorities aren't investing in', through 'the right kind of agencies and agency partnerships' and 'opportunities to get people back into work'. She added that, at times, town councillors had 'a fight' to get the police 'interested in anything going on in the area'. Though keen to stress he was 'not being political', Cllr Jones told a similar story about disadvantaged areas of Stoke-on-Trent and its Staffordshire surrounds – implicitly invoking the 'North and South of the mind' by bluntly stating that 'no money was ever put into this town', whereas 'it's been pumped into other regions.' His biggest concern was the ongoing absence of investment in affordable housing locally, which he blamed on a combination of political short-termism and the greed of 'corporations and big businesses'. 'With every planning application the builders always come back half-way through building these properties and say, "we can't do [the] affordable housing"', he sighed. The company behind the latest local development had cut its quota of affordable homes 'from 100 to three' after securing planning permission, while the city council had just given consent to another planned estate, 'but the infrastructure isn't there', with little capacity at the local surgery and a school that now needed to extend to accommodate '300 more pupils'. 'Myself and other councillors think it's deliberate', he concluded, adding that 'nobody believes anything now', because 'no matter what the various political parties are doing, people say, "I'll believe it when I see it"'.

Another person convinced that politicians had consciously deprived post-industrial areas of investment was Stephen. Referring to the neglect of Leigh and 'many' similar towns and villages nearby, he argued they had been '*deliberately* left behind' historically – by a 'system' that was 'rigged' against them. Even today, with the Tories installed at Westminster, Leigh's constituency turning blue in 2019 and Boris Johnson's government repeatedly accused of targeting infrastructural investment at newly captured 'red-wall' seats, to incentivize them to keep voting Tory, he was sceptical that the town would benefit from upcoming bids to the recently launched 'Levelling Up Fund'.

But lack of attention from *government* was only part of the story, according to Caroline Flint. Instead, she argued, underinvestment was often the result of a vicious circle of long-term ministerial neglect combined with an inadequate private sector. She recalled how, even when the 1997–2010 'New Labour' administration had embarked on its large-scale school and hospital-building programme, which relied on public-private partnerships between the Treasury and commercial investors, Doncaster was so bereft of bigger companies that it 'lost out' – because 'the private capacity didn't exist' there in the same way it did in 'wealthier, corporate cities'. As a result, she and other local politicians had 'had to lobby for a change in funding policy to help build new schools our communities deserved too'.

Intriguingly, though, while anger over political inattention and underinvestment was often levelled at distant, unheeding politicians and bureaucrats, several interviewees stressed how it was directed just as often at *local* policy-makers as Whitehall Ministers or mandarins. Reflecting on Bideford's recent failed bid for a grant from a central government-directed 'Future High Streets Fund', Jude insisted that 'government should be helping us more', as 'they're not really giving us anything and so we're on our own.' However, she was also 'pointing the finger at' Torridge District Council, the local authority on which she sat as an Independent. Asked who (or what) her electors blamed for lack of jobs in her East-the-Water ward, following the closure of a succession of relatively large-scale local businesses, including factories manufacturing everything from toy snooker tables to cosmetic pencils, she was unhesitant: 'the council'. 'The East-the-Water councillors always feel they are fighting a battle with Bideford' for funds from both the town and district councils, she said, adding that this led to locals' anger being 'localized' – rather than directed towards London-based decision-makers. This perception that responsibility for underinvestment, lack of infrastructure and opportunities primarily rested with *local* political establishments – especially elected councillors – strongly echoed the findings of Mattinson's 'red-wall' focus-groups, which invariably blamed long-time Labour councils and MPs for service cutbacks and library closures, rather than Tory governments that had imposed austerity on them from afar.

LEFT BEHIND – OR SOMETHING ELSE?

To what extent, then, did interviewees *recognize* and/or *identify with* the term 'left behind' as a descriptor for the condition of their areas and communities, and was it a label they had heard others using – whether to characterize themselves, their neighbourhoods, or groups with which they associated? If not, what (if any) was their *preferred* language for describing their circumstances and those of people like them? 'That's a common term they [people] *do* actually use', said Jude, describing East-the-Water residents' views on the unequal distribution of resources between them, the rest of Bideford and the wider Torridge area. Describing Bideford overall as 'just about hanging on', she added that other people 'would see it as a dying town.' Though characterizing Stoke and its surrounding pottery communities in similar terms, Cllr Jones argued that the fact they were 'on a downhill slope' did not mean they had been 'overlooked' but rather that successive governments had *consciously* left them to fend for themselves – mistakenly assuming their strong historical industrial base meant they were self-supporting. 'Yes, we've been left behind', he said, adding that 'there were so many pottery manufacturers' that 'governments thought, "look how many companies there are!"' and 'it was only when all the threats from abroad came in that they saw it.'

Expanding on this idea, others argued it was *important* to be defined as left behind because this signalled a recognition that their communities had been neglected in the past – and were more deserving of future 'levelling up' than competing neighbourhoods that had been better treated. Evoking similar us-versus-them tensions, Ken and Margaret felt left behind was a more apt description for Belton and neighbouring villages than Great Yarmouth itself. 'Left behind is the language we use because it's true', said Ken, adding that 'the vast amount' of funding was put into 'Yarmouth seafront', instead of 'the villages'. Illustrating this, Margaret stressed how Belton was 'very much left behind' in respect of important 'little things', like 'road repairs and streetlights', that 'happen in the town but not in the country'. But perhaps the starkest example of a willingness to appropriate – even weaponize – the term 'left behind' for the benefit of a community was signalled by Daniel Fell, chief executive of Doncaster Chamber of Commerce, who revealed that it was 'one of those phrases I want to reserve the right to use myself if that's going to help leverage £25 million'.

Others representing groups they regarded as left behind reiterated their accusations that both governments and businesses had *deliberately* left them in this position. Describing asylum-seekers (especially undocumented arrivals) as among the most left-behind groups of all, Stuart said he understood the term as 'being *deliberately* left behind: just abandoned'. Alluding to recent governments' notorious 'hostile environment' policies towards refugees and asylum-seekers, he described them as 'a deliberate attempt to make things bad for people', so they would 'go away' – adding:

> I'm just aware of all the people you don't know and we don't know who are just left out, who right now are scared to go and get a COVID test. One thing I've seen going on is that part of this left-behind thing is creating a precariat, through *policy* – so you go to a car wash and you'll see it a lot in South Yorkshire, you'll see a lot of Kurdish guys doing this work [who were] probably without status … in some ways they've assimilated quite well into these former mining communities, where there's not a lot of money about, there's a lot of informal employment [and] if you're an employer your ideal employee is probably someone you can sack just like that.

Summing up the position of native and migrant workers alike as typified by *degrees* of precariousness, he added, 'there's competition at the bottom between people who are desperate.'

Interviewees querying or contesting the term 'left behind' generally did so because they disliked its underlying inference that their communities were somehow *responsible* for their circumstances – by wallowing in their misfortunes or failing to keep up with the modern world. 'Left behind by *whom*? That's the thing', Jean reflected, when prompted to consider the term's relevance to Stoke-on-Trent. 'There hasn't been the investment in the area … so I do recognize that term – "left behind"– but it's not something people here have done *willingly*, is it?', she said, invoking the concept of a North–South divide by adding, 'they [politicians and businesses] haven't thought it worthwhile to invest' because 'it's all been too much around the southern bit of England.' More dismissive still was fellow 'Stokie' Andrea, who said the term 'makes me quite cross', because 'sometimes I think it's a bit of an excuse: it's saying, "well, it's hard luck for them – that's your lot".' 'I don't want our place to be thought of like that', she said, adding that Stoke was 'not as bad as some places' and she was sick of it being portrayed in ways that made locals 'feel second rate'. Asked how she would prefer Stoke to be described, she said, 'Can we say "moving forward"? Could we move things forward and be brought into line with other places? I suppose our issue is we *are* left behind, but we don't want people to feel sorry for us, do we?' Fell also objected to the label's 'connotation of permanence', recalling 'the absolute bollocking' Boris Johnson had received for applying it to Doncaster as a 'reminder that these areas don't *want* to be left behind!'

To others, the floating signification of the term carried more overtly stigmatizing connotations, recalling other labels politicians and media had used to patronize (or demonize) disadvantaged groups. For Jade, mention of the term 'left behind' triggered an association with 'the "scroungers" label', leading her to reflect that there had 'always been this kind of culture of "us versus them"' directed towards people 'on benefits' – though COVID had shown that 'anything can happen to anybody', as even once 'very privileged' people had been forced to 'rely on the state'. Similar associations were drawn by Ele Hicks, policy manager for Diverse Cymru, a charity supporting people across Wales facing inequalities relating to everything from age and disability to race, gender and sexuality. 'Someone has to have *done* the leaving behind', she argued, adding that this label was just the latest example of the media's predilection for a 'blame culture' and myths about the 'cycle of poverty'. Proposing 'seldom heard' as a more appropriate descriptor for those with often complex, intersectional disadvantages whom she represented, Ele argued that, once labels like 'left behind' were 'invented', 'we end up with a term that's still *blaming* the poor.'

Both Bryant and Flint also aired misgivings. While Flint conceded it was a 'helpful shortcut by national commentators, media and politicians to describe two speeds of British economy – North versus South; city versus town', she argued it would be 'more relevant to talk about former mining communities, who hate the term "deprived community", or small towns'. In a lengthy criticism of the way in which the term had been lazily applied – by London-based journalists and in-denial Remainers alike – as a discursive shorthand which failed to capture the essence of why areas like Don Valley felt unheard, she added:

> After the referendum there was much talk about the 'left-behind communities' but it allowed commentators and politicians to avoid what these communities wanted: more control on immigration and to leave the EU. Of course, Don Valley communities want a greater slice of the cake from London, the South and their regional city neighbours. It bothers people [that] their banks and high streets are in decline and another bus service has been cut. These concerns encouraged some to think that diverting discussion to a more general economic malaise and how leaving the EU would make that worse would somehow change these Leave voters' minds. But you can't get permission to be heard on poverty, homelessness, free broadband and the rest of the Labour manifesto when Labour isn't listening and delivering on their most important demand. Even after Labour's defeat in 2019 politicians hid behind the 'left-behind' narrative rather than face the fact that Labour's second referendum/Remain position was the primary reason we lost 'red-wall seats' and majorities tumbled in many others.

For Bryant – who preferred the terms 'post-industrial' or 'peripheral economy' to describe areas like Rhondda – a primary concern was to avoid left-behind discourse becoming internalized by his constituents as a 'grievance machine'. Force-feeding disadvantaged people narratives of hopelessness could, he argued, discourage ambition and convince them they were doomed to lives of failure. Describing 'victimhood' as a 'vicious circle' and 'inequality' as a force 'that holds the whole of the country back', he echoed Keri's remarks about the self-fulfilling nature of negative portrayals. 'If you think people in Rhondda are portrayed badly on television', he said, 'you might be less likely to think, "I want to be a barrister"'.

FROM LEFT BEHIND TO RIGHT AHEAD? GREEN SHOOTS AND FUTURE HOPES

What, then, were the medium- to longer-term prospects for these (disputably) left-behind areas and their often multifaceted, diverse and intersecting communities? For all the deep-seated inequalities and other challenges almost all interviewees agreed their towns and neighbourhoods faced, many of those elected or appointed to *represent* them saw at least some grounds for optimism. While Leigh was wrestling with huge conundrums over how to rejuvenate swathes of land left contaminated by centuries of mining and milling to provide for families in desperate need of affordable housing, one of the most heartening developments Dane had observed was how some investors had been 'repurposing mills' – whether as retail outlets, housing, or hubs for a mix of 'for-profit' and 'voluntary and community businesses'. Under powers bestowed by Whitehall on the Greater Manchester Combined Authority and its elected mayor, Andy Burnham (the town's ex-MP), the borough council had also intervened to moderate the impact of years of austerity by setting up 'some big community-led organizations' to 'take on things the council couldn't do' anymore.

Fell described Doncaster's position as a similar mix of 'glass half-full' and 'glass half-empty': while the town was blighted by pockets of 'third- or fourth-generation unemployment' and still sometimes 'defines itself by the things it can't do, not by the things it can', he pointed to a recent Centre for Cities report ranking it the fourth fastest-growing town in England and reeled off a list of upcoming 'transformational' projects – from a new airport, shopping centre and theatre to 'significant investment' in its world-famous racecourse. Although the town's good 'connectivity' meant that many of its biggest employers were warehouses and out-of-town distribution centres – and there were 'multinational companies' whose 'most senior employee in Doncaster' was 'the warehouse manager' – it also benefited from 'brilliant civic-minded employers', like Edlington-based Polypipe.

Similarly positive stories emerged about the resilience of community spirit. If solidarity no longer existed in poorer areas of post-industrial Stoke or Wigan, then no one seemed to have told Janet's Bentilee Volunteers or the Leigh Neighbours Project. While confessing her frustration with other people in 'early retirement' (like herself) who were less inclined to 'put something back', Janet had assembled a band of committed activists who increasingly found themselves providing vital grassroots services no longer offered by a cuts-ravaged city council. These included everything from a donation-based furniture-cum-white goods store for those unable to afford essentials like sofas or fridges, to a youth club, activities for excluded schoolchildren and a learning and activity group for adults with learning disabilities. For Susan, meanwhile, the communitarian values driving the work of Leigh's volunteers were demonstrated in everyday encounters across the town. 'The people in Leigh are very friendly', she said, recalling how a visitor from Warrington attending a then recent community festival had told her, 'I love coming to Leigh, because people talk to you.'

What emerged from all these anecdotes was a sense that, even in neighbourhoods riven by ingrained inequalities, unfit infrastructure and simmering tensions between groups competing for the meagre resources and opportunities available, substantial numbers of people (perhaps the majority) were committed to doing what they could to hold their communities together – battling to unite them in a shared recognition that the *causes* of their disadvantages lay elsewhere, not among those on neighbouring streets or estates fighting for the same scraps from the top table as themselves. Allied to this was a sense from many accounts that neighbourhoods that had once been easily compartmentalized as 'white working class', even mono-ethnic or monocultural, were becoming increasingly variegated – if more rapidly in some cases than others. Summing up this feeling of complex communities struggling to both adapt and stabilize at the same time, often with limited help from outside, Keri insisted that Edlington was (warts and all) 'a really good place to live in terms of community'; one where 'people really do pull together.' In a phrase that might almost have been invented to describe left-behind neighbourhoods, whether real or imagined, she added, 'it really is a lovely community: it just has its issues.'

Conclusion
Towards a manifesto for 'unite and rule'

Popular narratives about politics and society depend for their power on how closely they resonate with our lived experiences and our perceptions of what aligns us with (and distinguishes us from) our fellow citizens. Our sense of connectedness to the body politic often rests on our ability to identify with particular 'in-groups' – invariably in competition with, or opposition to, one or more 'out-groups'. Although we may sometimes view competing groups with sympathy, even empathy, the insular and polarizing worlds we frequently inhabit as social, economic, political – and media – actors can have the effect of reducing them to 'others': objects of curiosity, consternation, resentment, ridicule, or blame. In the years encapsulating the UK's 2016 Brexit referendum, a new popular imaginary emerged as a locus for such sentiments, one which would come to define the terms of political debate around British society, economy and culture for years to come: the left behind.

Though consistently associated with monocultural post-industrial towns populated by an under-siege, dispossessed 'traditional' working class – a homogeneous imaginary largely racialized as white – the left-behind concept has become increasingly intangible since it was first popularized in the elite discursive spaces of think-tank reports and academic monographs almost a decade ago. In the swirling slipstreams of the referendum and subsequent elections, settled early definitions have increasingly been challenged by political and media actors eager to appropriate and weaponize the left-behind narrative (and left-behind communities themselves) for their own ideological and commercial ends. Today, the term 'left behind' (applied adjectivally or as a noun) is no more than a floating signifier. Sketched in bold strokes, it is a nebulous rhetorical shorthand interchangeable with words like 'marginalized' or 'disadvantaged'. Yet it swiftly becomes subject to intriguing semantic and associative variations when deployed more narrowly and in other contexts – especially in the service of specific political projects. Thus, while media and political discourse was initially dominated by economistic definitions foregrounding the *material* inequalities affecting the left behind, over time this thesis has been challenged by rival diagnoses. Chief among these is a culturalist narrative focusing on the decline in wider society of traditional values ascribed to left-behind communities – including a complex intermeshing of hyper-local and national patriotism.

This culturalist reading has increasingly been exploited by the populist Right to appropriate the left behind as a divisive concept: constructing it as one 'side' in a long-rumbling, but ever-more explosive, 'culture war' between liberal and conservative, metropolitan and provincial, young and old voters with (supposedly) fundamentally incompatible ideas about their country and its place in the world. Given the neoliberal ideologies of many of those most keen to promote and inflame this culture war, it is surely not fanciful to view this thesis as (at least in part) a convenient vehicle for discursive displacement: a distraction from the true drivers of left-behind discontentment, principally austerity, underinvestment and economic inequality, that they are reluctant to address.

Taking its cue from the term's original application (at least in the present epoch), Chapter 1 explored the evolution of two qualities persistently associated with the left-behind concept in media, political and academic discourse(s) since the prospect of Brexit first cast its ominous shadow over the public sphere during the Coalition years: the British working class and its intersection with historical currents of small-c (and, occasionally, big-C) 'blue-collar' conservatism. In doing so, it showed how the industrial foundations, and associated intergenerational certainties, seen to have once typified 'working-class Britain' were already quietly fracturing many decades before being assailed by Thatcherism, globalization and the wholesale ensuing neoliberalization of economy, society and government. It also explored an uncomfortable alternate genealogy of left-behind discourse, conceptualizing it as the latest branch in a centuries-old family tree of stigmatizing imaginaries that have sought to 'other' groups judged to be non-productive, burdensome, ignorant and/or behaviourally deviant. Viewed through this prism, the left-behind narrative slots into a dispiriting continuum of mythologies associating it with supposedly endemic unemployment and cycles of deprivation that have repeatedly cast large swathes of people onto a metaphorical societal scrapheap – from Victorian concepts like 'the residuum' and 'dangerous class' to the 'underclass', Tony Blair's 'workless class' and denizens of David Cameron's 'broken Britain'.

In framing socially excluded groups as 'the forgotten people' – a clear forerunner of today's left behind – New Labour at least had the grace to acknowledge they had been 'cut off from society's mainstream' by decades of underinvestment and lack of opportunity (bbc.co.uk, 1997). However, in explicitly linking the collapse of manufacturing jobs and 'old industries' with the plight of 'households where three generations have never had a job' (a claim strongly disputed by academics – see MacDonald et al., 2014), it constructed an implausible contradiction: positioning such communities as, simultaneously, both direct casualties of *sudden* mass job losses caused by de-industrialization and festering hotbeds of *intergenerational* worklessness.

Having excavated the antecedents and origins of left-behind discourse, Chapters 2 and 3 mapped out its mobilization in the context of the turbulent early life-cycle of Brexit: specifically, the three-and-a-half years between the referendum and the Labour Party's fabled 'red-wall' rout at the 2019 general election. While framing analysis demonstrated that the left-behind concept was predominantly portrayed in *economic* terms during this period (by politicians and press), in unpacking its transmutations over time it identified the early prominence of rival depictions, including a perhaps unsurprising pre- and immediate post-referendum focus on *political* disconnection: the sense that some voters rebelled against feeling left behind (or left *out*) not by macroeconomic forces but distant, unresponsive elites. More significant, however, was the creeping increase in *culturalist* frames constructing the left-behind condition as a state of mind or sense of identity relating as much to values and worldviews as material circumstances. This saw the growing proliferation of a strain of left-behind thinking that had first emerged, *before* the referendum, in the ruminations of political scientists concerned about the resurgence of right-wing populism – one associating the term with a diminishing (if still substantial) socially conservative working class, increasingly at odds with the liberal mores of younger middle-class graduates, or 'modern' Britons generally. Yet more prominent than either straight political or culturalist readings of the left-behind were *hybrid* representations diagnosing it as a consequence, symptom and/or expression of a *combination* of economic, political and/or cultural factors.

In the context of the years-long economic and political whirlwind culminating in Brexit, the concept of a socially conservative post-industrial (white) working class that felt left behind by Westminster politicians' slow-burn metropolitan drift, blamed (im) migration for pressures on jobs, housing and public services, and held out-of-touch political elites responsible for all of the above was first exploited by Nigel Farage and UKIP. Spying an opportunity to racialize the consequences of the 2007–08 financial crash and a divisive, ideologically driven austerity programme, he cynically stoked resentments whose underlying causes were economic and political in the service of a largely *culturally framed* campaign for a EU referendum (and British withdrawal) for which he had long agitated from the side-lines.

Nearly two years before the Brexit vote, Farage used a party conference speech in Doncaster (then Labour leader Ed Miliband's constituency) to stress-test the slogan that would toxify the messaging of both official and unofficial Leave campaigns – declaring, 'we must take back control of our border' (cited in Stewart, 2014). A year later, shortly before the launch of formal referendum campaigning, a fringe event at the same conference was headlined, 'Who stands up for the working class?' By the time of the referendum itself, UKIP's rhetoric had tipped into full-blown culture-war mode, amplified by an 'unofficial' Leave campaign which reached its baleful apotheosis a week before the historic vote – on the very same date that a Labour MP known for her work with refugees and migrants was murdered by a far-right white supremacist. In launching his now-notorious 'Breaking Point' poster, depicting a snaking queue of Syrian asylum-seekers (*not* intra-EU migrants) crossing the Croatia-Slovenia border (*not* entering Britain), Farage appeared intent on triggering a moral panic about invading foreigners indebted to a malign amalgam of racist imaginaries, from Enoch Powell's 1968 'Rivers of Blood' speech and various later 'crises' around the supposed criminality of young black men to images of swarming refugees in Nazi propaganda.

Four years on, eyeing similar political opportunities, Boris Johnson discursively co-opted the left behind to exploit fertile new recruiting grounds from which to annex Labour heartlands despairing at that party's confused, dissembling position on Brexit – promising to end parliamentary paralysis, implement the referendum result and 'level up' economic opportunities and infrastructure across the country by investing in areas long overlooked by Westminster and Whitehall. In the lead-up to the 2019 election, it suited the Tories to frame the newly christened 'red wall' primarily in *economic* terms, disingenuously portraying the areas it comprised as having been 'left behind by *Labour*' (and the EU), rather than successive Tory-led governments or the neoliberal settlement they had long championed (Davison, 2019). At times, this discourse resembled the double-think of Orwell's *1984*: for Winston Smith's fevered rewriting of the history of Oceania, and its supposed forever-war with Eastasia, read 'it was Labour/the EU, not Tory austerity, that closed SureStart centres and slashed benefits.' Pre-eminent in this discursive strand – articulated as vocally by the Conservative Party's 'Northern Research Group' as the All-Party Parliamentary Group for 'Left Behind' Neighbourhoods – has been the symbolic imaginary of a 'North and South of the mind', which, at times, has had as much to do with fuelling (real or exaggerated) divisions between Leavers and Remainers, graduates and non-graduates, and metropolitan urbanites and provincial townsfolk as identifying and addressing genuine material disparities between left-behind regions of 'the North' and the prosperous South-East.

As Tom Hazeldine recognized in his insightful 2021 book *The Northern Question*, the historically hardwired concept of a 'North–South divide' *does* have tangible, well-documented historical roots – even if the geographical fault-line separating these two super-regions remains fuzzy. In truth, though, 'the North' has not always been the poor relation. For all the 'low-wattage' nature of its 'regional identities' and supposed shared sense of 'cultural belonging', it has often been Britain's social and economic *engine*, driving its forward progress rather than wobbling wildly at its rear, like a clumsily towed trailer the prosperous South would happily see career off into the distance, abandoned and left behind (Hazeldine, 2021: 4). As he argues, the role of industrial northern communities in Britain's 'pioneering Industrial Revolution' was one with 'a stronger case for priority in the world-historical reckoning than anything the rest of the country can boast', excepting London's historic role as 'capital of empire and high finance'. Immediately after the First World War, the economies of the North and South East (including London) accounted for 30 and 35 per cent of UK gross domestic product (GDP) respectively, putting them 'roughly on level pegging' (ibid.: 1).

Since the 2019 election, the Tories' newly (re)discovered rhetorical affinity with working-class 'angels in marble' – and that of their socially conservative media cheerleaders – has increasingly morphed into propaganda designed to foment conflict over cultural issues, framed (with Downing Street's tacit approval) as a 'war on woke' by everyone from Johnson's own former paper, the *Daily Telegraph*, to the libertarian Campaign for Common Sense (Lehain, 2020). As Chapter 2's discourse analysis demonstrated, having collaboratively (or competitively) *defined* the left behind, politicians and media set out to *problematize* them, alternately defending their concerns about democratic deficits, economic abandonment, austerity and the impact of migration on wages and jobs, and deriding the misdirected fire they had trained at the EU and Labour, and their (supposedly) old-fashioned, prejudiced values. Initial reactions to the referendum saw commentators across the political spectrum strain to 'understand' and empathize with the left behind, as it became clear many communities fitting this loose descriptor had voted to leave the EU. Liberal-Left and/or Remainer commentators – often elite 'outsiders', with no long-standing connections to the areas and communities they strained to speak up for – generally emphasized economic factors contributing to their sense of neglect and disillusionment, with 'Lexiters' also stressing the democratic deficit/lack of accountability issues around the EU/distant politicians.

But while right-wing actors also initially acknowledged the economic dimensions, spying yet another opportunity to rewrite the left-behind narrative in pursuit of their own ideological ends, they swiftly became vociferous promoters of a rival thesis. As this version of events had it, the grievances and resentments that had spawned post-industrial areas' justifiable backlash against the status quo related less to macro-level structural economic inequalities than micro-level concerns about queue-hopping EU migrants/immigrants on NHS and housing 'waiting-lists', and a simmering clash of values between the cultural custodians of hard-pressed traditional communities and marauding waves of foreigners whose beliefs and behaviours were alien to them. According to this sub-Faragist 'culture-war' narrative, the schism between working-class voters and metropolitan elites (particularly Labour's leadership) had primarily been *caused* by a disconnect between bourgeois, socially liberal cosmopolitans and champagne socialists obsessed with 'woke' causes, and their patronized, taken-for-granted and/or despised (socially conservative) one-time core voters.

As culturalist frames grew in prominence, they were increasingly addressed (often defensively) by the liberal-Left itself, which found itself fighting a rear-guard offensive against values *ascribed* to the left behind in terms veering between confusion, condescension and contempt. All the while, Centrist Remainers were mired in a no-win discursive space: liberated to criticize a voting segment apparently lost to them electorally, while battling to uphold their better instincts not to dismiss the popular imaginary of such groups as nativist cultural throwbacks or, worse, racist 'Little Englanders'. Yet while it was easy to become distracted by and/or embroiled in this overheated debate, how credible *was* the 'culture-war' thesis when no two commentators seemed able to agree on a settled definition of the left behind – let alone the precise nature of the cultural upheavals that had so disempowered them? Moreover, how incongruous was it that many of those most vocally championing the left behind against the sneers and disgust of the (real or imagined) 'liberal elite' – from Farage to Johnson – were not working-class themselves but rather metropolitan 'outsiders' from vastly more privileged, elite-educated backgrounds, who had benefited personally, professionally and politically from precisely the same cultural (and economic) inequalities they now professed to disavow? Just as implausible was the spectacle of long-time evangelists for the neoliberal economics that had subjected so many left-behind areas to 'managed decline', de-industrialization and years of depressed wages, austerity and benefit cuts suddenly claiming to be standard-bearers of a new era of 'Levelling Up' – another empty signifier as elusive and devoid of meaning as the term 'left behind' itself.

Naturally, the most critical representations of Britain's left behind were to surface on social media. On the night of the referendum itself (one of two key discursive moments sampled for Chapter 4's Twitter and comment thread analysis), reactions to the mass Brexit vote in many post-industrial areas was broadly sympathetic to working-class voters – including on Left-leaning sites, among self-identifying liberal-Left commentators. The focus of debate and balance of sentiments among newspaper readers tended to strongly reflect the way left-behind groups were framed by articles they accompanied, suggesting that the 'version' of the left behind and/or degree of sympathy towards them conveyed by journalists exerted strong agenda-setting effects. But, significantly, though the left behind were constructed (at least partly) as an *economic* phenomenon on both Twitter and threads, even at this earliest stage there were signs of a fast-emerging recognition of the *cultural* dimensions of their condition, particularly on www.theguardian.com, where the articles' accompanying comments explicitly focused on the growing values divide between Labour and its traditional voters.

Over time, however, a stark divergence in understandings of what it meant to be (or to *have been*) left behind emerged between liberal and conservative sites. Self-identifying right-wing commentators broadly became more sympathetic towards the Brexit-backing working class – especially as the scale of their drift away from Labour emerged – while left-wingers grew more hostile. By far the most vitriolic and dismissive posts about such voters were found on Twitter, where, by the night of the 2019 election, commentators despairing at the fissures in Labour's 'red wall' began to drop any pretence of empathizing with left-behind voters – deriding them as everything from 'racist twats' to 'cretins' and 'utter fucking morons'. Conversely, in more conservative-inclined online spaces, such as www.thetimes.co.uk, there was a growing sense of affinity with – and responsibility towards – working-class voters framed as having 'lent' their votes to the Tories. More intriguingly, discussion of the 'classic' left-behind imaginary – post-industrial red-wall voters – was balanced by the emergence of an intriguing late variant of the Faragist idea of an anti-elite, *politically* left-behind mass movement: a construct, variously crystallized on social media as 'the people' or 'the silent majority', with which many posters associated *themselves*.

If Chapters 2–4 were concerned with the social construction and negotiation of left-behind *discourse* in the public sphere, Chapter 5 took an exploratory look at how the term is received and perceived by people from communities to which it has been applied. From ex-miners and millworkers to businesspeople, librarians, parish councillors and community activists, it found there was widespread identification with the concept – even among actors who (though living and working in areas tagged with the left-behind label) might themselves be described as middle class and/or materially comfortable. In both their reflections on the term's usefulness and wider observations about the challenges facing their communities, they collectively constructed a montage of 'dimensions of left-behindness', ranging from insecurities fuelled by precarious low-paid work, high-cost (but poor-quality) housing and mounting household debt, to a sense of dislocation caused by inadequate transport and communication infrastructure, to a feeling of being 'invisible' to distant, unresponsive politicians and bureaucrats – from Parliament and the EU to local MPs and councils. Crucially, there was also considerable agreement on many of these dimensions of disadvantage among people from seldom-heard groups largely omitted from the national conversation around the left behind, but arguably deserving of inclusion. These ranged from a Glaswegian daughter of Pakistani immigrants to charities representing migrants, BAME groups and/or the disabled.

Despite being drawn from a purposively sampled geographical spread of areas identified as 'left behind' in numerous previous studies and reports, these 50-plus interviews could only begin to unpack the concerns and perspectives of the multiple intersecting (and often far from monocultural) communities to which they were home. Nonetheless, beyond the fivefold taxonomy of left-behindness they articulated, important patterns emerged in relation to how people conceptualized the overall position of themselves, their communities and their surroundings. The issue of cultural clashes between 'indigenous' and immigrant populations *was* raised by some people, often without prompting: a veteran Labour councillor for Leigh mentioned sensitivities about different attitudes to disposing of household rubbish between long-time residents and a recently arrived Roma community, while a migrant support worker spoke of how police in South Yorkshire had remarked to him that it 'isn't a great idea' to house asylum-seekers in 'already "left-behind"' neighbourhoods where 'there's a swastika around the corner.' Overall, though, *economistic* diagnoses of the disadvantages affecting these communities undoubtedly dominated – with even the most candid interviewees largely rationalizing cultural tensions as *symptoms*, rather than causes, of problems they attributed (in one way or another) to de-industrialization, underinvestment, austerity and neoliberal economics. Put more prosaically: in the end, there were relatively few complaints about immigration, or incompatible values and customs, but there was plenty of moaning about buses!

TOWARDS MORE *INCLUSIVE* IMAGES OF EXCLUSION: EXPANDING THE LEFT-BEHIND IMAGINARY

If one abiding take-home message emerged from the nexus of meanings and associations ascribed to the term 'left behind' over time, it was that settled, universal definitions of the concept (and its 'causes') were hard to come by – and agreement about remedies for the left-behind condition even less so. But not only was the left-behind label the perfect floating signifier, allowing politicians and the press to tug it this way and that to suit their ideological, political and/or commercial purposes at any given moment: it often acted as the discursive trigger for passionate and, at times, vitriolic debates, both in the heated pressure-cooker spaces of social media and across the wider public sphere. In other words, the left behind has been toxified to become an invidious and incendiary imaginary – whether operationalized as a derogatory descriptor for a malodorous out-group of under-educated, nativist and/or welfare-dependent 'white trash', or as an expansive *in*-group with which many of the most vocal pro-Brexit commentators proudly associated *themselves* (however implausibly).

A consistent *absence* in left-behind discourse exposed by this analysis has been the welter of groups and individuals beyond the nebulous white working-class imaginary who might, with some justification, be described as forgotten, neglected, overlooked and economically and/or politically marginalized. If, for a moment, we broadly accept the validity of the term 'left behind' – the premise that, in a world constantly at war over words and bereft of a common language to describe most social phenomena, this label is as good as any – how *should* we define it? The received wisdom of the 1980s, 1990s and much of the Noughties was that globalized markets – for goods, services and labour – were both desirable and inevitable. As then Prime Minister Tony Blair famously declared in a 2005 Labour conference speech since viewed as a watershed moment in accelerating his party's drift away from its long-time working-class base, the unstoppable tide of globalization, low-cost imported labour and mobile capital was 'indifferent to tradition', 'unforgiving of frailty' and 'no respecter of past reputations': a 'reality', he argued, that British workers (and Labour itself) should embrace rather than oppose, by becoming 'swift to adapt, slow to complain, open, willing and able to change', so that they could '"own" the future' (Blair, 2005).

Blair's clinical prognosis both echoed and subverted the breathless evangelism of early proto-globalizers and Internet pioneers, with their excited proselytizing about the empowering cultural, socioeconomic and democratic possibilities of 'the global village' (McLuhan, 1964) and 'information superhighway' (Gore, 1994). Yet, wind forward nearly three decades and it is hard to see any tangible evidence for these benefits in the lives of multifaceted, but collectively disempowered, social groupings like the precariat: that amorphous army of zero-hours, gig-economy, temporary and/or part-time workers whose often vital contributions to society have only now begun to be recognized during our many warehoused months relying on doorstep deliveries and occasional supermarket outings in the throes of the COVID pandemic. Today's young, urban, cosmopolitan, (literally) mobile Deliveroo drivers may all be 'digital natives' – with smartphones in back pockets and levels of quotidian technical knowhow undreamt of in 'New Labour's' day – but in so many other ways they are shorn of the basic tools enabling them to play a full part in an unforgiving global marketplace, from regular, decent pay and legally enforceable employment rights to access to affordable housing and meaningful education and training opportunities.

None of this is to say anything of the *political* disenfranchisement affecting various groups – from supposedly 'undeserving' populations, including serving prisoners, 'undocumented' asylum-seekers and immigrants awaiting formal 'settled' status, to the manifestly 'deserving'. These include homeless people, those detained under mental health legislation and countless 'legitimate' intra-EU economic migrants who, for many years, have forged new lives for themselves and their families, worked alongside UK colleagues and paid UK taxes, yet been treated as second-class citizens, shorn of social security entitlements or voting rights for anything other than local and European elections – even during Britain's long years of EU membership. This is to say nothing of a rapidly emerging segment of the country's 'real' left behind: the disproportionate numbers of low earners, Black and minority-ethnic people and/or migrants who (for whatever reason) have not been vaccinated against COVID-19, and have found themselves ever more excluded from prosaic but important forms of social life through the creeping introduction of various forms of 'vaccine passport'.

At the time of writing, a lively debate was gathering steam about the chronic labour shortages emerging as Britain's economy finally restarted in the wake of the pandemic – and the impact of declining post-Brexit migrant worker flows was finally exposed. Day after day, the bosses of haulage firms, horticultural businesses and motor industry suppliers were on the airwaves despairing of their inability to recruit sufficient replacement employees from Britain, despite rising unemployment caused by COVID. Alighting on this, tabloid depictions of low-waged hospitality workers had begun to steer uncomfortably close to scrounger discourses of old – with one June 2021 *Daily Mail* headline ventriloquizing a hypocritical plea from Brexit-backing Wetherspoons pub-chain boss Tim Martin for a 'liberal' migration policy to stem staff shortages he blamed on 'British workers … happy "sitting on furlough getting 80% pay"' (Scully, 2021).

Yet what was largely missing from these reports, and accompanying analyses, was any adequate discussion of an uncomfortable truth: the fact that shelf-stackers, HGV drivers and fruit-pickers had long been subject to debilitating working conditions and/or risible piece-rates necessitating Herculean levels of effort and endurance to cover even their most basic living costs. Why should *anyone* – 'indigenous worker' or migrant – be prepared to work on such terms, and what do these dire shortages expose about the track-records of seldom-interrogated sectors in offering basic standards, from job security to paid holidays to a real living wage? As Felicity Lawrence put it in the *Guardian*, 'conditions, as much as pay, underlie the refusal of British workers to do these jobs' (Lawrence, 2021). They are not simply 'idlers who prefer their paddleboards to a bit of graft', as 'some cabinet ministers would have us believe'; rather, 'industry has made these vital jobs incompatible with any normal settled life', to such an extent that 'only desperate people, from poorer countries, will take them, and then only long enough to earn what they need to establish a better life back home, or long enough to learn English and move up the employment ladder in Britain.'

This leads neatly into discussion of that other key problem with commonplace characterizations of the left behind: the narrowness of their *ethnic* focus. Even away from the news media and political discourse – in the wider realms of popular culture – attempts to wrestle with the socioeconomic-cum-cultural condition of left-behindness have generally cast it as a state of post-industrial marginality. The BBC's self-explanatory *White* season – broadcast four years before the Brexit referendum and two before the term 'left behind' began being popularized – painted an archetypal picture of 'English national identity', as 'emblematically attached to members of the white working class', which sociologist Steph Lawler forcefully critiqued as '*extreme* whiteness' (emphasis added). This was a delineation of 'white' that had 'shifted its meaning' from 'something normal, normative and unmarked' to become 'a marked – and markedly problematic – category that is applied only to *some* white people', positioning them 'in the past', by 'marking' them as culturally/economically primitive (Lawler, 2012: 409). Much more recently, away from the multiracial scrounger-baiting of Channel 4's *Benefits Street* and its slew of prime-time imitators, the 2018 BAFTA-nominated documentary series *The Mighty Redcar* attempted to both humanize and contextualize the parlous economic position of the eponymous North Yorkshire steel port, while (as its title suggests) sounding a defiant battle-cry from younger people determined to build themselves – and their town – a brighter future. Hearteningly, at least two of the series' main protagonists were people of colour. Yet, in both this and the near-contemporaneous BBC3 drama *The Left Behind*, the editorial choices taken about precise regional focus dictated that the main cast of characters would remain predominantly white – even if the latter's narrative focus was a post-industrial South Wales precariat whose key players, suspicious and resentful of foreign migrants, flipped into rampaging racists by night. In bravely addressing the difficult issue of interracial tensions in the zero-hours job market, the film drew on what its accompanying publicity blurb described as 'deep research into the realities of life in "forgotten Britain"' (bbc.co.uk, 2019). But by returning to terrain familiar from pre-referendum warnings about the growing appeal of right-wing populism among alienated white working-class men (for example, Ford & Goodwin, 2014), it also reactivated a provocative and sensitive, if salient, stereotype: that of the aggressive, white working-class nativist.

Archetypal iterations of the left behind were still alive and well in public discourse as this book went to press – courtesy of a new US-style news channel, *GB News*, launched in June 2021 with a bombastic pledge to tell 'the stories that matter' to 'those that have been neglected'. The channel received risible early ratings and predictably hostile reviews, and by three months into its life had already lost its chairman and lead presenter, Andrew Neil. But it was mounting a steady, if stumbling, ascent by the end of the year – thanks, in large part, to the addition of a flagship peak-time show hosted by one Nigel Farage. Elsewhere, it was hardly possible to come across a mainstream media report on a social or cultural 'issue' – from NHS waiting times, to cuts to regional theatre budgets – without noting the initially strained and performative, but increasingly normalized, ways in which newsrooms had begun falling over themselves to seek out case studies beyond the time-honoured parameters of the M25 (thanks, in part, to handy tools like Zoom), with Rochdale and Grimsby accents becoming as commonplace as the off-the-shelf 'Queen's' and 'estuary English' of old.

Elsewhere, 'localism' and 'regionalism' were fast becoming new media buzzwords, thanks to emerging outlets from Edinburgh-based *NationalWorld*, an online UK-wide paper staffed almost entirely by regionally based reporters, to *The People's Newsroom*, a project backed by the Bureau of Investigative Journalism which aims to 'support the creation and sustainability of community projects that reimagine journalism' by recruiting new 'community newsroom leaders' among groups 'traditionally marginalised by the media' (thebureauinvestigates.com, 2021). Interviewed on BBC Radio 4's *The Media Show* about the purpose of his new Wales-based news-site, *Nation.Cymru*, founder Morgan Jones declared his mission was 'to decentralize' reporting, because London-based journalism no longer held 'power to account' in ways that were 'particularly useful ... to people in other parts of the UK' (bbc.co.uk, 2021b). 'We've heard levelling up already being mentioned: well, we need to level up the journalism in different parts of the UK, so that it tells the stories, and represents the needs, of people in different parts of the UK', he added.

If *GB News*'s 'shock jock-style' channel had *set out* to unsettle Britain's 'liberal elite', moreover, this had been precisely the effect *achieved* earlier in the year by a (since widely discredited) report by the Commission on Race and Ethnic Disparities. Defying its ostensible government remit to examine 'racial disparities in the UK', the report concluded that 'the system' was no longer 'deliberately rigged against ethnic minorities' (Sewell, 2021: 8). On the contrary, the term 'institutional racism' had been overused and the label 'BAME' was now unhelpful and 'demeaning', as it grouped 'all ethnic minorities together' and 'categorised' people of colour 'in relation to what we are not, rather than what we are: British Indian, British Caribbean and so on' (ibid.: 32). Most controversially, the report stressed how, based on 'a range of outcomes', the most heavily disadvantaged ethnic grouping was 'white working-class children', who 'trail behind their peers in almost all ethnic minority groups' – even if 'the extent of these disparities vary by area' (ibid.: 29). Yet if there is no such thing as racial disadvantage (or it is so wildly exaggerated), how might one explain the findings of a Public Accounts Committee report published that September, which revealed that unemployment among young black people had soared to 41.6 per cent in the final quarter of 2020 – more than three times the 12.4 per cent rate for whites (publications.parliament.uk, 2021b)?

The ongoing political emphasis on the plight of white working-class children was also picked up in a June 2021 report by the Conservative-dominated House of Commons Education Select Committee. Bearing a title normatively framing 'white working-class children' as 'the forgotten', this cast educational disadvantages experienced by young people from low-income backgrounds as endemic to a problematic ethno-class imaginary. By *explicitly* identifying under-achievement in schools as a white working-class problem, it *implicitly* aligned working-class disadvantage with white ethnicity. A more balanced and nuanced investigation – and one less informed by the new Tory obsession with cementing its recently assembled 'blue wall' – would have acknowledged that the material poverty with which it associated educational disadvantages also applied to many children of colour and that, in such cases, these were just fragments of a mosaic of intersecting inequalities (publications.parliament.uk, 2021a).

Equally contentiously, the report challenged the overuse of the term 'White privilege' in ongoing debates about postcolonialism and institutional racism, arguing that it could be 'alienating to disadvantaged White communities', contributing towards 'a systemic neglect of White people facing hardship who also need specific support' (ibid.). It was hard to disagree entirely with the report's concerns that impoverished white pupils might be adversely affected by 'hearing terms' like 'White privilege' normatively repeated 'as fact'. However, it missed the point by arguing that, purely by dint of their *educational* disadvantages, such children did not still have privileges over minority-ethnic classmates. As in the preceding 'racial disparities' report (which it heavily cited), there was a strong sense that the committee's near-exclusive preoccupation with white working-class disadvantage was calculated to further inflame, rather than alleviate, simmering 'culture-war' tensions.

Meanwhile, flying the flag for anti-woke sentiment elsewhere were early signs of a potential resurgence for the right-wing populism that had propelled earlier iterations of Faragism. Polling in September 2021 prompted political scientist Matthew Goodwin to warn on Twitter that 'the revolt on the right might be about to return', based on data showing that up to 10 per cent of 2019 Tory voters, dismayed by Johnson's centrism, had 'moved' to the reincarnated Brexit Party, Reform UK (Goodwin, 2021). Troublingly, Farage himself would soon appropriate Goodwin's phrase – penning a January 2022 *Telegraph* comment warning of 'a Ukip-style surge of discontent' in the 'Red Wall', under the headline 'A revolt on the Right is brewing – and I'm ready to be a part of it' (Farage, 2022). Meanwhile, scenting the threat on its right flank, Ministers signalled their intention to rocket-boost their agenda for reviving left-behind areas – symbolically rebranding the Ministry of Housing, Communities and Local Government the 'Department of Levelling Up, Housing and Communities' amid polls showing that fewer than one in five people had any idea what 'levelling up' actually meant (opinium.com, 2021).

Yet, for all these provocations, there was much to be cheered in the discursive turns taken by media conversations around the left behind in the early 'recovery phase' of the post-Brexit, late-COVID epoch. Amid the ever-multiplying think-pieces, discussion programmes, documentary inserts and talk-show topics focusing on the pandemic's impact on poverty and post-industrial economic disadvantage, a standout exchange came in the third programme in journalist John Harris's purposely selective odyssey for BBC Radio 4 around 'four places with a distinctive identity' in 'the story of the UK in 2021': *Citizens of Somewhere*. Interviewed at the site of Stoke-on-Trent's once iconic Spode pottery works, locally based playwright and former *Coronation Street* actor Deborah McAndrew described the loss of its ceramics industry as 'a very particular bereavement for the city', adding eloquently that 'young people growing up in a city that has experienced a massive cultural bereavement grow up with that ghost – even though they don't really know what it was' (bbc.co.uk, 2021a). Crystallizing the complex challenges involved in (re)connecting younger people with a once deeply ingrained industrial identity – precious to their elders – of which only fossilized reminders remain, McAndrew posed the question, 'how do you honour the loss that the older generation feel without burdening the young?' Clearly moved by her words, Harris elided from them what he described as a 'profound tension' for post-industrial, post-Brexit, post-COVID Britain as a *whole* – one we might all do well to consider in coming years: 'That's the question in the South Wales valleys, and it's the question in the old shipyards of Newcastle, and it's the question in the post-industrial parts of Scotland – that's the sort of "British Question", I think ... .

FROM DIVISION TO UNITY: DETOXIFYING DISCUSSION OF THE LEFT BEHIND

What, then, is the recipe for improving the quality of left-behind discourse – whether by cooling it down or dispensing with it entirely? A good start would be for media (and political) portrayals of disadvantaged groups to adopt more of the narrative *complexity* of *Citizens of Somewhere*, and less of the *alarmism* to which the eponymous film *The Left Behind* sometimes succumbed. As in more nuanced existing media and political analyses (of which there have been *some*), we need to move beyond narrow definitions of white working-class grievance, which invariably overemphasize difference and division, towards more inclusive, forward-looking narratives – rather like that attempted by *The Mighty Redcar* (or, for that matter, the more optimistic turns in Shane Meadows' BAFTA-winning state-of-the-nation drama, *This is England*). We need to tell stories focusing on the *similar*, even *shared*, lived realities of otherwise disparate communities experiencing inequality. To do this, however, will require creating much more public space for the voices of 'left-behind' people themselves

– and a sustained, society-wide effort to take down the tenor of debate a notch or two.

Another key objective must be to curb the shameless appropriation and *exploitation* of left-behind people as ammunition in relentless rounds of public mud-slinging; this means voting with our feet to reject cheap electoral point-scoring by politicians, and the sensationalist ramping-up of divisions for commercial purposes by everyone from the usual culprits (tabloids and hyper-partisan news-sites, yes, but also broadsheets and 24-hour news channels) to documentary-makers and dramatists. In the end, we *all* have a collective responsibility to open our minds to more nuanced, multidimensional understandings of economic disadvantage and its (often complex) relationships with additional, aggravating forms of inequality – while, crucially, finding a more inclusive, empathetic and tolerant public vocabulary with which to discuss it.

As in so many other areas of life – from contributing towards the cost of public services to supporting those in need – the primary responsibility for all of this must rest with those fortunate enough to have 'the broadest shoulders': in this case, the economic, social and/or cultural capital enabling them to get their voices heard. Those of us lucky enough *not* to be left behind have a duty of care to those who *are* – and we can exercise it by making ethical, *evidence*-based contributions to public discussion; more communitarian, less impulsive consumer choices (which papers to read, which links to share, which 'sellers' to buy from); giving our time and/or money through targeted donations and volunteering, whether through foodbanks, community regeneration projects or outreach activities for the isolated and lonely; and using our votes to reject *anyone* who seeks to profit politically by stoking division.

Above all else, however, we need to start treating everyone else with civility – including those with whom we profoundly disagree and have little instinctive affinity or connection. While long-term, sustainable, socially just solutions to deep-seated problems of disadvantage will inevitably cost money – and must always, ultimately, involve the hand of government – we can all do our bit to both stand up for and empower those less fortunate than ourselves; to put back what we can (financially or in kind); and, above all, avoid passing by on the other side, in ethos or action, when we witness others in distress. To paraphrase a recent political leader often derided for his naivety – but full of an enviable optimism about our capacity to reshape society for the common good – 'we don't *have* to be unequal', life 'doesn't *have* to be unfair' and 'poverty *isn't* inevitable' (Corbyn, quoted in Mason, 2015). To this ambitious (but achievable) list of retorts to cast-iron shibboleths we might usefully add another: in societies as rich as ours, no one *has* to be left behind.

Appendix
Research methodologies

FRAMING ANALYSIS

The Lexis Library database of UK newspapers was used to collect a series of relevant datasets spanning all national and regional papers across five snapshots – or 'discursive "events"' (Wodak, 2001: 65) – between 23 June 2016 and 27 December 2019. These were: the two months between 23 June and 22 August 2016, commencing with the date of the European Union referendum; the three-month period beginning with the activation of Article 50 of the Treaty of Lisbon on 29 March 2017 and encompassing the 'snap' general election; the two months between 4 December 2018 and 3 February 2019; the month of 3 May–2 June 2019, encapsulating local and European elections, and the two-month period leading to the 2019 general election and subsequent Queen's Speech. Hansard searches were combined into one dataset for the whole period. The keyword search combination was 'left behind' and 'Brexit'.

Searches were conducted using the Lexis 'moderate similarity' filter to first group together identical pieces published multiple times (on the same date, by a single paper) and manually sift out duplicates. Collectively, Lexis searches produced a corpus of 662 print and online articles spread over the five snapshots. Hansard searches generated 270 parliamentary speeches and other contributions mentioning the term 'left behind' in the context of Brexit. In coding articles' frames, a two-stage approach was applied, beginning with immersion in the datasets (in this case, an initial read-through): a process known as 'inductive category development' (Mayring 2000: 3). This necessitated refining (and increasing) the number of categories during the exploratory read-through, as unexpected variations emerged: for example, the early appearance of some articles comprised largely of quotes from people from 'left-behind' communities necessitated introducing a 'voices of the left behind' category. Six categories of newspaper frame were finally identified: 'economic', 'cultural', 'political', 'hybrid', 'voices of the left behind' and 'incidental'. Only the first four applied to Hansard. Initial content-based analysis quantified the totals for each frame detailed in Tables 2.1 and 2.2.

To ensure initial coding was reliable enough to be replicated, one-tenth of each sample (67 articles and 27 Hansard records) were re-coded eight months after initial analysis, producing matches of 96 per cent and 100 per cent respectively. Two of the three articles coded differently the second time were re-coded from 'cultural' to 'political', based on a re-reading of the primary focus of their analysis of the Brexit result – as a consequence of disconnection from political elites, not elite values. The third was re-coded from 'cultural' to 'hybrid' for similar reasons: on repeat reading, it was felt to reflect concerns about both elites *and* elite values.

CRITICAL DISCOURSE ANALYSIS

Following the initial framing analysis, another analytical method was applied to a much smaller, more selective, sub-sample of newspaper articles and Hansard records that expressed explicit opinions about 'left-behind' areas/groups and/or factors contributing to communities feeling or becoming left behind. This was a form of critical discourse analysis (CDA) drawing on the discourse-historical approach (DHA), which 'attempts to integrate a large quantity of available knowledge about the historical sources and the background of the social and political fields in which discursive "events" are embedded' (Wodak, 2015: 3). DHA applies three related 'aspects' of social critique: a 'text or discourse-immanent' approach, which focuses on identifying inconsistencies and paradoxes in texts; 'sociodiagnostic critique', which aims to decode the persuasive/manipulative character of discursive practices, and a 'future-related prospective' approach, which aims to improve communication by critiquing problematic discourse – for example, stigmatizing language (ibid.). In supplementing framing analysis with CDA, the intention was to add a deeper layer of qualitative analysis to a small sample of texts chosen to illustrate various ways in which the left-behind concept was problematized by the media-political commentariat. As it was not an objective to quantify *how many* articles/Hansard records adopted such approaches, this analysis was entirely qualitative and no quantitative tabular data was produced.

SENTIMENT ANALYSIS

Initial sampling of all UK-wide national newspapers' coverage of the five discursive events identified only a few titles that published comments beneath their articles in each case. Sampling was eventually confined to threads published in response to the two key democratic events in the lifetime of Brexit: the 2016 referendum itself and the 2019 general election. The samples were extracted from three national news-sites that carried threads on both these occasions and that, taken together, offered a broadly representative spread of the political balance of the UK national newspaper market: www.theguardian.com, website of centre-left quality newspaper the *Guardian*; www.thetimes.co.uk, the online version of centre-right quality newspaper *The Times*, and www.thesun.co.uk, the web platform of right-wing red-top the *Sun*.

Initial datasets generated were manually cleaned up to remove comments irrelevant to the primary focus of analysis: the framing and conceptualization of rebelling voters. As some articles generated hundreds of comments, it was necessary to rationalize the datasets prior to analysis, by confining the final samples to only the first few pages of posts and prioritizing those that were 'most liked' or 'most rated'. The final sample for snapshot 1 across all three titles numbered 354, and the total for snapshot 2 was 285. Comments were coded using manual sentiment analysis techniques. Stage one involved identifying the range of discursive categories present in the sample by applying Mayring's 'inductive category development' approach (2000) and Pfeil and Zaphiris's rationale that this 'offers a way to capture the essence of the communication within an online community' (2010: 7). Posts were eventually coded across seven categories, spanning the full range of 'pro-', 'anti-' and neutral sentiments observed in relation to the left behind and/or a wider category of (supposedly) 'voiceless' voters frequently described as 'the people' that emerged from the initial immersion phase. These categories were: 'defending left behind', 'defending "will of the people"', 'neutral comment on left behind', 'left behind duped', 'left behind backward', 'posts critical of "the people"', and 'other posts about voters'. After fine-tuning the categories, the final tallies for each were quantified.

The Twitter datasets were sampled, using Twitter's own 'advanced search' function, around the same two snapshots used for comment threads – the 2016 referendum and 2019 election – and an identical analytical method and coding categories were used. Only tweets directly addressing and/or expressing a view on the relationship between 'left-behind' and/or other previously 'voiceless' voters and the referendum/election were included in the final sample – necessitating a lengthy process of manually cleaning up the datasets to remove tweets that simply retweeted or posted a link to an article (or similar), without commenting on it, or the many tweets that diverged into debating wider questions about society, economy and/or politics, rather than explicitly taking pro-, anti-, or neutral positions on the left-behind question. However, as the initial search using the keyword combination 'Brexit' and 'left behind' for 23–24 June 2016 (referendum night) produced only very small samples of relevant tweets, the final search terms for this date were expanded to 'left behind' plus 'any of' the following: 'Brexit', 'European Union', 'EU', 'referendum' and 'ref'. Snapshot 2 generated a sufficiently large sample for the night of the 2019 poll – 12–13 December 19 – using the simple search terms 'left behind' (as 'exact phrase') plus 'Brexit'. Total numbers of tweets analysed for each discursive event were 96 for snapshot 1 and 79 for snapshot 2.

To ensure initial coding was reliable enough to be replicated, one-tenth of each sample was recoded eight months after initial analysis. Of the 65 comments recoded (36 for snapshot 1 and 29 for snapshot 2), all but 63 were coded the same way as previously – producing a 97 per cent match. Of the two posts re-coded (one for each snapshot), the first was re-categorized from 'neutral' to 'defending the left behind', while the second (initially coded as one of the 'other post about voters') was re-coded as 'defending the "will of the people"'. Re-coding of the Twitter dataset produced a 100 per cent match.

INTERVIEWS

Semi-structured interviews were conducted on Zoom or telephone with 30 individuals drawn from five local clusters offering a broadly representative geographical spread of left-behind communities in England and Wales. The locations chosen were the Don Valley, South Yorkshire (North-East England); the town of Leigh in Wigan, Greater Manchester (North West); Great Yarmouth and surrounding villages in eastern England; the area around Stoke-on-Trent, Staffordshire (Midlands); the town of Bideford in the district of Torridge, North Devon (South West), and the Rhondda valley in South Wales. Subjects interviewed ranged from MPs and councillors to community activists, retired miners, unemployed people and those with disabilities. Interviewees were identified using a form of purposive sampling combined with snowballing. Prospective subjects were initially approached based on characteristics that could be seen to qualify them as broadly 'representative' voices of their areas/communities (Lavrakas, 2008): for example, councillors elected to represent voters and officials selected to lead local chambers of commerce as representatives of their local business sectors. Flyers advertising for interviewees from low-income groups, including unemployed and disabled people, were posted on the social media accounts of local organizations, such as community associations and foodbanks. The interviewer then used snowball sampling to widen the interview sample, by asking interviewees to refer him to additional contacts who might meet criteria not covered by his initial pool. Additional testimony was later drawn from another pool of 20 interviews conducted for a separate project focusing on the lived experiences of people from left-behind groups in Scotland (funded by the Political Studies Association).

The semi-structured interviews involved a mix of open questions, supplementaries and attempts to creatively rephrase enquiries that initially met with inconclusive answers to encourage interviewees to be more explanatory. One approach was to encourage them to 'narrativize' their responses by illustrating them with personal anecdotes (Hollway & Jefferson, 2000: 35). For Zoom interviews, the researcher drew inspiration from Geertz's writings on 'thick description' – in particular, his contention that affectations, including 'winks and twitches', are often as significant as spoken words (Geertz, 1973: 6–7).

References

Aaronovitch, D. (2017) 'The under-30s are the real "left behinds"', *The Times*, 31 May, www.thetimes.co.uk/article/the-under-30s-are-the-real-left-behinds-hxsvs7cgf, accessed 27 August 2021.

Abrams, M. (1961) 'Social class and British politics', *Public Opinion Quarterly*: 342–350.

Ainsley, C. (2018) *The New Working Class: How to Win Hearts, Minds and Votes*. Bristol: Policy Press.

Aldrick, P. (2016) 'Brexit crisis offers an opportunity to reshape the economy for benefit of all', *The Times*, 2 July, www.thetimes.co.uk/article/brexit-crisis-offers-an-opportunity-to-reshape-the-economy-for-benefit-of-all-k5jrx6vwx

Alford, R. (1963) 'Party and society: The Anglo-American democracies', *American Political Science Review*, 59(4): 1008–9.

Anderson, P.J. (2004) 'A flag of convenience? Discourse and motivations of the London-based Eurosceptic press', in R. Harmsen and M. Spiering (eds) *Euroscepticism: Party Politics, National Identity and European Integration*, New York: Rodopi, 151–70.

Antonucci, L., Horvath, L., Kutiyski, Y. and Krouwel, A. (2017) 'The malaise of the squeezed middle: Challenging the narrative of the "left behind" Brexiter', *Competition & Change*, 21(3): 211–29.

Armitage, J. (2016) 'Brexit: CBI chief tells UK government to tell EU nationals in London they can stay', *Evening Standard*, 30 June, www.standard.co.uk/news/uk/cbi-chief-promise-eu-nationals-working-in-london-they-can-stay-in-the-uk-a3284606.html, accessed 27 August 2021.

Barbulescu, R., Favell, A., Khan, O., Paraschivescu, C., Samuels, R. and Varela, A. (2019) *Class, Race and Inequality in Northern Towns*. Leeds: University of Leeds and Runnymede Trust.

Baston, L. (2019) 'The myth of the red wall', *The Critic*, 18 December, http://thecritic.co.uk/the-myth-of-the-red-wall/, accessed 27 August 2021.

bbc.co.uk (1997) 'Blair's speech: Single mothers won't be forced to take work', www.bbc.co.uk/news/special/politics97/news/06/0602/blair.shtml, accessed 27 August 2021.

bbc.co.uk (2011) 'Toxteth riots: Howe proposed "managed decline" for city', www.bbc.co.uk, 30 December, www.bbc.co.uk/news/uk-england-merseyside-16355281, accessed 27 August 2021.

bbc.co.uk (2012) 'British workers "among worst idlers", suggest Tory MPs', www.*bbc.co.uk*, 18 August, www.bbc.co.uk/news/uk-politics-19300051, accessed 11 January 2022.

bbc.co.uk (2019) 'The Left behind', www.bbc.co.uk/programmes/p07f4j35, accessed 22 February 2022.

bbc.co.uk (2021a) *Citizens of Somewhere: Stoke-on-Trent*, www.bbc.co.uk, 2 September, www.bbc.co.uk/sounds/play/m000z6rp, accessed 7 September 2021.

bbc.co.uk (2021b) *The Media Show: Making the News 'Less' London*, www.bbc.co.uk, 1 September, www.bbc.co.uk/programmes/m000z6d4, accessed 17 September 2021.

Beatty, C. and Fothergill, S. (2016) *Jobs, Welfare and Austerity: How the Destruction of Industrial Britain Casts a Shadow over the Present-day Public Finances*. Sheffield: Sheffield Hallam University, http://shura.shu.ac.uk/14603/1/cresr30th-jobs-welfare-austerity_Final%20published%20Report.pdf, accessed 27 August 2021.

Beatty, C., Fothergill, S. and Gore, T. (2011) *Tackling Worklessness in Britain's Weaker Local Economies*. Sheffield: Sheffield Hallam University, http://shura.shu.ac.uk/26329/1/tackling-worklessness-britains-weaker-economies.pdf, accessed 27 August 2021.

Becker, S.O., Fetzer, T. and Novy, D. (2017) 'Who voted for Brexit? A comprehensive district-level analysis' *Economic Policy*, 32(92): 601–50.

Behr, R. (2016) 'Brexit earthquake has happened and the rubble will take years to clear', *The Guardian*, 24 June, www.theguardian.com/politics/2016/jun/24/brexit-earthquake-has-happened-the-rubble-will-take-years-to-clear, accessed 27 August 2021.

Biressi, A. and Nunn, H. (2013) *Class and Contemporary British Culture*. Berlin: Springer.

Bhambra, G.K. (2017) 'Brexit, Trump, and "methodological whiteness": On the misrecognition of race and class', *British Journal of Sociology*, 68(S1): 214–S232.

Blackburn, M. (2016) 'We need to make sure Brexit truly liberates this region, not do us further damage', 24 June, www.gazettelive.co.uk/news/teesside-news/we-need-make-sure-brexit-11520138, accessed 27 August 2021.

Blair, T. (2005) 'Tony Blair's conference speech 2005', *The Guardian*, 27 September, www.theguardian.com/uk/2005/sep/27/labourconference.speeches, accessed 2 September 2021.

Blanchard, J. (2016) 'Labour heartlands give huge backing to Brexit as the North votes to Leave', www.mirror.co.uk, 24 June, www.mirror.co.uk/news/uk-news/labour-heartlands-give-huge-backing-8271074, accessed 27 August 2021.

Blond, P. (2010) *Red Tory: How Left and Right have Broken Britain and How we Can Fix It*. London: Faber & Faber.

Booth, W. (2014) *In Darkest England and the Way Out*. Cambridge: Cambridge University Press.

Bourdieu, P. & Wacquant, L. (2002) 'Sobre as artimanhas da razão imperialista', *Estudos Afro-Asiáticos*, 24: 15–33.

Butler, D.E. and Rose, R. (1959) 'The British general election of 1951', *Canadian Journal of Economics and Political Science*, 20(3): 398–400.

Butler, P. (2016) 'Would-be Tory leaders pose as champions of the poor – after six years of cuts', *The Guardian*, 5 July, www.theguardian.com/society/2016/jul/05/would-be-tory-leaders-champion-poor-cuts-brexit-inequality, accessed 27 August 2021.

Cecil, N. (2016) 'Jeremy Corbyn reveals blueprint for a more caring Britain as Labour row intensifies', *Evening Standard*, 4 August, www.standard.co.uk/news/politics/jeremy-corbyn-reveals-blueprint-for-a-more-caring-britain-as-labour-row-intensifies-a3311946.html, accessed 27 August 2021.

Chu, B. (2016) 'Brexit means Brexit? Not for Cornwall – it's only kept up with the rest of Britain thanks to EU funding', *The Independent*, 2 August.

Coates, K., and Silburn, R. (1981) *Poverty: The Forgotten Englishmen*. London: Penguin Books.

Cockburn, P. (2019) 'Nationalism is transforming the politics of the British Isles', www.unz.com, 28 December, www.unz.com/pcockburn/2019/12/, accessed 27 August 2021.

Cohen, S. (1972) *Folk Devils and Moral Panics*. London: Paladin.

Coman, J. (2020) 'Labour would do well to rediscover its Conservative side', *The Guardian*, 8 December, www.theguardian.com/commentisfree/2020/dec/08/labour-conservative-values-liberal-left-working-class-voters, accessed 27 August 2021.

Conboy, M. and Steel, J. (2010) 'From "we" to "me": The changing construction of popular tabloid journalism', *Journalism Studies*, 11(4): 500–510.

Conservativehome.com (2016) 'Michael Gove's launch statement: Full text', 1 July, www.conservativehome.com/parliament/2016/07/michael-goves-launch-statement-full-text.html, accessed 27 August 2021.

Cork, T. (2017) 'How Bristol's Remain voters misunderstood why people voted for Brexit', 24 May, www.bristolpost.co.uk/news/bristol-news/how-bristols-leave-voters-misunderstood-73689, accessed 27 August 2021.

Cornillie, B. (2009) 'Evidentiality and epistemic modality: On the close relationship between two different categories', *Functions of Language*, 16(1): 44–62.

Crewe, I. (1986) 'On the death and resurrection of class voting: Some comments on How Britain Votes', *Political Studies*, 34(4): 620–38.

Crouch, C. (2020) *Post-democracy after the Crises*. London: John Wiley & Sons.

Cruddas, J. (2021) *The Dignity of Labour*. Bristol: Policy Press.

Cumming, E. (2019) 'Mrs Brown's Boys Christmas special, review: This panto is pure Brexit telly', *The Independent*, 26 December, www.independent.co.uk/arts-entertainment/tv/reviews/mrs-browns-boys-review-christmas-special-bbc-brexit-brendan-ocarroll-a9259306.html, accessed 27 August 2021.

Curtice, J. (2016) 'What the EU referendum results tell us about Brexit Britain', *The Independent*, 24 June, www.independent.co.uk/voices/eu-referendum-results-brexit-what-they-tell-us-about-britain-a7100286.html, accessed 27 August 2021.

Curtis, P. (2010) 'Gordon Brown calls Labour supporter a "bigoted woman"', 28 April, www.theguardian.com/politics/2010/apr/28/gordon-brown-bigoted-woman, accessed 27 August 2021.

Dabirimehr, A. and Fatmi, M.T. (2014) 'Laclau and Mouffe's theory of discourse', *Journal of Novel Applied Sciences*, 3(11): 1283–7.

Daily Mail (2019) 'Now repay voters for building the Blue Wall', 17 December, https://www.pressreader.com/uk/daily-mail/20191217/281801400855219, accessed 27 August 2021.

Daley, J. (2019) 'The people have got their revenge against the hateful Remainer diehards', *Daily Telegraph*, 14 December, www.telegraph.co.uk/politics/2019/12/14/people-have-got-revenge-against-hateful-remainer-diehards/, accessed 27 August 2021.

Davenport, A. and Zaranko, B. (2020) 'Levelling up: where and how?' in *IFS Green Budget 2020*. London: Institute for Fiscal Studies.

Davison, D. (2019) 'Dehenna Davison: We have to reward our new voters and make blue collar the new Tory buzzword', www.thesun.co.uk, 15 December, www.thesun.co.uk/news/10554617/reward-new-voters-blue-collar/, accessed 7 September 2021.

Deacon, A. (1978) 'The scrounging controversy: public attitudes towards the unemployed in contemporary Britain', *Social Policy & Administration*, 12(2): 120–35.

Dearden, L. (2017) 'Theresa May prompts anger after telling nurse who hasn't had pay rise for eight years: "There's no magic money tree"', 3 June, *The Independent*, www.independent.co.uk/news/uk/politics/theresa-may-nurse-magic-money-tree-bbcqt-question-time-pay-rise-eight-years-election-latest-a7770576.html, accessed 27 August 2021.

De Vries, R., Baumberg Gieger, B., Scullion, L., Summers, K., Ermiston, D., Ingold, J., Robertshaw, D., and Young, D. (2021) *Solidarity in a Crisis? Trends in Attitudes to Benefits During COVID-19*, https://62608d89-fc73-4896-861c-0e03416f9922.usrfiles.com/ugd/62608d_ffc54112b28141fdb85a9e9474120452.pdf, accessed 14 September 2021.

Delestre, I., Joyce, R., Rasul, I. and Waters, T. (2020) *Income Protection Policy during COVID-19: Evidence from Bank Account Data*. London: Institute for Fiscal Studies.

Doane, D. (2016) 'Brexit was a backlash against globalisation – the poorest are being left behind everywhere', 26 June, *The Guardian*, www.theguardian.com/global-development-professionals-network/2016/jun/26/brexit-was-a-backlash-against-globalisation-the-poorest-are-being-left-behind-everywhere, accessed 27 August 2021.

Domokos, J. (2018) 'Made in Stoke-on-Trent: Local people inspired our documentary. Tell us what you think', www.theguardian.com, 8 January, www.theguardian.com/cities/2018/jan/08/made-in-stoke-on-trent-documentary-guardian-readers, accessed 27 August 2021.

Dorling, D. (2016) 'Brexit: the decision of a divided country' *British Medical Journal*, 354, www.bmj.com/content/354/bmj.i3697.full, accessed 27 August 2021.

Dorling, D. (2020) 'Want to understand the Covid map? Look at where we live and how we work', *The Guardian*, 29 November, www.theguardian.com/commentisfree/2020/nov/29/want-to-understand-the-covid-map-look-at-where-we-live-and-how-we-work, accessed 27 August 2021.

Duffy, B., Hewlett, K., Hesketh, R., Benson, R. and Wager, A. (2021) *Unequal Britain: Attitudes to Inequalities after Covid-19*. London: King's College London.

Duxbury, G. (2019) 'We need to rebuild Britain through local communities', *Daily Express*, 16 January, www.express.co.uk/comment/expresscomment/1073043/

brexit-news-local-communities-government-brexit-deal, accessed 27 August 2021.

Eatwell, R. and Goodwin, M. (2018) *National Populism: The Revolt against Liberal Democracy*. London: Penguin UK.

El-Gingihy, Y. (2016) 'Triggering Article 50 will plunge the UK into turmoil – and the EU with it. It's mutually assured destruction', 5 July, *The Independent*, www.independent.co.uk/voices/brexit-article-50-triggered-eu-membership-turmoil-europe-marine-le-pen-fascism-a7120216.html, accessed 27 August 2021.

Elliott, F. and Coates, S. (2016) 'Britain votes for Brexit', www.thetimes.co.uk, 24 June, www.thetimes.co.uk/article/closest-call-for-britain-5rcrxnjho, accessed 22 February 2022.

Elliott, F., Wright, O., Waterfield, B. and Devlin, K. (2019) 'UK election result: Boris Johnson offers olive branch after Tory win', *The Times*, 13 December, www.thetimes.co.uk/article/uk-election-results-exit-poll-predicts-johnson-majority-5xphhbwor, accessed 27 August 2021.

Embury, P. (2020) *Despised: Why the Modern Left Loathes the Working Class*. London: Polity Press.

Encyclopedia.com (2020) 'Embourgeoisement', www.encyclopedia.com/social-sciences/dictionaries-thesauruses-pictures-and-press-releases/embourgeoisement, accessed 27 August 2021.

Entman, R.M. (1993) 'Framing: toward clarification of a fractured paradigm', *Journal of Communication*, 43(4): 51–8.

Essletzbichler, J., Disslbacher, F. and Moser, M. (2018) 'The victims of neoliberal globalisation and the rise of the populist vote: a comparative analysis of three recent electoral decisions', *Cambridge Journal of Regions, Economy and Society*, 11(1): 73–94.

Evans, G. (2017) 'Brexit Britain: Why we are all post-industrial now', *American Ethnologist*, 44(2): 215–19.

Fairclough, N. and Wodak, R. (1997) 'Discourse as social interaction, in T. Van Dijk (ed.) *Discourse as Social Interaction*, London: Sage, 258–84.

Farage, N. (2022) 'A Revolt on the Right is brewing and I'm ready to be part of it', www.telegraph.co.uk, 7 January, www.telegraph.co.uk/news/2022/01/07/revolt-right-brewing-ready-part/, accessed 11 January 2022.

Fenews.co.uk (2020) 'Rishi Sunak's spending review 2020 speech', 25 November, www.fenews.co.uk/press-releases/59235-spending-review-2020-speech, accessed 27 August 2021.

Ferguson, J. (2019) 'Ruth Davidson targets Tory led Scotland that ends SNP "grudge and grievance" politics', *Daily Record*, 5 May, www.dailyrecord.co.uk/news/politics/ruth-davidson-blasts-snp-grudge-14997879, accessed 27 August 2021.

Ferrari, N. (2019) 'Theresa May needed to be tough, not stubborn', *Express*, www.express.co.uk/comment/columnists/nick-ferrari/1132338/brexit-theresa-may-eu-deal-resignation, accessed 19 February 2022.

Field, F. (1989) *Losing Out? The Emergence of Britain's Underclass*. Oxford: Blackwell.

Fieldhouse, E., Green, J., Evans, G., Mellon, J., Prosser, C., de Geus, R. and Bailey, J. (2021) *Electoral Shocks: The Volatile Voter in a Turbulent World*. Oxford: Oxford University Press.

Flinders, M. (2017) 'A new political language needed for world in flux', *Yorkshire Post*, 22 June, www.yorkshirepost.co.uk/news/politics/matthew-flinders-new-political-language-needed-world-flux-1774980, accessed 27 August 2021.

Ford, R. (2017) 'A Conservative landslide is likely, but no election is risk free', *The Guardian*, 23 April, www.theguardian.com/politics/2017/apr/22/theresa-may-no-election-is-risk-free-brexit-divisions, accessed 27 August 2021.

Ford, R. and Goodwin, M. (2014) *Revolt on the Right*. Abingdon: Routledge.

Fowler, R. (1991) *Language in the News: Discourse and Ideology in the Press*. London: Routledge.

Frankova, M. (2000) 'Divided Englishness: The North and South of the mind', *Looking into England Papers*, 11(5).

Fraser, G. (2016a) 'Brexit brought democracy back – now we need to start listening to each other', *The Guardian*, 24 June, www.theguardian.com/commentisfree/2016/jun/24/brexit-democracy-i-voted-leave-divisions-campaigns, accessed 27 August 2021.

Fraser, G. (2016b) 'Labour is partly to blame for the racists' capture of the EU debate', *The Guardian*, 30 June, www.theguardian.com/commentisfree/belief/2016/jun/30/labour-is-partly-to-blame-for-the-racists-capture-of-the-eu-debate, accessed 27 August 2021.

Fraser, G. (2017) 'Theresa May has signed, sealed and delivered Article 50. Our writers respond', 29 March, www.theguardian.com/commentisfree/2017/mar/29/theresa-may-article-50-eu-panel, accessed 27 August 2021.

Freedland, J. (2016a) 'Welcome to the age of Trump', *The Guardian*, 19 May, www.theguardian.com/us-news/2016/may/19/welcome-to-the-age-of-trump, accessed 27 August 2021.

Freedland, J. (2016b) 'For the 48%, this was a day of despair', *The Guardian*, 25 June, www.theguardian.com/commentisfree/2016/jun/25/48-britain-regrexit-voted-remain, accessed 27 August 2021.

Freyas-Tamure, K. (2016) 'Pro-"Brexit" city of Sunderland glad to poke establishment in the eye', *New York Times*, 27 June, www.nytimes.com/2016/06/28/world/europe/european-union-brexit-sunderland-britain-cameron.html, accessed 27 August 2021.

Friedman, S. (2014) 'The price of the ticket: Rethinking the experience of social mobility', *Sociology*, 48(2): 352–68.

Froud, J., Johal, S., Law, J., Leaver, A. and Williams, K. (2011) *Rebalancing the Economy (or Buyer's Remorse)*, Manchester: CRESC, University of Manchester.

Gallo, A. (2016) 'Leaving is not the right fix, it will expose Britain's weaknesses', *The Times*, 28 June, www.thetimes.co.uk/article/leaving-is-not-the-right-fix-it-will-expose-britains-weaknesses-spw296vx9, accessed 27 August 2021.

Geertz, C. (1973) *Thick Description: Toward an Interpretive Theory of Culture*. New York: Basic Books.

Gitlin, T. (1980) *The Whole World is Watching*. Berkeley: University of California Press.

Glasman, M. (2016) 'Things don't only get better: Why the working class fell out of love with Labour', 3 November, *New Statesman*, www.newstatesman.com/politics/2016/11/things-dont-only-get-better-why-working-class-fell-out-love-labour, accessed 27 August 2021.

Glasman, M. (2020) 'A Blue Christmas', www.bluelabour.org, 24 December, www.bluelabour.org/home/a-blue-christmas, accessed 27 August 2021.

Golding, P. and Middleton, S. (1982) *Images of Welfare: Press and Public Attitudes to Poverty*. Oxford: Robertson.

Goldthorpe, J.H., Lockwood, D., Bechhofer, F. and Platt, J. (1968) *The Affluent Worker: Political Attitudes and Behaviour*. Cambridge: Cambridge University Press.

Goodhart, D. (2017) *The Road to Somewhere: The New Tribes Shaping British Politics*. London: Penguin.

Goodwin, M. (2016) 'Labour's traditional voters no longer share its progressive values', *The Guardian*, 23 June, www.theguardian.com/commentisfree/2016/jun/23/labour-traditional-voters-progressive-values-working-class-ukip, accessed 27 August 2021.

Goodwin, M. (2019) 'The Strange death of Labour Britain', *The Times*, 2 June, www.thetimes.co.uk/article/the-strange-death-of-labour-britain-8npfmgqnn, accessed 27 August 2021.

Goodwin, M. (2021) @GoodwinMJ, 10 September, https://mobile.twitter.com/goodwinmj/status/1436259133993496578, accessed 17 September 2021.

Goodwin, M.J. and Heath, O. (2016) 'The 2016 referendum, Brexit and the left behind: An aggregate-level analysis of the result', *The Political Quarterly*, 87(3): 323–32.

Gore, A. (1994) 'Information superhighway', www.c-span.com, 29 March, www.c-span.org/video/?55624-1/information-superhighway, accessed 2 September 2021.

gov.uk (2019) *Queen's Speech 2019*, www.gov.uk/government/speeches/queens-speech-2019, accessed 27 August 2021.

gov.uk (2020) *Universal Credit Statistics, 29 April 2013 to 9 January 2020*, www.gov.uk/government/statistics/universal-credit-29-april-2013-to-9-january-2020/universal-credit-29-april-2013-to-9-january-2020, accessed 27 August 2021.

gov.uk (2021a) *Universal Credit Statistics, 29 April 2013 to 14 January 2021*, www.gov.uk/government/statistics/universal-credit-statistics-29-april-2013-to-14-january-2021/universal-credit-statistics-29-april-2013-to-14-january-2021#:~:text=The%20headline%20statistics%20for%20Universal,4.2%20million)%20received%20a%20payment, accessed 27 August 2021.

gov.uk (2021b) *Benefit Cap: Number of Households Capped to February 2021*, www.gov.uk/government/statistics/benefit-cap-number-of-households-capped-to-february-2021/benefit-cap-number-of-households-capped-to-february-2021, accessed 27 August 2021.

Gove, M. (2017) 'Now we'll find out what Mayism stands for', *The Times*, 21 April, www.thetimes.co.uk/article/now-we-ll-find-out-what-mayism-stands-for-6qt7g3v62, accessed 27 August 2021.

Graham, J. (2018) *Brexit: The Uncivil War*. London: Baffin Media.

Grice, A. (2016) 'David Cameron wanted to unite us – he's just shown how divided we really are', *The Independent*, 24 June, www.independent.co.uk/voices/brexit-eu-referendum-result-david-cameron-latest-live-britain-leaves-european-union-a7099216.html, accessed 27 August 2021.

Grieve, D. (2019) 'Even in Tory heartlands, Boris Johnson was merely the lesser of two evils', *The Guardian*, 23 December, www.theguardian.com/commentisfree/2019/dec/23/tory-boris-johnson-labour, accessed 27 August 2021.

Griffith, P. and Glennie, A. (eds) (2014) *'Alien Nation? New Perspectives on the White Working Class and Disengagement in Britain*. London: Institute for Public Policy Research. www.ippr.org/files/publications/pdf/alien-nation_Oct2014.pdf, accessed 27 August 2021.

Groundwork.org.uk (2021) 'About us', www.groundwork.org.uk/about-groundwork/, accessed 27 August 2021.

Habermas, J., Lennox, S. and Lennox, F. (1974) 'The public sphere: An encyclopedia article [1964]' *New German Critique*, 3: 49–55.

Hall, M. (2019) 'Boris Johnson to supercharge business by dumping EU state aid rules after Brexit', *Daily Express*, 30 November, www.express.co.uk/news/politics/1211185/general-election-news-boris-johnson-brexit-buy-british, accessed 27 August 2021.

Hall, S., Critcher, C., Jefferson, T., Clarke, J. and Roberts, B. (1978) *Policing the Crisis: Mugging, the State and Law and Order*. London: Macmillan.

Halikiopoulou, D. and Vlandas, T. (2017) 'Voting to leave: Economic insecurity and the Brexit vote', in *The Routledge Handbook of Euroscepticism*, Abingdon: Routledge, 444–55.

Hansard (2016a) 'European Council', 29 June, https://hansard.parliament.uk/Lords/2016-06-29/debates/29475315-0B49-48C6-92D5-24FBDCF70BF4/EuropeanCouncil?highlight=%22the%20alternatives%20offered%20by%20the%20leave%20campaign%22#contribution-9424A7F4-002F-4BD6-907D-8741C6DD27F6, accessed 27 August 2021.

Hansard (2016b) 'Outcome of the European Union referendum', 5 July, https://hansard.parliament.uk/Lords/2016-07-05/debates/FA935259-4199-4220-B9C3-6E93C4D17514/OutcomeOfTheEuropeanUnionReferendum?highlight=%22constantly%20worried%20about%20their%20jobs%2C%20the%20roof%20over%20their%20head%22#contribution-D11BC9B0-60AE-4893-BCC0-09EAE90C41B3, accessed 27 August 2021.

Hansard (2016c) 'Parliamentary scrutiny of leaving the EU', 12 October, https://hansard.parliament.uk/Commons/2016-10-12/debates/F327EC64-3777-4D40-A98D-BEC2E11763A2/ParliamentaryScrutinyOfLeavingTheEU?highlight=%22deep%20disillusionment%20with%20the%20political%20processes%22#contribution-BCA4B515-9D77-480B-9CA7-EFE159CB88D0, accessed 27 August 2021.

Hansard (2016d) 'Intergenerational fairness in government policy', 26 October, https://hansard.parliament.uk/Lords/2017-10-26/debates/32675A96-51FC-44C7-B0E7-0A2F71974DCD/IntergenerationalFairnessInGovernmentPolicy?highlight=%22costing%20us%20an%20arm%20and%20 a%20leg%20as%20they%20tread%20water%22#contribution-781888AC-EC45-4B25-BB76-575B71142803, accessed 30 December 2021.

Hansard (2016e) 'National life: shared values and public policy priorities', 2 December, https://hansard.parliament.uk/Lords/2016-12-02/debates/37E807CF-3A7E-4060-B139-8A30257E770F/NationalLifeSharedValuesAndPublicPolicyPriorities?highlight=%22frustrated%20and%20angry%20left%20behind%22#contribution-5D96BE48-5D46-4118-9B59-1B0DB721456A, accessed 27 August 2021.

Hansard (2016f) 'The Government's plan for Brexit', 7 December, https://hansard.parliament.uk/Commons/2016-12-07/debates/CA09D9B2-9634-41C8-8979-8B9CD82DBB8F/TheGovernmentsPlanForBrexit?highlight=%22contempt%20for%20those%20who%20have%20legitimate%20concerns%22#contribution-9A5228E0-EFAF-4AE4-9A7D-64B721866A33, accessed 30 December 2021.

Hansard (2017a) 'Leaving the EU: Security, law enforcement and criminal justice', 18 January, https://hansard.parliament.uk/Commons/2017-01-18/debates/D3BD1E6E-0C8F-4294-BFCB-4A542A16BBB5/LeavingTheEUSecurityLawEnforcementAndCriminalJustice?highlight=%22wanted%20to%20leave%20the%20european%20union%20for%20three%20reasons%22#contribution-1006CEBD-BA45-4564-98A8-DEF5EFB531FF, accessed 27 August 2021.

Hansard (2017b) 'Charter for Budget Responsibility', 24 January, https://hansard.parliament.uk/Commons/2017-01-24/debates/FB3A0D9B-8ECC-48B8-90EB-87B894788672/CharterForBudgetResponsibility?highlight=%22starved%20of%20investment%20for%20decades%22#contribution-1B0590CD-23AA-487D-BDC5-F5749644EF37, accessed 27 August 2021.

Hansard (2017c) 'European Union (Notification of Withdrawal) Bill', 1 February, https://hansard.parliament.uk/Commons/2017-02-01/debates/5B0251FC-94E6-4216-8830-4F85E0EC2250/EuropeanUnion(NotificationOfWithdrawal)Bill?highlight=%22economically%2C%20politically%20and%20socially%20excluded%22#contribution-26BC2AF0-D402-4C59-A2C3-42039ECEEE87, accessed 27 August 2021.

Hansard (2017d) 'President Trump: State visit', 20 February, https://hansard.parliament.uk/Commons/2017-02-20/debates/34847E5C-8B14-46E6-8251-AE99526CC011/PresidentTrumpStateVisit?highlight=%22reverse%20the%20democratic%20decision%22#contribution-09B4005C-E37D-4D93-B5BB-DC23B5B30787, accessed 27 August 2021.

Hansard (2017e) 'European Union (Notification of Withdrawal) Bill', 20 February, https://hansard.parliament.uk/Lords/2017-02-20/debates/30224DBB-4C77-4D65-A591-699EB7F99981/EuropeanUnion(NotificationOfWithdrawal)Bill?highlight=%22trust%20in%20british%20politics%20and%20politicians%20is%20at%20a%20terrible%20low%22#contribution-FB8BDA28-7CD5-4250-9487-832EC91CB6E4, accessed 27 August 2021.

Hansard (2017f) 'Budget resolutions', 9 March, https://hansard.parliament.uk/Commons/2017-03-09/debates/C2A7F416-1A88-4896-93DD-A857967F3401/BudgetResolutions?highlight=%22a%20chosen%20 few%2C%20in%20certain%20chosen%20areas%22#contribution-92E48B50-2181-45A1-9920-2222A468B400, accessed 27 August 2021.

Hansard (2017g) 'Queen's Speech', 29 June, https://hansard.parliament.uk/Lords/2017-06-29/debates/9A69A4EF-E7C3-45DD-B16F-077F0C77D154/Queen%E2%80%99SSpeech?highlight=%22often%2C%20when%20we%20talk%20about%20those%20who%20are%20uneducated%22#contribution-004765C8-86D9-419B-9500-35BBD776EED5, accessed 27 August 2021.

Hansard (2017h) 'Exiting the European Union and global trade', 6 July, https://hansard.parliament.uk/Commons/2017-07-06/debates/B1351616-A3BA-4A62-AEA7-7A77F80D733B/ExitingTheEuropeanUnionAndGlobalTrade?highlight=%22ensure%20that%20no%20one%20is%20left%20behind%20by%20the%20pace%20of%20change%22#contribution-EE57AF0D-0F7B-406E-8321-13EA901B87A6, accessed 27 August 2021.

Hansard (2017i) 'Ways and Means', 6 September, https://hansard.parliament.uk/Commons/2017-09-06/debates/9E3B339B-20C2-4479-9910-78EA09CA84D9/WaysAndMeans?highlight=%22global%20economy%22%20%22on%20the%20move%22#contribution-CB849E57-FDCC-4239-BC45-1A5EE7658B06, accessed 27 August 2021.

Hansard (2017j) 'European Union (Withdrawal) Bill', 11 September, https://hansard.parliament.uk/Commons/2017-09-11/debates/B10868CD-F096-47A2-84EE-A902C8A271BE/EuropeanUnion(Withdrawal)Bill?highlight=%22because%20we%20demonstrated%20our%20trust%20in%20the%20public%E2%80%99s%20judgment%20in%20voting%20to%20leave%22#contribution-64991D0F-2911-438A-A715-218564E6FB23, accessed 27 August 2021.

Hansard (2017k) 'Transport in the North', 6 November, https://hansard.parliament.uk/Commons/2017-11-06/debates/DC905F80-1791-4A37-880F-4EB9B958F9A0/TransportInTheNorth?highlight=%22to%20back%20northern%20powerhouse%20rail%22#contribution-A12FFC0E-64B7-4B7A-9E77-D01C7E6453A9, accessed 27 August 2021.

Hansard (2017l) 'Deafness and hearing loss', 30 November, https://hansard.parliament.uk/Commons/2017-11-30/debates/59353F2C-DA5B-4EA6-A8A9-640BC46C1D8A/DeafnessAndHearingLoss?highlight=%22left%20behind%2C%20ignored%20and%20told%20that%20they%20could%20not%20work%22#contribution-CDEA532D-1DAB-4105-ADBF-0849FF69C9F2, accessed 27 August 2021.

Hansard (2018a) 'Yorkshire devolution', 9 January, https://hansard.parliament.uk/Commons/2018-01-09/debates/A258E72B-52AF-4DC3-9513-3AE8AF89AF03/YorkshireDevolution?highlight=%22tired%20of%20being%20left%20behind%22#contribution-C1C223B2-233D-469C-8C5F-3DDA3718C675, accessed 27 August 2021.

Hansard (2018b) 'European Union (Withdrawal) Bill', 19 March, https://hansard.parliament.uk/Lords/2018-03-19/debates/47210FF1-A5B4-4CC6-895D-8F4C1838316D/EuropeanUnion(Withdrawal)Bill?highlight=%22%E2%80%98voices%20of%20the%20poorer%20regions%20of%20england%22#contribution-38A05EEB-58E8-4BD6-92ED-20C6A3EB859F, accessed 27 August 2021.

Hansard (2018c) 'Strengthening the union', 23 July, https://hansard.parliament.uk/Commons/2018-07-23/debates/5D428934-DE7E-4952-911F-AA644C63F21B/StrengtheningTheUnion?highlight=%22while%20at%20the%20same%20time%20cutting%20their%20budgets%20and%20limiting%20their%20powers%22#contribution-ADA855FB-A93D-40B6-A1A9-C0B71E7A48C2, accessed 27 August 2021.

Hansard (2018d) 'Constitutional convention', 13 December, https://hansard.parliament.uk/Lords/2018-12-13/debates/BEE4FA8E-B1EF-4700-BC97-89C92727A82C/ConstitutionalConvention?highlight=%22never-ending%20austerity%20and%20widening%20inequality%22#contribution-B8AE1B6A-2DE4-4FD8-BA63-978A1D17D1F7, accessed 27 August 2021.

Hansard (2019a) 'Social mobility: North-West', 9 January, https://hansard.parliament.uk/Commons/2019-01-09/debates/39AE2BAA-CF44-4FA2-B8D7-3E3FDBD1C79D/SocialMobilityNorth-West?highlight=%22comprehensive%20plan%22%20%22no%20place%20is%20left%20behind%22#contribution-DFE21327-7282-47C7-B1F8-7159AA21F3CA, accessed 27 August 2021.

Hansard (2019b) 'European Union (Withdrawal) Act', 10 January, https://hansard.parliament.uk/Commons/2019-01-10/debates/159740E3-991B-4DF4-A29C-D04B2F1CE10F/EuropeanUnion(Withdrawal)Act?highlight=%22jobs%20were%20going%20to%20portuguese%20workers%22#contribution-F49B0AAF-3C45-428A-8496-1306B730BA47, accessed 27 August 2021.

Hansard (2019c) 'Brexit: Withdrawal Agreement and Political Declaration', 14 January, https://hansard.parliament.uk/Lords/2019-01-14/debates/96C63DAC-0F16-49AA-8EDF-1F69D1D05A5F/BrexitWithdrawalAgreementAndPoliticalDeclaration?highlight=%22solve%20lack%20of%20infrastructure%20investment%2C%20the%20housing%20crisis%22#contribution-C9AE2B7B-EA58-422C-93AF-616518B95620, accessed 27 August 2021.

Hansard (2019d) 'Trade Bill', 4 February, https://hansard.parliament.uk/Lords/2019-02-04/debates/0CBE2153-AECA-4FDC-89BE-33AC0F3D4017/TradeBill?highlight=%22the%20evidence%20points%20to%20the%20need%20not%20to%20stop%20the%20beneficial%20flow%20of%20economic%20migrants%22#contribution-8B5D200C-B09F-414D-9FBD-AD6216C1587F, accessed 27 August 2021.

Hansard (2019e) 'Stronger Towns Fund', 4 March, https://hansard.parliament.uk/Commons/2019-03-04/debates/B9137B37-AC0F-411E-A7C8-FA3C385C8739/StrongerTownsFund?highlight=%22other%20towns%2C%20such%20as%20blackpool%22#contribution-49CAF5A2-96EE-45B5-AB07-236598A495E4, accessed 27 August 2021.

Hansard (2019f) 'Shared Prosperity Fund', 14 May, https://hansard.parliament.uk/Commons/2019-05-14/debates/5BD70352-F634-4E81-ADF5-1E81833BFF48/SharedProsperityFund?highlight=%22our%20people%22%20%22too%20chaotic%22#contribution-D0A884BF-BD5F-4775-BAFF-E5A28EC8509F, accessed 27 August 2021.

Hansard (2019g) 'Future of seaside towns', 1 July, https://hansard.parliament.uk/Lords/2019-07-01/debates/126DE39B-1B97-4F0B-BBE5-FCA096286A03/

FutureOfSeasideTowns?highlight=%22reverse%20the%20decline%22%20%22our%20nation%E2%80%99s%20story%22#contribution-2C8F3931-5484-4472-BA35-B457618465A3, accessed 27 August 2021.

Hansard (2019h) 'Topical questions', 1 October, https://hansard.parliament.uk/Commons/2019-10-01/debates/634E6487-76E3-4C6B-90F0-DDE0ED32B06C/TopicalQuestions?highlight=%22fiscal%20policy%20steps%22%20%22coalfield%20communities%22#contribution-F4F2D5FB-3200-418A-ADB8-094952EB14E6, accessed 27 August 2021.

Hansard (2019i) 'The Economy', 24 October, https://hansard.parliament.uk/Commons/2019-10-24/debates/867C435E-2BE9-47E9-B0F8-F55B628BDCDA/TheEconomy?highlight=%22set%20out%20an%20electioneering%20position%22#contribution-D9BB2BD8-AB3A-4CB7-ABB6-F80A49B6DB93, accessed 27 August 2021.

Hansard (2019j) 'Debate on the address', 19 December, https://hansard.parliament.uk/Commons/2019-12-19/debates/66EEE94D-F200-4889-90AC-5EE34753AC3E/DebateOnTheAddress?highlight=%22not%20only%20enshrine%20but%20enhance%20workers%E2%80%99%20rights%22#contribution-0619F3C1-0B3D-4B0B-9056-25F063CCF6C1, accessed 27 August 2021.

Hansard (2019k) 'European Union (Withdrawal Agreement) Bill', 20 December, https://hansard.parliament.uk/Commons/2019-12-20/debates/FE5B9762-F298-457B-8306-98D2D1D3519B/EuropeanUnion(WithdrawalAgreement)Bill?highlight=%22left%20behind%20by%20the%20excesses%20of%20the%20free%20market%22#contribution-AE8B5ACA-E1AE-4E01-9C4F-2DAF451904C6, accessed 27 August 2021.

Hansard (2020a) 'Productivity', 7 January, https://hansard.parliament.uk/Commons/2020-01-07/debates/A9F24C6C-F5DD-41CE-B35C-AAC6E2E90FB7/Productivity?highlight=%22unleash%20the%20potential%20of%20the%20whole%20country%22#contribution-06E6F7E7-B189-453D-8037-7587F219451D, accessed 27 August 2021.

Hansard (2020b) 'Socio-economic inequality: Equality Hub', 22 July, https://hansard.parliament.uk/Commons/2020-07-22/debates/DDF3C945-2E47-44AD-A54B-6F74D77A9C86/Socio-EconomicInequalityEqualityHub?highlight=%22has%20set%20out%20his%20vision%20to%20level%20up%20and%20spread%20opportunity%20across%20the%20country%2C%20and%20the%20equality%20hub%20will%20play%20an%20important%20part%20in%20realising%20that%20vision%20by%20rigorously%20analysing%20where%20the%20real%20inequality%20in%20britain%20is%20today%22#contribution-432F69EA-66F8-4DF0-B00F-E19E11DDF742, accessed 11 January 2022.

Harker, J. (2019) 'I'm a remainer. So why do I feel more and more sympathy with leave voters?' *The Guardian*, 12 January, www.theguardian.com/politics/commentisfree/2019/jan/12/brexit-remainer-leave-voters-labour-northern-people, accessed 27 August 2021.

Harris, J. (2020) *The Guardian*, 'Beyond the Red Wall by Deborah Mattinson and The Northern Question by Tom Hazeldine – review', 24 September, www.theguardian.com/books/2020/sep/24/beyond-the-red-wall-by-deborah-mattinson-and-the-northern-question-by-tom-hazeldine-review, accessed 27 August 2021.

Haylett, C. (2001) 'Illegitimate subjects? Abject whites, neoliberal modernisation, and middle-class multiculturalism', *Environment and Planning D: Society and Space*, 19(3): 351–70.

Hazeldine, T. (2021) *The Northern Question: A History of a Divided Country*. London: Verso.

Heath, A. (2000) 'Were traditional Labour voters disillusioned with New Labour? Abstention at the 1997 general election', *British Elections & Parties Review*, 10(1): 32–46.

Heath, A. (2019) 'This is our last chance to save Brexit – and even democracy itself', *Daily Telegraph*, 11 December, www.telegraph.co.uk/politics/2019/12/11/last-chance-save-brexit-even-democracy/, accessed 27 August 2021.

Heath, A., Jowell, R. and Curtice, J. (1986) 'Understanding electoral change in Britain', *Parliamentary Affairs*, 39(2): 150–64.

Hesp, M. (2019) 'Walking to vote against incoming tide', *Western Daily Press*, 25 May.

Hollway, W. and Jefferson, T. (2000) *Doing Qualitative Research Differently: Free Association, Narrative and the Interview Method*. London: Sage.

Howell, P. and Johnson, D. (2020) 'Foreword' in *Communities of Trust: Why We Must Invest in the Social Infrastructure of "Left Behind" Neighbourhoods*. London: Local Trust and All Party Parliamentary Group on 'Left Behind' Neighbourhoods.

Hudson, K. (2019) *Lowborn: Growing Up, Getting Away and Returning to Britain's Poorest Towns*. London: Chatto and Windus.

Hull Daily Mail (2016) 'The People voted to leave and now we must deal with whatever the future brings', *Hull Daily Mail*, 15 July.

Inglehart, R.F. and Norris, P. (2016) Trump, Brexit, and the rise of populism: Economic have-nots and cultural backlash, *Harvard JFK School of Government Faculty Working Papers Series*, Cambridge, MA: 1–52.

Ipsos-MORI (2016) 'NRS data uncovers a rise in Britain's middle class', 1 March, www.ipsos.com/ipsos-mori/en-uk/nrs-data-uncovers-rise-britains-middle-class, accessed 12 January 2022.

itv.com (2016) 'Foreign NHS workers must be assured their jobs are safe after Brexit, says health boss', www.itv.com, 19 July, www.itv.com/news/2016-07-19/foreign-nhs-workers-must-be-assured-their-jobs-are-safe-after-brexit-says-health-boss, accessed 27 August 2021.

Iyengar, S. (1991) *Is Anyone Responsible? How Television Frames Political Issues*. Chicago, IL and London: University of Chicago Press.

Jensen, T. (2014) 'Skivers/strivers and the classificatory politics of welfare reform', in *Youth, Community and Urban Regeneration Seminar Series, University of Limerick, Department of Sociology* (Vol. 9), Limerick: University of Limerick.

Johnson, B. (2019) 'The message of the European election results is clear. If we go on like this, we will be dismissed', *Daily Telegraph*, 27 May, www.telegraph.co.uk/politics/2019/05/26/win-back-public-must-show-can-deliver-pledges/, accessed 27 August 2021.

Kabaservice, G. (2019) 'Britain may be completely different to the US – but we can still learn from its election', *The Guardian*, 18 December, www.theguardian.com/commentisfree/2019/dec/18/britain-election-us-corbyn-sanders-trump-johnson, accessed 27 August 2021.

Kellner, D. (2017) 'Brexit plus, whitelash, and the ascendency of Donald J. Trump', *Cultural Politics*, 13(2): 135–49.

Kellner, P. (2017) 'Public opinion and the depth of Labour's crisis', *The Political Quarterly*, 88(1): 20–29.

Kelly, M. (2016a) 'EU referendum result: Where did it all go wrong for the Remain campaign in the North East', www.chroniclelive.co.uk, 24 June, www.chroniclelive.co.uk/news/north-east-news/eu-referendum-result-go-wrong-11522341, Accessed 27 August 2021.

Kelly, M. (2016b) 'Northern Powerhouse – supercharge it says Tory leadership hopeful', www.chroniclelive.co.uk, 4 July, www.chroniclelive.co.uk/news/north-east-news/northern-powerhouse-supercharge-says-tory-11565041, accessed 27 August 2021.

Khan, S. (2019) 'If May stays at Number 10, I'm starting Project Hope, the positive case for Remain', *The Guardian*, 13 January, www.theguardian.com/politics/2019/jan/13/eu-brexit-referendum-positive-case-remain-sadiq-khan, accessed 27 August 2021.

Kirby, D. (2020) 'Coronavirus latest: Greater Manchester Mayor Andy Burnham urges MPs to call for more Tier 3 lockdown support', www.inews.co.uk, inews.co.uk/news/politics/greater-manchester-mayor-andy-burnham-urges-mps-more-tier-3-lockdown-support-776885, accessed 27 August 2021.

Kreidler, C.W. (1998) *Introducing English Semantics*. London: Routledge.

Lavrakas, P. (2008) 'Purposive sample', in *Encyclopaedia of Survey Research Methods*. London: Sage.

Lawler, S. (2012) 'White like them: Whiteness and anachronistic space in representations of the English white working class', *Ethnicities*, 12(4): 409–26.

Lawrence, F. (2021) 'The empty shelves crisis isn't just down to Covid and Brexit – it's been decades in the making', *The Guardian*, 17 September, www.theguardian.com/commentisfree/2021/sep/17/empty-shelves-covid-brexit-britain-lorry-drivers?CMP=Share_iOSApp_Other, accessed 20 September 2021.

Lehain, M. (2020) 'Why woke won't win (but be wary anyway)', *Campaign for Common Sense*, 19 October, https://campaigncommonsense.com/blog/why-woke-wont-win-but-be-wary-anyway/, accessed 1 September 2021.

Lentin, A. (2019) 'All the talk of racism in this election reveals how little we understand it', *The Guardian*, 10 December, www.theguardian.com/commentisfree/2019/dec/10/racism-election-defined, accessed 27 August 2021.

Lessmann, C. and Seidel, A. (2017) 'Regional inequality, convergence, and its determinants: A view from outer space', *European Economic Review*, 92: 110–32.

Lind, M. (2020) *The New Class War: Saving Democracy from the Metropolitan Elite*. London: Penguin.

Lichfield, J. (2019) 'Stoke, the city that Britain forgot', *Unherd*, 20 November, https://unherd.com/2019/11/stoke-the-city-that-britain-forgot/ , accessed 27 August 2021.

Local Trust (2019) *Left Behind? Understanding Communities on the Edge*, https://localtrust.org.uk/insights/research/left-behind-understanding-communities-on-the-edge/, accessed 27 August 2021.

Lopez, A., Detz, A., Ratanawongsa, N. and Sarkar, U. (2012) 'What patients say about their doctors online: A Qualitative content analysis', *Journal of General Internal Medicine*, 27(6): 685–92.

Los, B., McCann, P., Springford, J. and Thissen, M. (2017) 'The mismatch between local voting and the local economic consequences of Brexit', *Regional Studies*, 51(5): 786–99.

Lott, T. (2016a) 'The privilege of the elite fuelled the anger of the leave voters', *The Guardian*, 28 June, www.theguardian.com/lifeandstyle/2016/jun/28/the-privilege-of-the-elite-fuelled-the-anger-of-the-leave-voters, accessed 27 August 2021.

Lott, T. (2016b) 'We've betrayed Britain's working-class children', *The Guardian*, 15 July, www.theguardian.com/lifeandstyle/2016/jul/15/weve-betrayed-britains-working-class-children, accessed 27 August 2021.

MacAskill, K. (2019) 'Brexit-induced contempt for politicians is risk to democracy', *The Scotsman*, 9 May, www.scotsman.com/news/opinion/columnists/kenny-macaskill-brexit-induced-contempt-politicians-risk-democracy-1417988, accessed 27 August 2021.

MacDonald, R., Shildrick, T. and Furlong, A. (2014) 'In search of "intergenerational cultures of worklessness": Hunting the Yeti and shooting zombies', *Critical Social Policy*, 34(2): 199–220.

Macwhirter, I. (2016) 'It's been a slog but it was right to hold a vote on Europe', *The Herald*, 23 June, www.heraldscotland.com/opinion/14574030.iain-macwhirter-slog-right-hold-vote-europe/, accessed 27 August 2021.

Malik, K. (2021) 'It's too easy to lapse into stereotypes when we talk about "red wall" seats', *The Guardian*, 3 January, www.theguardian.com/commentisfree/2021/jan/03/its-too-easy-to-lapse-into-stereotypes-when-we-talk-about-red-wall-seats?CMP=Share_iOSApp_Other, accessed 27 August 2021.

Marx, K. (1911) *A Contribution to the Critique of Political Economy*. Chicago: C.H. Kerr.

Marx, K. and Engels, F. (1977) *The Communist Manifesto*, 12th edn, London: Penguin Books.

Mason, R. (2015) 'Jeremy Corbyn's victory speech: What he said, what he meant', *The Guardian*, 14 September, www.theguardian.com/politics/ng-interactive/2015/sep/14/jeremy-corbyns-victory-speech-what-he-said-what-he-meant, accessed 7 September 2021.

Mattinson, D. (2020) *Beyond the Red Wall*. London: Biteback Publishing.

Mayring, P. (2000) 'Qualitative content analysis', *Forum: Qualitative Social Research*, 1(2), https://ci.nii.ac.jp/naid/10026506554/, accessed 21 February 2022.

McColm, E. (2019) 'Momentum takes Labour to the brink of extinction', *The Scotsman*, 15 December, www.scotsman.com/news/opinion/columnists/euan-mccolm-momentum-takes-labour-brink-extinction-1399707, accessed 27 August 2021.

McDonnell, A. and Curtis, C. (2019) 'How Britain voted in the 2019 general election', www.yougov.co.uk, 17 December, https://yougov.co.uk/topics/politics/articles-reports/2019/12/17/how-britain-voted-2019-general-election, accessed 27 August 2021.

McConnell, I. (2019) 'Scottish electorate sees economic truth that eludes Johnson voters amid this wilful damage of Brexit', *The Herald*, 20 December, www.heraldscotland.com/business_hq/18113651.ian-mcconnell-scottish-electorate-sees-economic-truth-eludes-johnson-voters-amid-wilful-damage-brexit/, accessed 27 August 2021.

McCurdy, C., Gardiner, L., Gustafsson, M. and Handscomb, K. (2020) *Painting the Town Blue: Demography, Economy and Living Standards in the Political Geographies Emerging from the 2019 General Election*. London: Resolution Foundation.

McKenzie, L. (2015) *Getting by: Estates, Class and Culture in Austerity Britain*. Bristol: Policy Press.

McKenzie, L. (2017) 'The class politics of prejudice: Brexit and the land of no-hope and glory', *The British Journal of Sociology*, 68 (S1): 265–80.

McKenzie, L. (2019) 'The British class system is in great shape', *IPPR Progressive Review*, 26(3): 230–37.

McKenzie, R.T. and Silver, A. (1968) *Angels in Marble: Working Class Conservatives in Urban England*. Chicago: University of Chicago Press.

McLuhan, M. (1964) *Understanding Media: The Extensions of Man*. New York: McGraw-Hill.

Messiou, K. (2012) *Confronting Marginalisation in Education: A Framework for Promoting Inclusion*. London: Routledge.

Morris, I. (2017) 'Left behind in the Brexit capital?' *Forbes*, 10 August, www.forbes.com/sites/stratfor/2017/08/10/left-behind-in-the-brexit-capital/?sh=34828acd6ba2, accessed 27 August 2021.

Morrison, J. (2017) 'Finishing the "unfinished" story: Online newspaper discussion threads as journalistic texts', *Digital Journalism*, 5(2): 213–32.

Morrison, J. (2019a) *Scroungers: Moral Panics and Media Myths*. London: Zed Books.

Morrison, J. (2019b) 'Re-framing free movement in the countdown to Brexit? Shifting UK press portrayals of EU migrants in the wake of the referendum', *British Journal of Politics and International Relations*, 21(3): 594–611.

Moynihan, D.P. (1967) 'The Moynihan Report: The negro family: The case for national action', in L. Rainwater and W.L. Yancey (eds) *The Moynihan Report and the Politics of Controversy*. Cambridge, MA: MIT Press, 39–124.

Mudde, C. (2004) 'The populist zeitgeist', *Government and Opposition*, 39(4): 541–63.

Murray, C. (1989) 'Underclass: The Crisis deepens', in R. Lister, J.C. Brown, A. Walker, N. Deakin, P. Alcock, M. David, M. Phillips, S. Slipman and A. Buckingham (eds) (1996) *Charles Murray and the Underclass: The Developing Debate*. London: IEA Health and Welfare Unit.

Murray, C. (1995) 'The emerging British underclass', in R. Lister, J.C. Brown, A. Walker, N. Deakin, P. Alcock, M. David, M. Phillips, S. Slipman and A. Buckingham (eds) (1996) *Charles Murray and the Underclass: The Developing Debate*. London: IEA Health and Welfare Unit.

Nandy, L. (2019) 'Workington Man is London's latest stereotype for the northern voters it neglects', *The Guardian*, 31 October, www.theguardian.com/commentisfree/2019/oct/31/workington-man-swing-voter-north-rugby-league-towns, accessed 27 August 2021.

Newton Dunn, B. (1988) *Why the Public Should be Worried by the EEC's Democratic Deficit*. London: European Democratic Group.

Newton Dunn, T. (2019) '"I was frightened": Chancellor Sajid Javid reveals he was spat on by racist thugs as he chats about growing up in 1970s Britain', *The Sun*, 5 December, www.thesun.co.uk/news/10492660/sajid-javid-growing-up-1970s-britain/, accessed 27 August 2021.

Nixon, S. (2016) 'It's not just confusion here – the EU didn't plan for Brexit either', *The Times*, 7 July, www.thetimes.co.uk/article/simon-nixon-lwtkzonxt, accessed 27 August 2021.

Nomis (2021a) 'Labour market profile – Great Yarmouth', www.nomisweb.co.uk/reports/lmp/la/1946157234/printable.aspx, accessed 27 August 2021.

Nomis (2021b) 'Labour market profile – Rhondda Cynon Taff', www.nomisweb.co.uk/reports/lmp/la/1946157398/report.aspx, accessed 27 August 2021.

Nomis (2021c) 'Labour market profile – Stoke', www.nomisweb.co.uk/reports/lmp/la/1946157171/report.aspx?town=stoke, accessed 27 August 2021.

Nomis (2021d) 'Labour market profile – Glasgow City', www.nomisweb.co.uk/reports/lmp/la/1946157420/report.aspx, accessed 27 August 2021.

Nordlinger, E.A. (1967) *The Working-class Tories: Authority, Deference and Stable Democracy*. Berkeley: University of California Press.

Nurse, A. and Sykes, O. (2019) 'It's more complicated than that!: Unpacking "Left Behind Britain" and some other spatial tropes following the UK's 2016 EU referendum', *Local Economy*, 34(6): 589–606.

Observer (2016) 'The *Observer* view on the EU referendum', www.theguardian.com, 26 June, For 30 years, the 'left-behind' (the working poor, the 'strivers', the zero-hours workers) have waited for a new economic reality based on fairness and equality to rebalance the effects of late capitalism as it advantaged a smaller and smaller number of people with grotesque income inequalities. This time, they were led to believe that a correction was at hand, accessed 21 February 2022.

O'Grady, F. (2016) 'I wanted to stay, but now we need to help working people in a post-EU Britain', *The Guardian*, 24 June, www.theguardian.com/commentisfree/2016/jun/24/working-people-eu-britain-brexit, accessed 27 August 2021.

O'Grady, S. (2019) 'The usual political rules are history – these are the key questions for this general election', *The Independent*, 30 October, www.independent.co.uk/voices/general-election-boris-johnson-dominic-cummings-workington-man-weather-brexit-a9178416.html, accessed 27 August 2021.

O'Neill, B. (2016) 'In defence of the crowd', 18 November, https://brendanoneill.co.uk/, accessed 27 August 2021.

ONS (Office for National Statistics) (2020) *Labour Market Overview, UK: November 2020*, www.ons.gov.uk/employmentandlabourmarket/peopleinwork/employmentandemployeetypes/bulletins/uklabourmarket/november2020, accessed 27 August 2021.

ONS (Office for National Statistics) (2021) *Effects of Taxes and Benefits on UK Household Income: Financial Year Ending 2020*, file:///C:/Users/james/-Downloads/Effects%20of%20taxes%20and%20benefits%20on%20UK%20household%20income%20financial%20year%20ending%202020.pdf, accessed 27 August 2021.

Opinium.com (2021) *The Political Report 5 August 2021*, 5 August, www.opinium.com/wp-content/uploads/2021/08/Opinium-Political-Report-5th-August-2021.pdf, accessed 20 September 2021.

Partington, R. (2020) 'UK government to pay 80% of wages for those not working in coronavirus crisis', *The Guardian*, 20 March, www.theguardian.com/uk-news/2020/mar/20/government-pay-wages-jobs-coronavirus-rishi-sunak, accessed 27 August 2021.

Payne, S. (2021) *Broken Heartlands: A Journey through Labour's Lost England*. London: Macmillan.

Payne, S. and Wright, R. (2020) 'Labour accuses Johnson of stoking "culture war" to distract from failings', *Financial Times*, www.ft.com/content/06ffc5a1-44e5-45aa-a05f-d83ec84c77ab, accessed 27 August 2021.

Pfeil, U. and Zaphiris, P. (2010) 'Applying qualitative content analysis to study online support communities', *Universal Access in the Information Society*, 9(1): 1–16.

Pidd, H. (2020) 'Over 50 Tory MPs in northern England press PM for roadmap out of lockdown', *The Guardian*, 26 October, www.theguardian.com/world/2020/oct/26/over-50-tory-mps-in-northern-england-press-pm-for-roadmap-out-of-lockdown accessed 27 August 2021.

Pope, C. (2016) 'Campaign chief Trickett demands snap election amid Tory chaos', www.labourlist.org, 11 July, https://labourlist.org/2016/07/campaign-chief-trickett-demands-snap-election-amid-tory-chaos/, accessed 27 August 2021.

publications.parliament.uk (2021a) *The Forgotten: How White Working-class Pupils have been Let Down, and How to Change It*, https://publications.parliament.uk/pa/cm5802/cmselect/cmeduc/85/8502.htm, accessed 8 September 2021.

publications.parliament.uk (2021b) *DWP Employment Support*, https://publications.parliament.uk/pa/cm5802/cmselect/cmpubacc/177/17702.htm, accessed 8 September 2021.

Pyke, C. (2019) '"Fund to aid Wales" regional economy is doubled to £3m', *Western Mail*, 14 May.

Rahim, Z. (2019) 'John Bolton says UK "first in line" for trade deal with US', *The Independent*, 13 August, www.independent.co.uk/news/uk/politics/john-bolton-boris-johnson-us-trade-deal-donald-trump-a9055141.html, accessed 27 August 2021.

Rawnsley, A. (2016) 'Brexit: A journey into the unknown for a country never before so divided', *The Observer*, 26 June, www.theguardian.com/commentisfree/2016/jun/26/brexit-eu-referendum-disunited-kingdom, accessed 27 August 2021.

Rawnsley, A. (2020) 'Rishi Sunak reverted to Tory type when he chose to leave the poor behind', *The Observer*, 29 November, www.theguardian.com/commentisfree/2020/nov/29/rishi-sunak-reverted-to-tory-type-when-he-chose-to-leave-world-poor-behind accessed 27 August 2021.

Razaq, A., Harrison, D., Karunanithi, S., Barr, B., Asaria, M. and Khunti, K. (2020) *BAME Covid Deaths: What do we Know? Rapid Data and Evidence Review: 'Hidden in Plain Sight'*. Oxford: Centre for Evidence-based Medicine.

Reed, J. (2016) 'Farage exits, but now Ukip voters are centre stage', *Yorkshire Evening Post*, 4 July.

Reilly, K. (2016) 'Read Hillary Clinton's "basket of deplorables" remarks about Donald Trump supporters', *Time*, 10 September, https://time.com/4486502/hillary-clinton-basket-of-deplorables-transcript/, accessed 27 August 2021.

Restad, H. (2016) 'Donald Trump's calls to "Make America great again" show that American Exceptionalism is still a powerful idea', *Impact of American Politics & Policy Blog*, http://eprints.lse.ac.uk/65942/1/blogs.lse.ac.uk-Donald%20Trumps%20calls%20to%20Make%20America%20great%20again%20show%20that%20American%20Exceptionalism%20is%20still%20a%20powerful%20(1)%5B1%5D.pdf, accessed 27 August 2021.

Riis, J. (2009) *How the Other Half Lives*. New York: Norton and Company.

Roach, A. (2020) 'Boris Johnson warns "things will be tough" as he hails Rishi Sunak's new job scheme as "best thing for growth in this country"', *Evening Standard*, 24 September, www.standard.co.uk/news/politics/boris-johnson-tough-times-rishi-sunak-jobs-scheme-a4555336.html, accessed 27 August 2021.

Roberts, G. (2019) 'Glyn Roberts: Why we need to reboot Northern Ireland plc', *belfasttelegraph.co.uk*, 23 May, www.belfasttelegraph.co.uk/opinion/news-analysis/glyn-roberts-why-we-need-to-reboot-northern-ireland-plc-38139600.html, accessed 21 February 2022.

Robinson, F. and Gregson, N. (1992) 'The "underclass": A class apart?' *Critical Social Policy*, 12(34): 38–51.

Rodríguez-Pose, A. (2018) 'The revenge of the places that don't matter (and what to do about it)', *Cambridge Journal of Regions, Economy and Society*, 11(1): 189–209.

Rose, J. (2001) *The Intellectual Life of the British Working Classes*. New Haven: Yale University Press.

Ruzza, C. and Pejovic, M. (2019) 'Populism at work: The language of the Brexiteers and the European Union', *Critical Discourse Studies*, 16(4): 432–48.

Ryan, F. (2019) 'The Suffering caused by austerity helped fuel Brexit – and will only get worse', *The Guardian*, 23 May, https://www.theguardian.com/commentisfree/2019/may/23/austerity-brexit-suffering-eu-anger, accessed 27 August 2021.

Said, E.W. (1978) *Orientalism*. New York: Vintage Books.

Savage, M. (2015) *Social Class in the 21st Century*. London: Penguin.

scotsman.com (2016) 'In full: Nicola Sturgeon's post-Brexit speech to the IPPR', 25 July, www.scotsman.com/news/politics/full-nicola-sturgeons-post-brexit-speech-ippr-1471418, accessed 27 August 2021.

Scully, E. (2021) 'Now Brexit cheerleading Wetherspoon boss Tim Martin calls for more EU migration to help bars and restaurants cope with staffing crisis – as business leader says British workers are happy "sitting on furlough getting 80% pay"', *Daily Mail*, 2 June, www.dailymail.co.uk/news/article-9643421/Brexit-cheerleading-Wetherspoon-boss-Tim-Martin-calls-EU-migration.html, accessed 3 September 2021.

Serna, A., Gerrikagoitia, J.K., Bernabé, U., and Ruiz, T. (2017) 'Sustainability analysis on urban mobility based on social media content', *Transportation Research Procedia*, 24: 1–8.

Sewell, T. (2021) 'Foreword from the chair' in *Commission on Race and Ethnic Disparities: The Report*. Available at: https://assets.publishing.service.gov.uk/government/uploads/system/uploads/attachment_data/file/974507/20210331_-_CRED_Report_-_FINAL_-_Web_Accessible.pdf, accessed 21 February 2022.

Sibley, D. (1995) *Geographies of Exclusion: Society and Difference in the West*. London: Psychology Press.

Skeggs, B. (2004) *Class, Self, Culture*. Abingdon: Psychology Press.

Smith, E. (2019) '"They don't know we're here": In Britain's most pro-Brexit town, voters are still angry and disillusioned', www.cnbc.com, 28 November, www.cnbc.com/2019/11/28/in-boston-britains-most-pro-brexit-town-voters-are-fed-up.html, accessed 27 August 2021.

Snoussi, D. and Mompelat, L. (2019) *'We Are Ghosts': Race, Class and Institutional Prejudice*. London: Runnymede Trust.

Sobolewska, M. and Ford, R. (2020) *Brexitland: Identity, Diversity and the Reshaping of British Politics*. Cambridge: Cambridge University Press.

socialistworker.co.uk (2008) 'BBC's white season is founded on racist lies', www.socialistworker.co.uk, 4 March, https://socialistworker.co.uk/reviews-and-culture/bbc-s-white-season-is-founded-on-racist-lies/, accessed 10 January 2022.

Sokol, J. (2008) *There Goes My Everything: White Southerners in the Age of Civil Rights, 1945–1975*. New York: Vintage.

Sparrow, A. (2022) 'More than half of UK's black children live in poverty, analysis shows', *The Guardian*, 2 January, www.theguardian.com/world/2022/jan/02/more-than-half-of-uks-black-children-live-in-poverty-analysis-shows, accessed 11 January 2022.

Spencer, A. and Oppermann, K. (2020) 'Narrative genres of Brexit: the Leave campaign and the success of romance', *Journal of European Public Policy*, 27(5): 666–84.

Standing, G. (2011) *The Precariat: The New Dangerous Class*. London: Bloomsbury.

Stewart, L. (2014) 'Nigel Farage speaks to the UKIP party conference', www.bbc.co.uk, 26 September, www.bbc.co.uk/news/uk-england-29382604, accessed 1 September 2021.

Stone, J. (2016a) 'Brexit: 5 things we learned from a night that shook Europe', *The Independent*, 24 June, www.independent.co.uk/news/uk/politics/brexit-explained-what-eu-referendum-britain-uk-voters-polls-results-a7100411.html, accessed 27 August 2021.

Stone, J. (2016b) 'Opposition call for early general election following Theresa May "coronation"', *The Independent*, 11 July, www.independent.co.uk/news/uk/politics/opposition-parties-call-for-early-general-election-following-theresa-may-coronation-a7130896.html, accessed 27 August 2021.

sunderlandecho.com (2016) 'Sunderland hits back to New York Times "slur" article', 30 June, www.sunderlandecho.com/news/sunderland-hits-back-new-york-times-slur-article-367014, accessed 27 August 2021.

Sveinsson, K.P. (2009) *Who Cares about the White Working Class?* London: Runnymede Trust.

telegraph.co.uk (2019) 'A post Brexit Britain must restore the hopes of Leavers who felt left behind', *Daily Telegraph*, 26 January, www.telegraph.co.uk/opinion/2019/01/26/post-brexit-britain-must-restore-hopes-leavers-felt-left-behind/, accessed 27 August 2021.

thebureauinvestigates.com (2021) 'What is the people's newsroom?', www.thebureauinvestigates.com/explainers/what-is-the-peoples-newsroom, accessed 21 February 2022.

theguardian.com (2016) 'The Guardian view on the EU referendum: The Vote is in, now we must face the consequences', *The Guardian*, 24 June, www.theguardian.com/commentisfree/2016/jun/24/the-guardian-view-on-the-eu-referendum-the-vote-is-in-now-we-must-face-the-consequences, accessed 27 August 2021.

theguardian.com (2019a) 'The Guardian view on general election 2019: A fleeting chance to stop Boris Johnson in his tracks', *The Guardian*, 10 December, www.theguardian.com/commentisfree/ng-interactive/2019/dec/10/the-guardian-view-on-general-election-2019-a-fleeting-chance-to-stop-boris-johnson-in-his-tracks, accessed 27 August 2021.

theguardian.com (2019b) 'The Guardian view on the 2019 election result: A new political landscape', *The Guardian*, 13 December, www.theguardian.com/commentisfree/2019/dec/13/the-guardian-view-on-the-2019-election-result-a-new-political-landscape, accessed 27 August 2021.

thenorthernecho.co.uk (2019) '"Stop stereotyping the North as Brexitland", say four Labour MPs', *Northern Echo*, 30 April, www.thenorthernecho.co.uk/news/17580613.stop-stereotyping-north-brexitland-say-four-labour-mps/, accessed 27 August 2021.

Thompson, E.P. (1968) *The Making of the English Working Class*. London: Pelican Books.

Thomson, A. and Sylvester, R. (2016) 'People aren't being listened to. Like Theresa, I want to put that right', *The Times*, 16 July, www.thetimes.co.uk/article/people-aren-t-being-listened-to-like-theresa-i-want-to-make-that-right-50vg2b2c7, accessed 27 August 2021.

Tobin, L. (2016) 'Credit Suisse boss says Brexit vote "is due to bad education in UK"', *Evening Standard*, 4 July, www.standard.co.uk/news/politics/brexit-vote-is-due-to-bad-education-in-uk-says-top-banker-a3287371.html, accessed 27 August 2021.

Tolhurst, A., Newton Dunn, T., and Hawkes, S. (2016) 'See EU later! Britain votes to LEAVE the EU on a dramatic night as Nigel Farage declares "victory for ordinary people"', *The Sun*, 23 June, www.thesun.co.uk/news/1332742/britain-votes-to-back-brexit-and-leave-the-eu-on-historic-night-as-nigel-farage-declares-victory-for-ordina ry-people/, accessed 27 August 2021.

Tombs, R. (2019) 'Extreme remainers are driven by a misguided pessimism about Britain's future', *Daily Telegraph*, 21 May, www.telegraph.co.uk/politics/2019/05/21/extreme-remainers-driven-misguided-pessimism-britains-future/, accessed 27 August 2021.

Torrance, D. (2016) 'History will not treat David Cameron lightly', *The Herald*, 25 June, www.heraldscotland.com/opinion/14579730.david-torrance-history-will-not-treat-david-cameron-kindly/, accessed 27 August 2021.

Toynbee, P. (2016) '*Guardian* writers on the vote to leave', *The Guardian*, 24 June, www.theguardian.com/commentisfree/2016/jun/24/eu-referendum-our-panel-on-the-vote-for-brexit, accessed 27 August 2021.

Tressell, R. (2004) *The Ragged Trousered Philanthropists*. London: Penguin Classics.

Trilling, D. (2019) 'This election may be the end of Farage, but not of Faragism', *The Guardian*, 18 November, www.theguardian.com/commentisfree/2019/nov/18/elelction-farage-brexit-party-leader, accessed 27 August 2021.

Tyler, I. (2013) *Revolting Subjects: Social Abjection and Resistance in Neoliberal Britain*. London: Zed Books Ltd.

Vine, A. (2016) 'Brexit reveals the stark contrasts of a divided nation', *Yorkshire Evening Post*, 27 June, www.yorkshireeveningpost.co.uk/news/politics/andrew-vine-brexit-reveals-stark-contrasts-divided-nation-617862, accessed 27 August 2021.

Virdee, S. and McGeever, B. (2018) 'Racism, crisis, Brexit', *Ethnic and Racial Studies*, 41(10): 1802–19.

Wacquant, L. (2008) 'Territorial stigmatization in the age of advanced marginality', in J. Houtsonen and A. Antikaenen (eds) *Symbolic Power in Cultural Contexts: Uncovering Social Reality*, Rotterdam: Sense, 43–52.

Wearden, G. (2019) 'Davos 2019: Do the global elite have the will to fix the world's problems?', *The Guardian*, 19 January, www.theguardian.com/business/2019/jan/19/davos-world-economic-forum-elite-globalisation-china-slowdown-problems, accessed 27 August 2021.

Weldon, D. (2021) 'The Red Wall reconsidered: The Truth behind the Tories' northern strongholds', *The Economist*, 31 May, www.economist.com/britain/2021/03/31/the-truth-behind-the-tories-northern-strongholds, accessed 7 January 2022.

Welshman, J. (2007) *From Transmitted Deprivation to Social Exclusion: Policy, Poverty and Parenting*. Bristol: Policy Press.

Welshman, J. (2013) *Underclass: A History of the Excluded: 1880–2000*. London: Hambledon Continuum.

Western Mail (2016) 'Hope springs eternal amid EU vote bereavement backlash: "It's not dishonourable or undemocratic to campaign for the Brexit vote to be overturned", argues leader of the Remain campaign in Wales, Geraint Talfan Davies', *Western Mail*, 8 July.

Whiteley, P. and Clarke. H.D. (2016) 'Brexit: Why did older voters choose to leave the EU?', *The Independent*, 26 June, www.independent.co.uk/news/uk/politics/brexit-why-did-old-people-vote-leave-young-voters-remain-eu-referendum-a7103996.html, accessed 27 August 2021.

Wiggan, J. (2012) 'Telling stories of 21st century welfare: The UK Coalition government and the neo-liberal discourse of worklessness and dependency', *Critical Social Policy*, 32(3): 383–405.

Williams, Z. (2019) 'Labour has been catapulted into conflict. That's not necessarily a bad thing', *The Guardian*, 13 December, www.theguardian.com/commentisfree/2019/dec/13/labour-conflict-party-defeat, accessed 27 August 2021.

Wilson, W.J. (ed.) (1993) *The Ghetto Underclass*. London: Sage.

Winter, P. (2019) 'Lord Chris Haskins to step down as chairman of Humber LEP', *Hull Daily Mail*, 13 September, www.hulldailymail.co.uk/news/business/lord-chris-haskins-humber-lep-3316268, accessed 27 August 2021.

Wismayer, H. (2016) 'Why the Brexit vote is so close', www.cnn.com, 22 June, https://edition.cnn.com/2016/06/21/opinions/brexit-campaign-disaffection-wismayer/index.html, accessed 27 August 2021.

Wodak, R. (2001) 'The discourse-historical approach', in R. Wodak and M. Meyer (eds) *Methods of Critical Discourse Analysis*, London: Sage, 63–94.

Wodak, R. (2015) 'Critical discourse analysis, discourse-historical approach', in K. Tracy, C. Ilie and T. Sandel (eds) *The International Encyclopedia of Language and Social Interaction*, Chichester: John Wiley and Sons, 1–14.

Wring, D. and Ward, S. (2020) 'From bad to worse? The media and the 2019 election campaign', *Parliamentary Affairs*, 73(S1): 272–87.

Index